AIRLINE OPERATIONS AND SCHEDULING

To
My mother, Sohayla, Sina, Shiva and Sarah

Airline Operations and Scheduling

MASSOUD BAZARGAN

ASHGATE

© Massoud Bazargan 2004

All rights reserved. No part of this publication may be reproduced, stored in a retrieval system, or transmitted in any form or by any means, electronic, mechanical, photocopying, recording or otherwise without the prior permission of the publisher.

Massoud Bazargan has asserted his right under the Copyright, Designs and Patents Act, 1988, to be identified as author of this work.

Published by
Ashgate Publishing Limited
Gower House
Croft Road
Aldershot
Hampshire GU11 3HR
England

Ashgate Publishing Company
Suite 420
101 Cherry Street
Burlington, VT 05401-4405
USA

Ashgate website: http://www.ashgate.com

British Library Cataloguing in Publication Data
Bazargan, Massoud
    Airline operations and scheduling
    1.Airlines - Management 2.Aeronautics, Commercial
    3.Airlines - Reservation systems 4.Operations research
    5.Airlines - Timetables 6.Scheduling
    I.Title
    387.7'068

Library of Congress Cataloging-in-Publication Data
Bazargan, Massoud.
    Airline operations and scheduling / by Massoud Bazargan.
        p. cm.
    Includes bibliographical references and index.
    ISNB 0-7546-3616-X
  1. Airlines--Management. 2. Aeronautics, Commercial. 3. Airlines--Reservation systems. 4. Operations research. 5. Airlines--Time tables. I. Title.

    TL552.B38 2004
    387.7'068--dc22
                                                              2004007443

ISBN 0 7546 3616 X

Reprinted 2005

Printed and bound in Great Britain by MPG Books Ltd, Bodmin, Cornwall

Contents

List of Figures   *vii*
List of Tables   *ix*
Preface   *xii*

1   Introduction   1

PART I
PLANNING OPTIMIZATION

2   Network Flows and Integer Programming Models   7

3   Flight Scheduling   30

4   Fleet Assignment   40

5   Aircraft Routing   59

6   Crew Scheduling   81

7   Manpower Planning   100

PART II
OPERATIONS AND DISPATCH OPTIMIZATION

8   Revenue Management   109

9   Gate Assignment   132

10   Airline Irregular Operations   140

PART III
COMPUTATION COMPLEXITY AND SIMULATION CASE STUDIES

11   Computational Complexity and Heuristics   159

12   Start-up Airline Case Study   163

13   Simulation Case 1   172

14   Simulation Case 2   187

Appendix 201

Index *203*

List of Figures

2.1	Basic elements of a network	7
2.2	Flow between two nodes	8
2.3	Directed flow	8
2.4	Undirected flow	8
2.5	Supply node	8
2.6	Demand node	9
2.7	Transshipment node	9
2.8	A network showing three paths from A to G	9
2.9	A cycle	10
2.10	Connected Network	10
2.11	Network with flight times between city pairs	11
2.12	Graphical solution for the Shortest Path Problem	12
2.13	Network presentation for minimum cost flow	13
2.14	Solution to minimum cost flow	14
2.15	Network presentation from source to destination	16
2.16	Network presentation for multi-commodity problem	19
2.17	Solution to multi-commodity problem	20
2.18	Solution showing three disjoint sequences or sub-tours	27
2.19	Solution showing two sub-tours after adding first breaking constraint	27
3.1	A sample airline network with two hubs and nine spokes	31
3.2	The hierarchy of airline planning	34
3.3	Ultimate Air route network	36
4.1	An example of a time-space network	44
4.2	Demand distribution and passenger spills	46
4.3	Example of aircraft balance	49
4.4	Time-space network for LAX	51
5.1	B737-800 one-day routing	63
5.2	B737-800 two-day routing	64
5.3	B737-800 three-day routing	65
5.4	B757-200 five-day routing with no opportunity for overnight maintenance at the JFK hub	66
6.1	A typical pairing with duty periods, sits within duty periods, overnight rests and sign-in and sign-out times	83
8.1	Nested and non-nested airline seat allocations	111
8.2	Normal probability distribution for demand with shaded area representing demand exceeding a certain level	112
8.3	Expected marginal revenue for full-fare paying passengers	115
8.4	Seat protections and booking levels for three fare classes under the nested seat allocation model	117
8.5	EMSR for the four-fare-class example	118

8.6	A simple network representing passengers with different origin-destination itineraries	120
8.7	Network diagram for the multi-leg example	121
9.1	C Concourse at SFO	133
9.2	Assignment of gates to flights	136
10.1	Time band network for the case study	142
10.2	Time band approximation network	144
12.1	Flight network for the start-up airline	164
12.2	Arrival/departure of flights at each airport	170
12.3	Airline's network and aircraft routing	171
13.1	Equipment type	175
13.2	Through flights on a typical day	176
13.3	Maintenance cycle for *through flights* (narrow body, mid body-domestic, mid body-international and wide body aircraft)	180
13.4	Total technician requirements for each sub-shift in a day	181
13.5	Average percentage utilization of technicians in a day	182
13.6	Total number of technicians with unfinished jobs in any shift	184
14.1	Forecasts for number of operations (landings and take-offs) at KTLH on a five-year basis	190
14.2	Forecast for SATS operations	191
14.3	Forecast for SATS, existing and total operations for KTLH	191
14.4	KTLH runway, taxiway and terminal layout	193
14.5	Daily arriving, departing and total flight operation at KTLH	194
14.6	Delay distribution for baseline scenario	195
14.7	Dissection of delays at KTLH	195
14.8	Runway usage at KTLH	196
14.9	Change in peak hourly movements for 2002-2025 study time	197
14.10	Changes in peak delay distribution time for 2002-2025	197
14.11	Change in dissection of delay 2002-2025	198
14.12	Change in runway utilization 2002-2025	199

List of Tables

1.1	Number of U.S. certificated (DOT) airlines in the years 1976 - 2002	2
2.1	Maximum number of flights per city-pair for Shuttle Hopper Airways	16
2.2	Distance-matrix between cities	22
2.3	Binary-matrix showing cities covered by each hub	23
2.4	Sequence of flights to cities in cargo airline network	26
2.5	Final tour sequence of flights with distances	28
3.1	A sample flight schedule	31
3.2	Load factor and expected revenue	35
3.3	Flight schedule for Ultimate Air	37
3.4	Destination in miles, demand means and standard deviations for Ultimate Air network	38
4.1	Fleet diversity for select airlines	40
4.2	US major carriers' unit revenues and expenses, by region	42
4.3	US major carriers' unit revenues and expenses, by fleet-type	43
4.4	Arrival/departure flights for LAX	50
4.5	Optimal number of aircraft grounded overnight at each airport	53
4.6	Fleet assignment for Ultimate Air	54
4.7	Total daily cost for various aircraft combinations	55
5.1	B737-800 Fleet Assignment	61
5.2	B757-200 Fleet Assignment	62
5.3	Sample three-day routing for B757-200 fleet	67
5.4	Sample three-day routing for B737-800 fleet	68
5.5	Routing candidates for flight 125	70
5.6	Feasible eight aircraft solution for the 757-200 fleet	72
5.7	Flights 105 and 125	72
5.8	Revised schedule for flight 105	72
5.9	One of the optimal solutions with six aircraft	73
5.10	Overnight stays at JFK for the optimal solution	73
5.11	Solution for aircraft routing of 737-800 fleet with 12 aircraft	74
5.12	Flight schedule for B737-800 stranded flights	75
5.13	Revised flight schedule for B737-800 stranded flights	75
5.14	Aircraft routing solution for B737-800 with revised schedule	76
5.15	B737-800 fleet schedule with major modifications	77
5.16	Aircraft routing for B737-800 with nine aircraft	78
6.1	Crew cost for US major carriers	81
6.2	All legal crew pairings for B757-200 fleet	86
6.3	Sample one-day crew pairing for B737-800 fleet	87
6.4	Sample two-day crew pairing for B737-800 fleet	87
6.5	Solution to crew pairing for B757-200 fleet	89
6.6	Solution to crew pairing for B737-800 fleet	90

6.7	Possible weekly crew roster combinations for Ultimate Air	93
6.8	Three sample rosters for B757-200 fleet	94
6.9	Solution to crew rosters for B757-200 fleet	96
6.10	Solution to crew rosters for B737-800 fleet	97
7.1	Check-in counter agents requirement at JFK for Ultimate Air	101
7.2	Index for shifts (j)	101
7.3	Index for days of the week (i)	102
7.4	Solution to manpower planning	104
8.1	Example of non-nested and nested airline seat allocations	111
8.2	Probability and expected marginal revenue for each seat in the fare class	113
8.3	Fare classes, demand distributions and fare levels for a flight	118
8.4	Protected number of seats for each fare class over lower classes	119
8.5	Demand and fare levels for the multi-leg example	122
8.6	Solution to the deterministic network seat allocation example	123
8.7	Probabilistic demand for the network seat allocation example	125
8.8	Expected marginal revenue for the probabilistic network seat allocation example	126
8.9	Solution to the probabilistic network seat allocation example	127
8.10	Seat allocations on flight-leg AH	128
9.1	Passenger flow	134
9.2	Distance matrix	134
9.3	Traveling distances	135
9.4	Solution to gate assignment	136
9.5	Revised assignments of gates to flights	137
10.1	Flight schedule and aircraft routing	141
10.2	Cancellation cost for flight legs	143
10.3	Non-zero delay costs	146
10.4	Solution for Scenario 1	150
10.5	Detailed and final solution for Scenario 1	150
10.6	Solution for Scenario 2	151
10.7	Detailed and final solution for Scenario 2	152
10.8	Solution for Scenario 3	153
10.9	Detailed and final solution for Scenario 3	153
11.1	Network and crew size for select airlines	160
12.1	List of airports and their codes for case study	163
12.2	Proposed routes and their frequencies	165
12.3	Three sample routes	166
12.4	Solution for the case	168
12.5	Flight schedule and aircraft routing for the case study	169
13.1	Number of through flights in a day	176
13.2	Total number of checks scheduled on each equipment type daily	177
13.3	Man-hours, ground time and technician requirements for *day holds* and *remains overnights* (RON)	177

13.4	*Service Check (SVC)* man-hours, ground time and technician requirements for *through flights*	178
13.5	*Level 3 Service Check (SC3)* man-hours, ground time and technician requirements for *through flights*	178
13.6	Shift and sub-shift schedules at Newark	178
13.7	Average number of aircraft serviced by each technician in each shift	181
13.8	Number of technicians with unfinished jobs at the end of each shift	183
13.9	Optimal shift schedule	184

Preface

Background

This book is the result of developing an MBA course on Airline Planning and Operations at the College of Business at Embry-Riddle Aeronautical University. The course was initiated based on feedback received from alumni, mainly working at airlines, as well as students undertaking the author's operations research and operations management classes. The feedback indicated that a follow-up course to these courses specifically focused towards airline scheduling based on optimization methodologies would be very appealing to them, and the aviation audience. The idea of developing such a course was additionally encouraged by the College's airline industry advisers. The development of the course was long and time consuming. The reason was that due to its unique nature, there were limited suitable texts; and related materials are very technical, thus, beyond the scope of an MBA class. This course was developed and offered in Spring 2002. The students undertaking this course motivated the author to write a text focused at the materials in this course. This book attempts to achieve a number of goals as follows:

- Introduce the importance and complexity of planning and operations at the airlines.
- Operations research techniques are extremely important tools for planning the operations in airlines. There is a large number of technical papers on airline optimization models. However, this literature is very advanced and therefore of interest only to a limited audience. This book attempts to fill this gap by simplifying the models and applying them to relatively simple examples thus exposing them to a larger audience.
- There has been a growing concern among the operations research community that the materials offered in OR courses at MBA or senior undergraduate business classes are too abstract, outdated, and at times irrelevant to today's fast and dynamic world. This book seeks to provide alternative and hopefully relevant materials for such courses.

Intended Audience

This book is intended to serve both as a textbook and as supporting material for graduate and undergraduate business, management, transportation, and engineering students. Currently the airlines spend a long time training and acquainting new recruits with the planning and scheduling processes of various operations. This book can serve as an additional resource for such training. Other aviation audiences such as general aviation, flight schools, International Air Transport Association (IATA), and International Civil Aviation Organization (ICAO) training course instructors, executive jets, chartered flights, air-cargo and package delivery companies, and airline consultants, may find the materials in this book relevant and useful.

Required Background

The main background requirement on the part of the reader for a major portion of this book is basic familiarity with linear and integer programming. This topic is widely covered in many disciplines at colleges and universities at different levels. Chapters 4 and 8 require some basic understanding of statistics in general and normal distribution in particular.

Adopting This Book as a Text

The author has offered the contents of this book in an MBA course as follows:
The students are grouped into teams, three students per team, each team representing operation managers of an airline company. As the course progresses, the teams are responsible for creating their own airlines, selecting routes, flight networks, fleet diversity, aircraft routings, maintenance locations, hub and spoke systems, air and ground crew scheduling, and gate assignments. The students need to conduct, thorough research on passenger demand on city pairs, fleet cost, crew cost, determine ASM, CASM, RASM, yield, etc for their airlines. The teams should address how to determine their fares (revenue management) and how they accommodate unexpected interruptions in their flight schedule (irregular operations). If the teams are familiar with simulation software such as Arena (www.arenasimulation.com) then they enjoy simulating the operation of each airport within their network to assess the smooth operations such as adequate number of check-in counters, availability of gates, baggage handlers, etc. The teams make a final presentation of their airlines and submit a comprehensive report detailing these operations.

Acknowledgements

I was very lucky to be constantly helped, supported and encouraged by so many people throughout writing this book. I would like to thank my patient and hard working assistants and friends Manolo Centeno and Rohan Dudley. I would like to sincerely thank James Buckalew, Oscar Garcia, Tom Reich, Michael Gialouris, Glenn Martin, and Scott Wargo, for helping me with the industry side of the airline operations. I would like to thank Candas Ozdogu, Mauricio Angel, Deniz Saka, Pavel Hosa, Werner Leidenfrost, John Owens, Michelle Williams, Baohong Jiang and Shaun Londono for their help. I am also grateful to Dr. Yu at the University of

Texas, Austin, and my colleagues at Embry-Riddle Aeronautical University, especially Drs. Petree and Reynolds for their support.

Finally, I would like to thank my wife Sohayla, my son Sina and daughters Shiva and Sarah for their patience, understanding and support throughout the writing of this book.

Massoud Bazargan

Chapter 1

Introduction

Introduction

The Airline Deregulation Act of 1978 in the United States paved the way for major structural changes to the airlines industry. Airlines became free to select their route system as well as fares. This prompted a rush of new airlines to the market. With this Act, suddenly the competition was not only from those pre-deregulation airlines, but also from new entrants. The airlines were no longer protected and if they wanted to stay in the market they had to manage their operations more intelligently. The airlines use numerous resources to provide transportation service for their passengers. It is the planning and efficient management of these resources that determines the survival or demise of the airlines. This industry is an excellent example of survival of the fittest. Table 1.1 shows the number of certificated airlines from 1976-2002 in the United States. This table also presents the number of airlines that were closed or merged with other airlines as well as newly established ones. As the table implies, the airlines operate in a very dynamic and uncertain environment. Furthermore low flexibility to respond to changes due to tightly coupled resources and tight and limiting FAA regulations generates additional restrictions for this industry leading to a complex environment for the airlines (Yu 1998). To handle this complexity, robust and efficient planning tools and techniques are required. Operations Research tools and techniques have played an important role in handling such complexities.

Operations Research and Airlines

Airlines have been using Operations Research techniques since the 1950s (Barnhart and Talluri 1997). These models have had tremendous impact on planning and managing operations within airlines. The advances in computer technology and optimization models resulted in tackling more complex problems and solving them in a much shorter span of time within the airlines. The vast contribution of these models lead to the establishment of Operations Research departments in many airlines saving them millions of dollars. These departments helped create an important professional society within the field of Operations Research. The Airline Group of the International Federation of Operational Research Societies (AGIFORS) is a professional society that seeks to advance, promote and apply Operations Research within the airline industry (see www.agifors.org). A brief browse through this website shows that operations research techniques have been successfully applied to many diverse problems such as revenue management, crew scheduling, aircraft routing, fleet planning, maintenance, etc, within the airline industry.

Table 1.1 Number of U.S. certificated (DOT) airlines in the years 1976-2002

Year	Total Number of U.S. Airlines	Closed or Merged	Newly Established
2002	67	3	7
2001	63	10	2
2000	71	13	9
1999	75	6	6
1998	75	12	8
1997	79	13	4
1996	88	6	9
1995	85	7	16
1994	76	8	14
1993	70	3	11
1992	62	4	12
1991	54	9	7
1990	56	7	4
1989	59	7	3
1988	63	4	5
1987	62	16	6
1986	72	15	17
1985	70	16	13
1984	73	16	21
1983	68	10	14
1982	64	28	14
1981	78	1	13
1980	66	1	13
1979	54	0	17
1978	37	10	5
1977	42	2	5
1976	39	4	1

Source: http://www.bts.gov/oai/employees/

Outline of This Book

This book explores a variety of optimization models adopted by airlines for scheduling and planning. The chapters discussing these models start with an example. The process of developing a mathematical model for this example is then explained. At the end of the chapter the general mathematical model is presented. The contents of this book is divided into three parts as follows:

Part 1 - Planning Optimization

- *Chapter 2 - Network Flows:* This chapter is intended as a review of the basic concepts in network flows and integer programming models. These models are adopted later on in the following chapters.

- *Chapter 3 - Flight Scheduling:* Construction of flight schedules is the starting point for all other airline optimization problems. This chapter discusses the construction of flight schedules for a fictitious airline. This schedule is then used in the following chapters to address fleet assignment, aircraft routing and crew scheduling and manpower planning.

- *Chapter 4 - Fleet Assignment:* Airlines typically operate a number of different fleet types, each having different characteristics and costs such as seating capacity, landing weights, and crew and fuel costs. This chapter introduces the basic fleet assignment model and its application to the fictitious airline.

- *Chapter 5 - Aircraft Routing:* This chapter presents the process of assigning individual aircraft to fly each flight segment assigned to a particular fleet. This chapter discusses mathematical models and their applications to the fictitious airline.

- *Chapter 6 - Crew Scheduling:* This chapter discusses the process of assigning crew to flight segments in two phases. First, crew pairing is introduced to determine which flight segments should be paired. The second phase, crew rostering, discusses how these pairings are assigned to the crew incorporating various rules and regulations.

- *Chapter 7 - Manpower Planning:* This chapter discusses manpower planning for ground crew through the fictitious airline case.

Part 2 - Operations and Dispatch Optimization

- *Chapter 8 - Revenue Management:* This chapter introduces revenue management, probabilistic models, and case studies.

- *Chapter 9 - Gate Assignment:* This chapter introduces the gate assignment mathematical model through a case study.

- *Chapter 10 - Irregular Operations:* When faced with a lack of resources and/or disruptions caused by various internal and external factors, airlines often are not able to fly their published flight schedule. This chapter provides introduction to irregular operations, delays, cancellations, a mathematical model for irregular operations and a case study.

Part 3 - Computation Complexity and Simulation

- *Chapter 11 - Computational Complexity:* This chapter discusses inherent computational complexity with the airline problems.

- *Chapters 12 - 14:* These chapters introduce case studies on a start-up airline, and utilize simulation approaches. Simulation studies have become an alternative and/or integrated part of mathematical models when faced with complex systems. Chapters 13 and 14 present the application of two simulation approaches to manpower planning and airport capacity planning.

- *Appendix:* provides the full name of the airports presented as their three/four letter codes in this book.

Software

Throughout this book references are made to software for solving linear/integer program models. Many of these models can be solved using student/trial versions of optimization software, which are typically available at colleges, universities and airlines. There are many software vendors who provide these student/trail versions free to download on their websites (see for example www.lindo.com or www.maximal-usa.com). For larger problems, which exceed the student/trial version limits, we used full version of MPL software (www.maximal-usa.com) with CPLEX solver (www.ilog.com).

References

Barnhart, C. and Talluri, K.T. (1997), *Airline Operations Research in Design and operation of civil and environmental engineering system*, edited by ReVelle C. and McGarity, A., Wiley, 435-469.
Yu, G. (1998), *Operations Research in the Airline Industry*, Kluwer Academic Publishers.

PART I
PLANNING OPTIMIZATION

Chapter 2

Network Flows and Integer Programming Models

Introduction

A large part of the problems that airlines face can be translated into network and integer programming models. These models are mentioned and used throughout this book. This chapter attempts to provide a review of some of the optimization models discussed in this book. It should be noted that these topics only represent a small selection of models from the vast area of network and integer programming techniques. For a complete discussion of various network models, interested readers are referred to the list of books referenced in this chapter.

Networks

A network (also referred to as graph) is defined as a collection of points and lines joining these points. There is normally some flow along these lines, going from one point to another. Figure 2.1 represents a network.

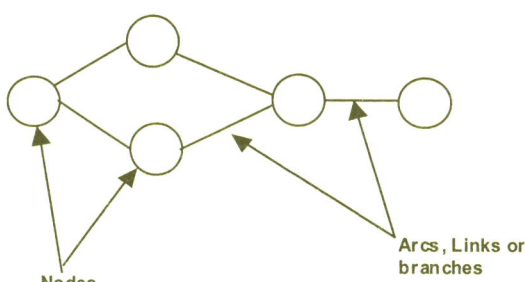

Figure 2.1 Basic elements of a network

Network Terminology

Before explaining the models, some terminologies commonly used in network study are described.

Nodes & Arcs: In a network, the points (circles) are called nodes and the lines are referred to as arcs, links or arrows (see Figure 2.1).

Flow: The amount of goods, vehicles, flights, passengers and so on that move from one node to another (see Figure 2.2).

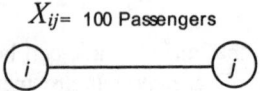

Figure 2.2 Flow between two nodes

Directed Arc: If the flow through an arc is allowed only in one direction, then the arc is said to be a directed arc. Directed arcs are graphically represented with arrows in the direction of the flow (see Figure 2.3).

Figure 2.3 Directed flow

Undirected Arc: When the flow on an arc (between two nodes) can move in either direction, it is called an undirected arc. Undirected arcs are graphically represented by a single line (without arrows) connecting the two nodes (see Figure 2.4).

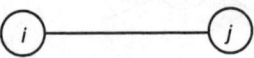

Figure 2.4 Undirected flow

Arc Capacity: The maximum amount of flow that can be sent through an arc. Examples include restrictions on the number of flights between two cities.

Supply Nodes: Nodes with the amount of flow coming to them greater than the amount of flow leaving them - or nodes with positive net flow. See Figure 2.5.

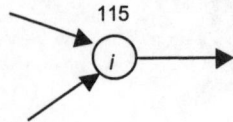

Figure 2.5 Supply node

Demand Nodes: Nodes with negative net flow or outflow greater than inflow, see Figure 2.6

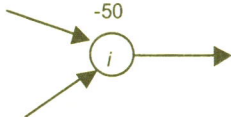

Figure 2.6 Demand node

Transshipment Nodes: Nodes with the same amount of flow arriving and leaving – or nodes with zero net flow, see figure 2.7

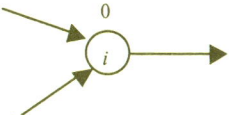

Figure 2.7 Transshipment node

Path: Sometimes two nodes are not connected by an arc, but could be connected by a sequence of arcs (see Figure 2.8). A path is a sequence of distinct arcs that connect two nodes in this fashion. Airliners utilize hubs to provide connections between city pairs in their network.

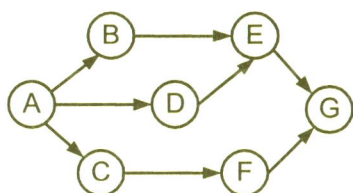

Figure 2.8 A network showing three paths from A to G

Source: Starting node in the path.

Destination: Last node in the path.

Cycle: A sequence of directed arcs, that begins and ends at the same node (see Figure 2.9). Examples include aircraft that start from an airport which is a maintenance base, and after flying to several destinations, end up at the same airport from which they departed.

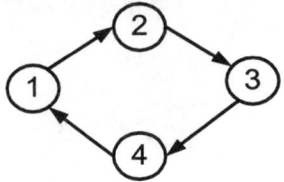

Figure 2.9 A cycle

Connected Network: A network in which every two nodes are linked by at least one path.

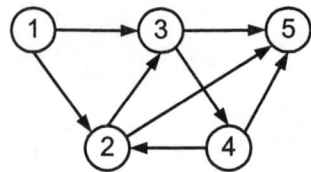

Figure 2.10 Connected Network

Network Flow Models

In this section, select network models that are used in this book are discussed. It is assumed that the reader is familiar with basic linear and integer programming.

Shortest Path (Route) Problem

This problem attempts to identify a path, from source to destination, within the network, that results in minimum transport time/cost. This particular problem should be especially attractive to cargo handlers and origin/destination scenarios (see Figure 2.11). The problem consists of a connected network with known costs for each arc in the network. The objective is to identify the path with the minimum cost between two desired nodes.

Example

Consider the following network shown in Figure 2.11 (adapted from Winston and Albright 2001). The nodes represent the cities, and the arcs are the flights. The numbers on the arcs represent the flight time in minutes between the city pairs. We want to determine the best route that results in the shortest flying time from node 1 (source) to node 10 (destination).

Network Flows and Integer Programming Models

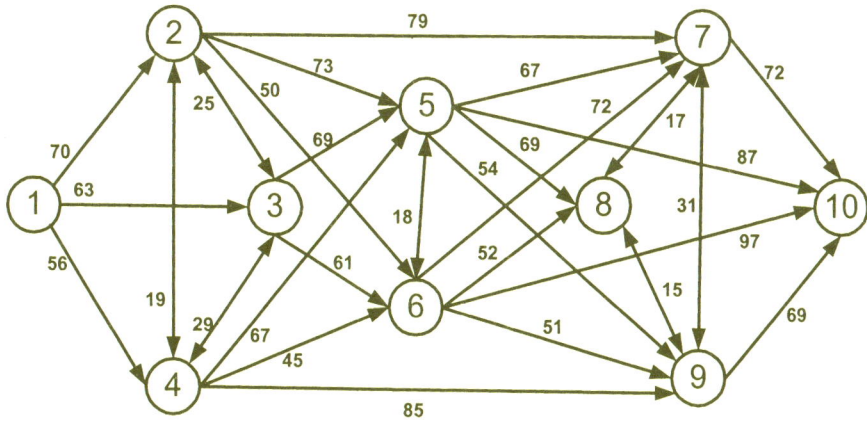

Figure 2.11 Network with flight times between city pairs

We assume the following binary (0-1) decision variable:
$$x_{i,j} = \begin{cases} 1 \text{ if arc } (i,j) \text{ is part of the solution} \\ 0 \text{ otherwise} \end{cases}$$

Then the objective function is to minimize the total flying cost as follows:

Minimize $70x_{1,2} + 63x_{1,3} + 56x_{1,4} + \ldots$

We have three sets of constraints as follows:

Source node: The flow must originate from node 1. To make sure that the flow (in this case our starting flight) leaves the source we must have:

$$x_{1,2} + x_{1,3} + x_{1,4} = 1$$

Transshipment nodes: Every other node (except source and destination) is a transshipment node. That is the net flow in these nodes should be zero. As an example node (2) in Figure 2.11 is a transshipment node. To address the constraint for this node we write:

$$x_{1,2} + x_{4,2} + x_{3,2} - x_{2,4} - x_{2,3} - x_{2,4} - x_{2,5} - x_{2,6} - x_{2,7} = 0$$

Similarly we write constraints for the other seven transshipment nodes.

Destination node: The flow must end up at the destination node (node 10). Therefore:

$$x_{5,10} + x_{6,10} + x_{7,10} + x_{9,10} = 1$$

Solving this problem using software, we find that the minimum cost is 198 minutes (56+45+97). The solution (route) for this example is presented in Figure 2.12.

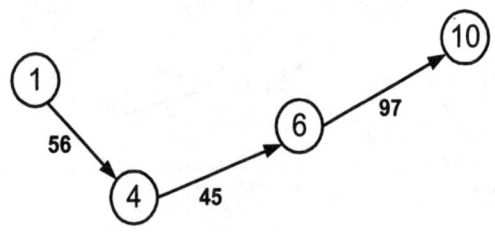

Figure 2.12 Graphical solution for the Shortest Path Problem

The general mathematical model for the Shortest Path Problem (SPP) is represented by a binary (0-1) integer programming as follows.

Sets
$\quad M$ = Set of nodes
Index
$\quad i,j,k$ = Index for nodes
Parameters
$\quad c_{i,j}$ = Cost of flow along the arc joining node i to node j
$\quad m$ = Destination node
Decision Variable
$$x_{i,j} = \begin{cases} 1 \text{ if arc } (i,j) \text{ is part of the path} \\ 0 \text{ otherwise} \end{cases}$$

Objective Function

$$\text{Minimize} \sum_{i \in M} \sum_{j \in M} c_{i,j} x_{i,j} \qquad (2.1)$$

Subject to

$$\sum_{j \in M} x_{1,j} = 1 \quad j \neq 1 \qquad (2.2)$$

$$\sum_{j \in M} x_{i,j} - \sum_{k \in M} x_{k,i} = 0 \qquad \text{For all } (\forall) \ i \neq 1 \text{ or } m \qquad (2.3)$$

$$\sum_{i \in M} x_{m,i} = -1 \qquad (2.4)$$

The objective function (2.1) attempts to minimize the total cost. Constraint (2.2) ensures that the flow is shipped from the source (supply) node. The set of constraints (2.3) impose that all other nodes (except the destination node) are transshipment nodes. Finally, constraints (2.4) ensure that the flow is received at the destination (demand) node.

Minimum Cost Flow Problem

The minimum cost flow network problem seeks to satisfy the requirements of nodes at minimum cost. This is a generalized form of transportation, transshipment, and shortest path problems. This problem assumes that we know the cost per unit of flow and capacities associated with each arc.

Example

Consider the following network presented in Figure 2.13 (adapted from Anderson et al. 2003). An airline is tasked with transporting goods from nodes 1 and 2 to nodes 5, 6 and 7 (see Figure 2.13). The airline does not have direct flights from the source nodes to the destination nodes. Instead, they are connected through its hubs in nodes 3 and 4. The numbers next to the nodes represent the demand/supply in tons. The numbers on the arcs represent the unit cost of transportation per ton. We want to determine the best way to transport the goods from sources to destinations so that the total cost is minimized. The aircraft flying to and from node 4 can carry a maximum of 50 tons of cargo.

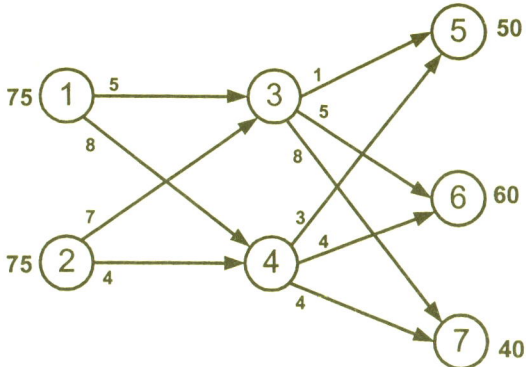

Figure 2.13 Network presentation for minimum cost flow

To formulate this problem consider the following decision variable:
　　$x_{i,j}$ = Amount of flow from node i to node j

The objective function is then:
Minimize $5x_{1,3} + 8x_{1,4} + 7x_{2,3} + ...$

We need to write one constraint for each node. For example, for node 1 we have:

$$x_{1,3} + x_{1,4} \leq 75$$

Similarly, we write constraints for the other six nodes. Note that the net flow for nodes 3 and 4 should be zero as these are transshipment nodes.

All the flights to and from node 4 can carry a maximum of 50 tons. Therefore, all the flow to and from this node must be limited to 50 as follows:

$x_{1,4} \leq 50$

$x_{2,4} \leq 50$

$x_{4,5} \leq 50$

$x_{4,6} \leq 50$

$x_{4,7} \leq 50$

Solving this problem using software generates a total minimum cost of $1,250. The solution for this problem is presented in Figure 2.14.

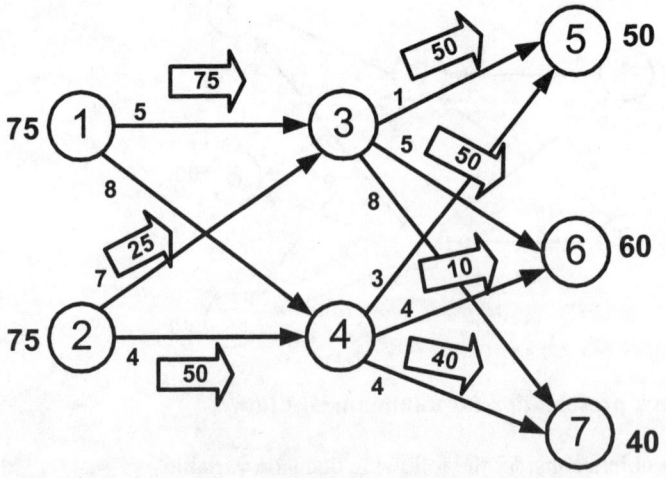

Figure 2.14 Solution to minimum cost flow

The general model is mathematically expressed as follows (Bazaraa et al. 1990).

Sets
  M = Set of nodes

Index
  i,j,k = Index for nodes

Parameters
  $c_{i,j}$ = Unit cost of flow from node i to the node j
  b_i = Amount of supply/demand for node i.
  $L_{i,j}$ = Lower bound on flow through arc (i, j)
  $U_{i,j}$ = Upper bound on flow through arc (i, j)

Decision Variable
  $x_{i,j}$ = Amount of flow from node i to node j

Objective Function

$$\text{Minimize} \sum_{i \in M} \sum_{j \in M} c_{i,j} x_{i,j} \quad (2.5)$$

Subject to

$$\sum_{j \in M} x_{i,j} - \sum_{k \in M} x_{k,i} = b_i \quad \forall\, i = 1, 2, .., M \quad (2.6)$$

$$L_{i,j} \le x_{i,j} \le U_{i,j} \quad (2.7)$$

The objective function (2.5) attempts to minimize the total cost of the network. Constraints (2.6) satisfy the requirements of each node by determining the amount of inflow and outflow from that node. The set of constraints (2.7) impose the lower and upper-bound restrictions along the arcs.

Maximum Flow Problem

The Maximum Flow problem is a special case of the Minimum Cost flow problem. It attempts to find the maximum amount of flow that can be sent from one node (source node) to another (destination node) when the network is capacitated, that is, the arcs in the network have a capacity restriction.

Example

This example is adapted from Winston and Venkataramanan (2003). An airline must determine the number of daily connecting flights that can be arranged between Daytona Beach (DAB), Florida and Lafayette (LAF), Indiana. Connecting flights must stop in Atlanta (ATL), Georgia and then make one more stop in either Chicago (ORD), Illinois or Detroit (DTW), Michigan. Due to its current policies with these airports, the airline has a maximum number of daily flights which it can operate between the city-pairs shown in Table 2.1.

Table 2.1   Maximum number of flights per city-pair for Shuttle Hopper Airways

City-Pairs	Maximum Number of Daily Flights
DAB - ATL	3
ATL - ORD	2
ATL - DTW	3
ORD - LAF	1
DTW - LAF	2

The airline wants to determine how to maximize the number of connecting flights daily from Daytona Beach, FL to Lafayette, IN respecting the current restrictions.

The following network represents this problem with arcs showing maximum daily flights along the city pairs.

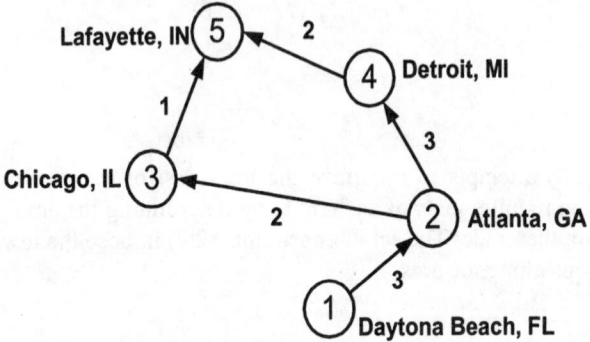

Figure 2.15 Network presentation from source to destination

To formulate the problem, let us assume the following decision variables:

$x_{i,j}$ = Number of flights (integer) from node i to node j
f = Number of daily flights from DAB to LAF

In this problem, the objective is to maximize the daily flights between DAB and LAF. Therefore:

Maximize f

Similar to the Shortest Path Problem, we have a set of constraints for source, transshipment and destination nodes:

Source node: DAB is our source node. f is the total flow leaving DAB, therefore:

$$x_{1,2} = f$$

Transshipment nodes: We write one constraint for each transshipment node. For example, for node 2 (ATL) we have:

$$x_{1,2} - x_{2,3} - x_{2,4} = 0$$

Similarly we write transshipment constraints for other nodes 3 and 4.

Destination node: The same number of daily flights f departing from DAB should now arrive at destination node LAF.

$$x_{25} + x_{35} = f$$

Arc capacity: The last set of constraints address the capacity of arcs as follows:

$$x_{12} \leq 3$$
$$x_{23} \leq 2$$
$$x_{24} \leq 2$$
$$x_{35} \leq 1$$
$$x_{45} \leq 2$$

Solving this problem generates a maximum flow of three daily flights between DAB and LAF as follows:

- 1 flight assigned to the DAB-ATL-ORD-LAF route, and;
- 2 flights assigned to the DAB-ATL-DTW-LAF route.

The general model is mathematically expressed as follows (Ahuja et al. 1993):

Sets
    M = Set of nodes
Index
    i, j, k = Index for nodes
Parameters
    $L_{i,j}$ = Lower bound on flow through arc (i, j)
    $U_{i,j}$ = Upper bound on flow through arc (i, j)

m = Destination node

Decision Variables:

$x_{i,j}$ = Amount of flow from node i to node j

f = Amount of flow from source node to destination node

Objective Function

$$\text{Maximize } f \qquad (2.8)$$

Subject to

$$\sum_{j \in M} x_{1,j} = f \qquad \Leftrightarrow \text{Origin Node} \qquad (2.9)$$

$$\sum_{i \in M} x_{i,j} - \sum_{k \in M} x_{j,k} = 0 \qquad \Leftrightarrow \text{Transshipment nodes} \qquad (2.10)$$

$$\sum_{i \in M} x_{i,m} = f \qquad \Leftrightarrow \text{Destination node} \qquad (2.11)$$

$$L_{ij} \leq x_{ij} \leq U_{ij}$$

The objective function (2.8) attempts to maximize flow from the source node (node 1) to the destination node (node m). The set of constraints (2.9) and (2.11) impose the outflow and inflow restrictions on the source and destination nodes. All other nodes are transshipment nodes. The set of constraints (2.10) imposes this restriction. Finally, constraints (2.12) restrict the flow along the arcs based on the imposed capacity.

Multi-Commodity Problem

All the network models explained so far assume that a single commodity or type of entity is sent through a network. Sometimes a network can transport different types of commodities. The Multi-commodity problem seeks to minimize the total cost when different types of goods are sent through the same network. The commodities may either be differentiated by their physical characteristics, or simply by certain attributes. The Multi-commodity problem is extensively used in transportation industry. In the airline industry, the Multi-commodity model is adopted to formulate crew-pairing and fleet assignment models.

Example

We modify the example that was presented for the Minimum Cost Flow problem discussed earlier to address the Multi-commodity model formulation. Figure 2.16 presents the modified example:

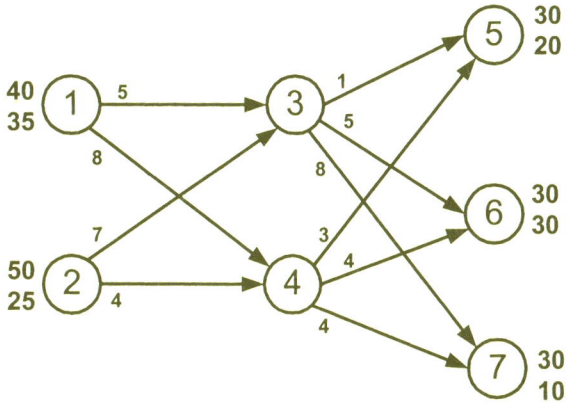

Figure 2.16 Network presentation for multi-commodity problem

As we see in this figure the scenario is very similar to the earlier case. The only difference is that instead of having only one type of cargo, in this case we have two types (two commodities). The numbers next to each node represent the supply/demand for each cargo at that node. As an example, node 1 supplies 40 and 35 tons of cargo to nodes 1 and 2 respectively. The transportation costs per ton are also similar. We want to determine how much from each cargo should be routed on each arc so that the total transportation cost is minimized.

To formulate this problem we assume the following decision variable:

$x_{i,j,k}$ = Amount of flow from node i to node j for commodity k

In this decision variable the indices i and j represent the nodes ($i,j = 1,..,7$) and k represents the type of commodity ($k = 1,2$).

The objective function is therefore:

Minimize $5x_{1,3,1} + 5x_{1,3,2} + 8x_{1,4,1} + 8x_{1,4,2} + ...$

We need to write one constraint for each node. For example, for node 1 we have:

$$x_{1,3,1} + x_{1,4,1} \leq 40$$
$$x_{1,3,2} + x_{1,4,2} \leq 35$$

We write similar constraint for the other six nodes.

Recall that all the flights to and from node 4 can carry a maximum of 50 tons. Therefore:

$$x_{1,4,1} + x_{1,4,2} \leq 50$$
$$x_{2,4,1} + x_{2,4,2} \leq 50$$
$$x_{4,5,1} + x_{4,5,2} \leq 50$$
$$x_{4,6,1} + x_{4,6,2} \leq 50$$
$$x_{4,7,1} + x_{4,7,2} \leq 50$$

Solving this problem using software generates a total minimum cost of $1150. The solution for this problem is presented in Figure 2.17.

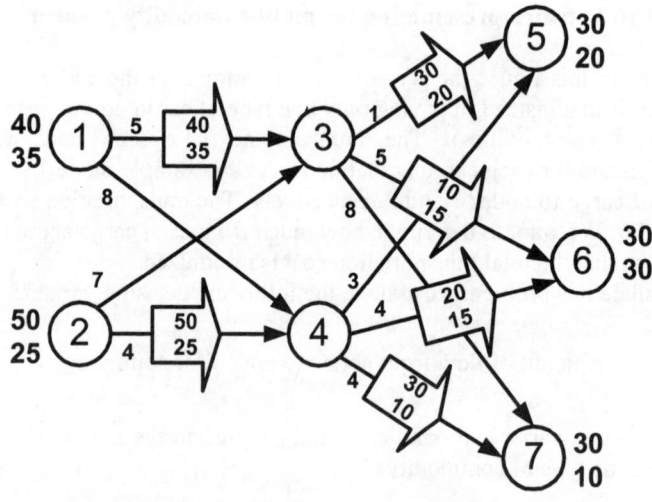

Figure 2.17 Solution to the multi-commodity problem

The general model is mathematically expressed as follows (Ahuja et al. 1993):

Sets
    M = Set of nodes
    K = Set of commodities

Indices

i, j, t = Index for nodes
k = Index for commodities

Parameters

$c_{i,j,k}$ = Unit cost of flow from node i to node j for commodity k,
$b_{i,k}$ = Amount of supply/demand at node i for commodity k
$u_{i,j}$ = Flow capacity on arc (i, j)

Decision Variable

$x_{i,j,k}$ = Amount of flow from node i to node j for commodity k

Objective Function

$$Min \sum_{k \in K} \sum_{i \in M} \sum_{j \in M} c_{i,j,k} x_{i,j,k} \tag{2.13}$$

Subject to

$$\sum_{t \in M} x_{i,t,k} - \sum_{t \in M} x_{t,i,k} = b_{i,k} \quad \text{For all } i \in M \text{ and } k \in K \tag{2.14}$$

$$\sum_{k \in K} x_{i,j,k} \leq u_{i,j} \quad \text{For all } i \in M \text{ and } j \in M \tag{2.15}$$

In this model, the objective function (2.13) seeks to minimize the total network cost over all nodes and all commodities. The set of constraints (2.14) and (2.15) satisfy the supply/demand of the node and impose capacity constraints on the arc.

Integer Programming Models

Integer programming models relate to certain types of linear programming in which all of the decision variables are required to be non-negative integers. The following represents a brief introduction to a small number of integer programming models adopted in the following chapters.

Set-Covering/Partitioning Problems

Set-covering problems relate to cases where each member of one set should be assigned/matched to member(s) of another set. Examples include the assignment of crew members to flights, aircrafts to routes, etc. The objective in a set-covering problem is to minimize the total cost of this assignment.

Example

The following is an example of set-covering adapted and modified from Winston and Venkataramanan (2003).

An airline wants to design its "hub" system (hub-and-spoke systems are discussed in Chapter 3). Each hub will be used for connecting flights to and from cities within a 1000 miles of the hub. The airline wants to serve the following cities: Atlanta, Boston, Chicago, Denver, Houston, Los Angeles, New Orleans, New York, Pittsburgh, Salt Lake City, San Francisco, and Seattle. The airline wants to determine the smallest number of hubs it will need in order to cover all of these cities. By cover, we mean each city should be within 1000 miles of at least one hub. Table 2.2 lists the distances between the cities.

Table 2.2 Distance-matrix between cities

		1	2	3	4	5	6	7	8	9	10	11	12
		AT	BO	CH	DE	HO	LA	NO	NY	PI	SL	SF	SE
1	AT	0	1037	674	1398	789	2182	479	841	687	1878	2496	2618
2	BO	1037	0	1005	1949	1804	2979	1507	222	574	2343	3095	2976
3	CH	674	1005	0	1008	1067	2054	912	802	452	1390	2142	2013
4	DE	1398	1949	1008	0	1019	1059	1273	1771	1411	504	1235	1307
5	HO	789	1804	1067	1019	0	1538	356	1608	1313	1438	1912	2274
6	LA	2182	2979	2054	1059	1538	0	1883	2786	2426	715	379	1131
7	NO	479	1507	912	1273	356	1883	0	1311	1070	1738	2249	2574
8	NY	841	222	802	1771	1608	2786	1311	0	368	2182	2934	2815
9	PI	687	574	452	1411	1313	2426	1070	368	0	1826	2578	2465
10	SL	1878	2343	1390	504	1438	715	1738	2182	1826	0	752	836
11	SF	2496	3095	2142	1235	1912	379	2249	2934	2578	752	0	808
12	SE	2618	2976	2013	1307	2274	1131	2574	2815	2465	836	808	0

We can now revise Table 2.2 above to identify which cities are covered by each hub. Simply replace all the distances in the above table by 1 if the distance is less than 1000 miles (covered) and 0 otherwise. Table 2.3 presents the revised matrix.

To formulate this problem, we define the following binary decision variable:

$$x_j = \begin{cases} 1 \text{ if city } j \ (1,2,..,12) \text{ is selected as a hub} \\ 0 \text{ otherwise} \end{cases}$$

We want to minimize the number of hubs, therefore the objective function is:

Minimize $x_1 + x_2 + ... + x_{12}$

Each city must be covered by at least one hub. Atlanta (Index 1), for example, is covered by cities 1, 3, 5, 7, 8 and 9 (see Table 2.3). Therefore, the constraint for Atlanta is:

$x_1 + x_3 + x_5 + x_7 + x_8 + x_9 \geq 1$ (Atlanta)

Table 2.3 Binary-matrix showing cities covered by each hub

		1	2	3	4	5	6	7	8	9	10	11	12
		AT	BO	CH	DE	HO	LA	NO	NY	PI	SL	SF	SE
1	AT	1	0	1	0	1	0	1	1	1	0	0	0
2	BO	0	1	0	0	0	0	0	1	1	0	0	0
3	CH	1	0	1	0	0	0	1	1	1	0	0	0
4	DE	0	0	0	1	0	0	0	0	0	1	0	0
5	HO	1	0	0	0	1	0	1	0	0	0	0	0
6	LA	0	0	0	0	0	1	0	0	0	1	1	0
7	NO	1	0	1	0	1	0	1	0	0	0	0	0
8	NY	1	1	1	0	0	0	0	1	1	0	0	0
9	PI	1	1	1	0	0	0	0	1	1	0	0	0
10	SL	0	0	0	1	0	1	0	0	0	1	1	1
11	SF	0	0	0	0	0	1	0	0	0	1	1	1
12	SE	0	0	0	0	0	0	0	0	0	1	1	1

Note that we use the greater than or equal to sign because a city can be covered by more than one hub. Similarly for Boston (Index 2), we have:

$x_2 + x_8 + x_9 \geq 1$ (Boston)

Hence, we can write similar constraints for all the other 10 cities.

Solving this binary integer program using software generates three hubs as follows:

Atlanta Covers Chicago, Houston, New Orleans, New York, and Pittsburgh;
Pittsburgh Covers Atlanta, Chicago, Boston, and New York;
Salt Lake City Covers Denver, Los Angeles, San Francisco, and Seattle.

We see that some cities are covered by more than one hub. As an example, Chicago is covered by both Atlanta and Pittsburgh hubs.

In the case where we want to cover each city by exactly one hub, all the inequalities in the above model become equal signs. This special case where each member of one set is covered exactly once is called *set-partitioning*.

If we run the above program with this restriction, i.e., changing all greater than or equal to signs with strictly equal to signs, we find that the minimum number of hubs to cover all cities exactly once is also three. The hubs are:

Boston Covers New York and Pittsburgh
New Orleans Covers Atlanta, Chicago and Houston
Salt Lake City Covers Denver, Los Angeles, San Francisco and Seattle

Therefore, as the name implies, set-partitioning attempts to make disjoint sets such that no member appears in two sets.

The general model for set-covering is as follows (Ignizio and Cavalier 1994):

Sets
$\quad M$ = Members of set 1
$\quad N$ = Members of set 2
Indices
$\quad i$ = Index for set 1
$\quad j$ = Index for set 2
Parameters
$\quad c_j$ = Cost associated with selecting member j
$$a_{i,j} = \begin{cases} 1 \text{ if member } j \text{ covers member } i \\ 0 \text{ otherwise} \end{cases}$$
Decision Variable
$$x_j = \begin{cases} 1 \text{ if member } j \text{ is selected} \\ 0 \text{ otherwise} \end{cases}$$

The integer binary programming model is as follows:

Objective Function

$$Min \sum_{j \in N} c_j x_j \qquad (2.16)$$

Subject to

$$\sum_{j \in N} a_{i,j} x_j \geq 1 \quad \text{For all } i \in M \qquad (2.17)$$

In this model, the objective function (2.16) seeks to minimize the total covering cost. The set of constraints (2.17) imposes that each member of set 1 is covered by at least one member of set 2.

The set-partitioning formulation of the above problem is similar, except that (2.17) is now re-written with a strictly equal to sign as follows:

$$\sum_{j \in N} a_{i,j} x_j = 1 \quad \text{For all } i \in M$$

Throughout this book both set-covering and set-partitioning models are used extensively. In these models references are made to matrices. By a set-covering or set-partitioning matrix, we mean a matrix of $a_{i,j}$ parameters where the members of one set (index i) is represented by rows and members of the other set (index j) is represented by columns as shown below. In this matrix a value of 1 means that the specific member in set 1 is covered by the specific member in set 2. A value of 0 means that this coverage does not exist.

$$\left\{ \begin{array}{l} \text{Members of} \\ \text{set 1 indexed by} \\ i \end{array} \right. \overbrace{\begin{pmatrix} 1 & 0 & \cdots \\ 0 & 0 & \cdots \\ \cdots & & \\ 1 & 1 & \cdots \end{pmatrix}}^{\text{Members of set 2 indexed by } j}$$

Traveling Salesman Problem

The Traveling Salesman problem is a classical problem in Operations Research, and has received considerable attention in the literature. It has vast applications in sequencing series of jobs or routes. The Traveling Salesman problem is as follows:

> Starting from his hometown, a traveling salesman wants to visit a series of cities just once, and finally return to his hometown. The problem is to determine the best sequence for visiting these cities so that the total cost (total distance or total time traveled) is minimized.

Despite the simplicity of the problem's scope, the solution to this problem is very challenging and falls among one of the most computationally intensive combinatorial problems (discussed further in Chapter 11). To clarify this problem, consider the following example.

Example

A cargo airline based in Atlanta (ATL) wants to determine the sequence of flights to cities in its network such that the total distance flown in its cycle is minimized. A restriction to this operation is that the flight sequences must start and end in

Atlanta. The cities in the airline's network, and their distances are presented in Table 2.4.

This case can be formulated as the Traveling Salesman problem. We define the following binary decision variable:

$$x_{i,j} = \begin{cases} 1 \text{ if city } j \text{ should immediately follow city } i \\ 0 \text{ otherwise} \end{cases}$$

Table 2.4 Sequence of flights to cities in cargo airline network

		1	2	3	4	5	6	7
		ATL	ORD	CVG	HOU	LAX	MON	JFK
1	ATL	-	702	454	842	2396	1196	864
2	ORD		-	324	1093	2136	764	845
3	CVG			-	1137	2180	798	664
4	HOU				-	1616	1857	1706
5	LAX					-	2900	2844
6	MON						-	396
7	JFK							-

The objective function is therefore to minimize the total distances flown:

$$\text{Minimize } 702x_{1,2} + 454x_{1,3} + \ldots$$

The first set of constraints is to make sure that each city is visited only once. For example, for Atlanta we have:

$$x_{1,1} + x_{2,1} + x_{3,1} + x_{4,1} + x_{5,1} + x_{6,1} + x_{7,1} = 1$$

We write similar constraints for the other six cities.

The second set of constraints must route the aircraft after visiting a city. Without these constraints, the aircraft will be stuck in one city. The constraint to route the aircraft after visiting Atlanta, for example, is as follows:

$$x_{1,1} + x_{1,2} + x_{1,3} + x_{1,4} + x_{1,5} + x_{1,6} + x_{1,7} = 1$$

We write similar constraints for the other six cities as well.

Solving this problem generates the following solutions:

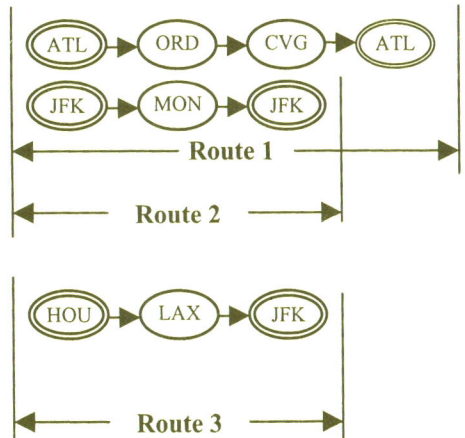

Figure 2.18 Solution showing three disjoint sequences or sub-tours

This solution shows three disjointed sequences. It does not offer the expected complete tour sequence among all of the seven cities. This is a common difficulty with the Traveling Salesman problem. Instead of one tour of all the cities, the solution generates sub-tours. To address this difficulty, the common approach is to prevent the formation of sub-tours. First, the problem is solved, and then we add additional constraints to break these sub-tours, if they are formed. As an example, we have the JFK-MON-JFK sub-tour in our solution. To break this sub-tour we add the following constraint in our model:

$$x_{6,7} + x_{7,6} \leq 1$$

We solve the problem once again, adding this new constraint. The following solution is generated:

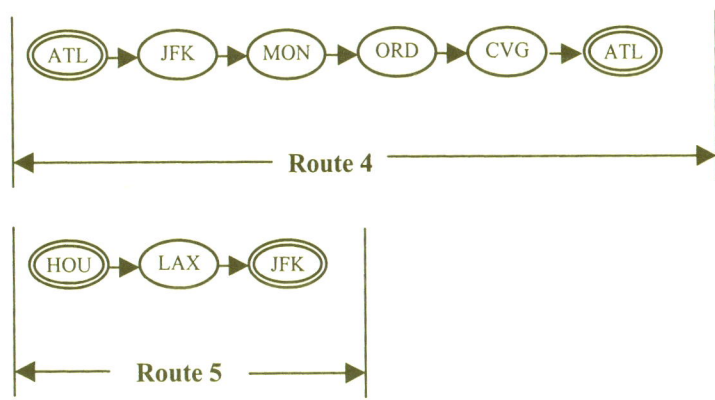

Figure 2.19 Solution showing two sub-tours after adding first breaking constraint

We now have two sub-tours. Hence, we add the following constraint to break the second sub-tour:

$$x_{5,4} + x_{4,5} \leq 1$$

Adding this constraint results in the following complete tour solution, presented in Table 2.5.

Table 2.5 Final tour sequence of flights with distances

Origin	Destination	Miles
ATL	CVG	454
CVG	JFK	664
JFK	MON	396
MON	ORD	764
ORD	LAX	2136
LAX	HOU	1616
HOU	ATL	842
	TOTAL	6872

The general model for the Traveling Salesman Problem, adapted from Ignizio and Cavalier (1994), is as follows:

Sets
N = Members' cities

Index
i, j = Index for cities

Parameters
$c_{i,j}$ = Cost of traveling from city i to city j

Decision Variable
$$x_{i,j} = \begin{cases} 1 \text{ if city } j \text{ follows city } i \\ 0 \text{ otherwise} \end{cases}$$

The integer programming model is as follows:

Objective Function
$$Min \sum_{i \in N} \sum_{j \in N} c_{i,j} x_{i,j} \tag{2.18}$$

Subject to

$$\sum_{j \in N} x_{i,j} = 1 \quad \text{for all } i=1,..., N \tag{2.19}$$

$$\sum_{i \in N} x_{i,j} = 1 \quad \text{for all } j=1,..., N \tag{2.20}$$

$$t_i - t_j + N x_{i,j} < N-1 \quad \text{for } i,j = 2,3,..,N \tag{2.21}$$

In this model, the objective function (2.18) seeks to minimize the total traveling cost. The set of constraints (2.19) ensure that each city i is followed by exactly one city j. Similarly, the set of constraints (2.20) ensure that each city j is visited exactly once. The set of constraints (2.21) impose the restriction on the sub-tours. Variables t_i and t_j are arbitrary fixed numbers used for breaking the sub-tours.

References

Ahuja, R., Magnanti, T. and Orlin, J. (1993), *Network Flows, Theory, Algorithm and Applications*, Prentince-Hall.

Anderson, D., Sweeney, D. and Williams, T. (2003), *Quantitative methods for business*, 9th edition, South-Western.

Bazaraa, M., Jarvis, J. and Sherali, H. (1990), Linear programming and network flows, Wiley.

Hillier, F. and Lieberman, G. (2001), *Introduction to Operations Research*, 7th edition, McGraw Hill.

Ignizio, J. and Cavalier, T. (1994), *Linear Programming*, Prentice Hall.

Schrage, L. (1997), *Optimization modeling with Lindo*, 5th edition, Duxbury.

Winston, W. and Albright, C. (2001), *Practical Management Science*, second edition, Duxbury.

Winston, W. and Venkataramanan, M. (2003), *Introduction to Mathematical programming*, 4th edition, Duxbury.

Chapter 3

Flight Scheduling

Introduction

Flight scheduling is the starting point for all other airline planning and operations (Yu and Thengvall 2002). The flight schedule is a timetable consisting of what cities to fly to and at what times. An airline's decision to offer certain flights will mainly depend on market demand forecasts, available aircraft operating characteristics, available manpower, regulations, and the behavior of competing airlines. The number of airports and flight frequencies served by an airline usually expresses and measures the physical size of the airline network (Janic 2000). For large air carriers, the flight scheduling group and route development may contain more than 30 employees (Kuzminski 1999).

Table 3.1 shows a small portion of the daily flight schedule for Delta Air Lines. The level of detail in constructing the flight schedule varies among the airlines, but it will be a complete schedule for a full cycle (Grandeau et al. 1998). A cycle is normally one day for domestic and one week for international services.

The schedule construction phase begins with the route system. The cities in the airline network determine the route system. The economics of an air carrier are driven by its route system. All the short- and long-term costs attributed to fleet, avionics, labor contracts and operations are tied to the route systems of an airline. The marketing department plays an important role in the construction of this schedule. Before the 1978 Airline Deregulation Act, airlines had to fly routes as assigned by the Civil Aeronautics Board (CAB) regardless of the demand for the service! During this period, most airlines emphasized long point-to-point routes. Since deregulation, airlines have gained the freedom to choose which markets to serve and how often to serve them. This change has led to a fundamental shift in most airlines' routing strategies from point-to-point flights to hub-and-spoke oriented networks (Etschamaier and Mathaisel 1985).

The schedule construction phase is a rough first schedule, which requires extensive modification to be both operationally feasible and economically viable (Etschamaier and Mathaisal 1985).

Table 3.1 A sample flight schedule

Carrier Flight #	Depart Time	Airport	Arrive Time	Airport
Delta 442	6:20:00 AM	ATL	7:39:00 AM	MCO
Delta 171	6:25:00 AM	ATL	7:46:00 AM	DFW
Delta 193	8:55:00 AM	CVG	10:28:00 AM	ATL
Delta 353	4:35:00 PM	CVG	6:10:00 PM	ATL
Delta 267	5:45:00 AM	DFW	8:52:00 AM	ATL
Delta 1264	7:45:00 PM	DFW	10:53:00 PM	ATL
Delta 1981	3:00:00 PM	JFK	5:28:00 PM	ATL
Delta 137	5:30:00 PM	JFK	8:40:00 PM	LAX
Delta 292	7:00:00 AM	LAX	2:20:00 PM	ATL
Delta 1886	3:15:00 PM	LAX	10:28:00 PM	ATL
Delta 929	7:35:00 AM	MCO	9:13:00 AM	ATL
Delta 622	10:05:00 AM	MCO	11:35:00 AM	ATL
Delta 2246	8:20:00 AM	MIA	10:13:00 AM	ATL
Delta 858	5:20:00 PM	MIA	7:22:00 PM	ATL

Source: www.delta.com

Hub-and-Spoke

Most airlines adopt some variation of a hub-and-spoke system. Major carriers operate up to five hubs, while smaller ones typically have one hub located at the center of the region they serve. Each hub has a set of cities that it serves, normally referred to as spokes. Figure 3.1 shows an airline network with Chicago O'Hare and Washington Dulles as hubs.

Figure 3.1 A sample airline network with two hubs and nine spokes

Air carriers normally assign large capacity non-stop flights between their hubs. Smaller airplanes are assigned to hub-and-spoke flights. Major advantages for the airlines adopting hub-and-spoke operations include higher revenues, higher efficiency, and lower number of aircraft needed as compared to point-to-point operations. Disadvantages of these operations include discomfort to the passengers, as they may require multiple connecting flights at different hubs, congestions and delays at hub airports, and higher personnel and operational costs for the airlines (Radnoti 2002).

Route Development and Flight Scheduling Process

There are two types of route development activities: *strategic* and *tactical*. Strategic development focuses on future schedules which may range from a few months to ten years depending on the air carriers' policies. Strategic developments respond to major changes in both business and operational environments. Tactical strategies on the other hand focus on short-term changes to the schedule and routes, sometimes on a daily basis. This is done by constantly monitoring markets, competitors and operations. The tactical strategy includes adding, dropping flights, and making changes to city-pair markets and their frequencies.

The following section briefly describes the phases of developing a flight schedule and the decisions made at each phase.

60+ Months	36-12 Months	12-3 Months	4-1 Months
Long Range Planning	Market Evaluations	Schedule Optimization	Schedule Issues

Long Range Schedule Planning

- Fleet diversity;
- Manpower planning;
- Protecting hubs;
- Adding or changing hubs;
- Adequate facilities at airports.

Market Evaluations

- Frequency and time of service to each market;
- Adding new and dropping existing markets;
- Pricing policies;
- Predicting competitors' behaviors;
- Code-sharing agreements and alliances.

Schedule Optimization

- Developing initial schedule based on available fleet;
- Assigning aircraft to flights;
- Evaluating facilities and manpower capabilities.

Schedule Issues

- Crew issues;
- Arrival departure times;
- Maintenance issues.

As described earlier, flight schedule construction is the basis for all other operations. It is therefore important to include detailed airline operations in the process of flight scheduling. This, however, creates a complex system with a large number of variables in the model (Grosche et al. 2001). Due to its complexity it is almost impossible to formulate the complete scheduling construction problem as a mathematical model. As a result, the schedule construction process is performed through a structured planning process involving various parts of the airline. This planning process is decomposed into sub problems with less complexity, which are solved sequentially. Chapters 4 to 6 present these sub problems.

One of the major drawbacks of this approach is that an individual sub problem's solution might not be good for the overall airline operations. To overcome this difficulty, the process of flight scheduling is performed on a feedback system. That is, if the solution to some sub problems are not desirable, the flight schedules are altered to see the impact of such changes. Figure 3.2 shows the process of flight schedule development and the hierarchy of various phases of airline planning. The chapters to follow show how this process is done.

Load Factor and Frequency

Average load factor plays an important role in determining the frequency of flights between city pairs. Load factor is the average percentage of aircraft seats which are filled with passengers. The parameters affecting load factors include flight times, frequency, type of service and of course, fare levels. It should be noted that a higher load factor does not necessarily translate into higher revenues for the airlines. As an example, Table 3.2 shows the fares, expected demands and load factors for a 150-seat Airbus 320. According to this table, an 85% load factor generates higher revenues of more than 100% for the airline! Demand and revenue management will be further discussed in Chapter 8.

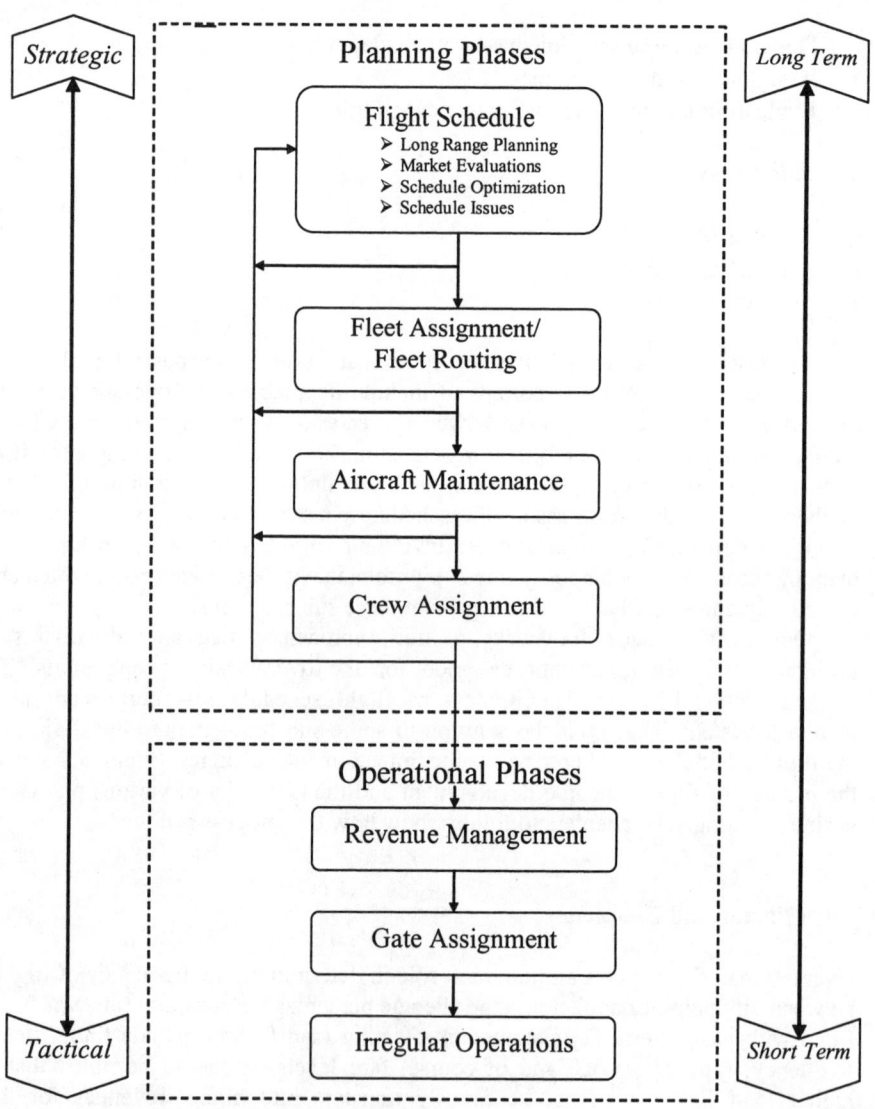

Figure 3.2 The hierarchy of airline planning

Table 3.2 Load factor and expected revenue

Average Fare	Expected Number of Passengers	Load Factor	Expected Revenue
$240	100	0.67	$24,000
$220	115	0.77	$25,300
$200	128	0.85	$25,600
$180	140	0.93	$25,200
$160	150	1.00	$24,000

The load factor is utilized to determine the frequency between city pairs. Let the forecasted daily number of passengers between two cities be *PAX* and the airline's policy on average load factor be *LF*. Further, let us assume the average aircraft capacity is *CAP*. Then the frequency (*FREQ*) of flights between these two cities is determined by:

$$FREQ = \frac{PAX}{CAP \times LF} \qquad (3.1)$$

As implied by the above equation, the load factor and frequency have an inverse relationship. It is up to the marketing and scheduling departments to actually assign these frequencies between city pairs to different times of the day/week.

Case Study

In this section a fictitious airline is presented. We will use this airline in the following chapters to introduce the various phases of planning within the airlines.

Ultimate Air is a new airline that provides service to the most important domestic business destinations from its hub at JFK in New York. The cities serviced from JFK are Boston (BOS), Los Angeles (LAX), San Francisco (SFO), Miami (MIA), Atlanta (ATL), Washington D.C. (IAD), and Chicago (ORD). Figure 3.3 shows the airline's network.

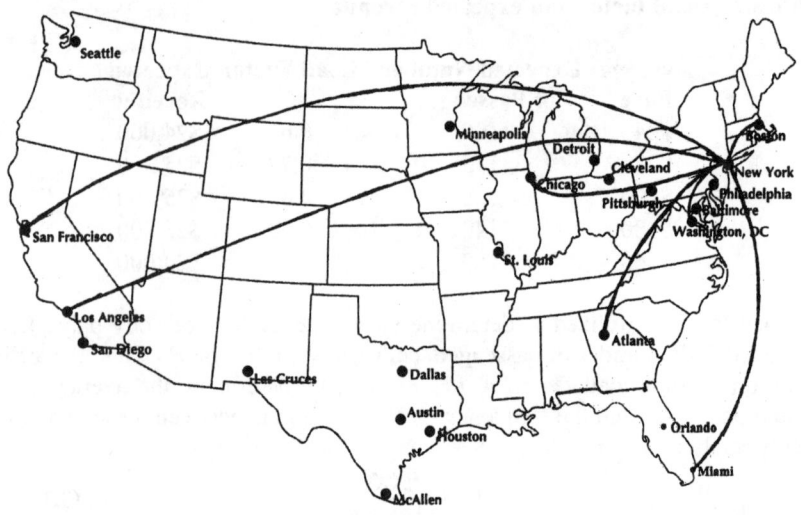

Figure 3.3 Ultimate Air route network

Based on forecasts, the airline's load factor policy, and marketing analysis, the airline has proposed providing three daily round trip flights from JFK to each city in the network. It has also developed a first draft of its schedule for the next quarter. The complete flight schedule route, incorporating the 42 flights per day, is presented in Table 3.3. All the arrival and departure times are local times.

Table 3.4 presents the demand distribution for each flight as well as distances between cities. It is assumed that demand for each flight is normally distributed with the given means and standard deviations.

Table 3.3 Flight schedule for Ultimate Air

Flight No.	Origin	Departure Time	Destination	Arrival Time	Flight Hours
101	LAX	5:00	JFK	13:30	5.5
104	SFO	5:05	JFK	13:35	5.5
116	BOS	6:15	JFK	7:45	1.5
140	JFK	6:20	IAD	7:20	1
125	JFK	7:25	SFO	9:55	5.5
107	ORD	7:30	JFK	10:30	2
122	JFK	7:35	LAX	10:05	5.5
137	JFK	7:40	BOS	9:10	1.5
110	ATL	8:10	JFK	10:40	2.5
119	IAD	8:15	JFK	9:15	1
113	MIA	9:10	JFK	12:10	3
131	JFK	9:30	ATL	12:00	2.5
102	LAX	9:45	JFK	18:15	5.5
105	SFO	9:50	JFK	18:20	5.5
117	BOS	10:00	JFK	11:30	1.5
128	JFK	10:05	ORD	11:05	2
134	JFK	10:35	MIA	13:35	3
141	JFK	12:00	IAD	13:00	1
108	ORD	12:20	JFK	15:20	2
138	JFK	12:30	BOS	14:00	1.5
111	ATL	13:10	JFK	15:40	2.5
120	IAD	14:25	JFK	15:25	1
114	MIA	14:30	JFK	17:30	3
132	JFK	14:35	ATL	17:35	2.5
118	BOS	15:00	JFK	16:30	1.5
129	JFK	15:05	ORD	16:05	2
135	JFK	15:10	MIA	18:10	3
142	JFK	15:15	IAD	16:15	1
103	LAX	15:20	JFK	23:50	5.5
106	SFO	15:25	JFK	23:55	5.5
126	JFK	15:30	SFO	18:00	5.5
123	JFK	16:00	LAX	18:30	5.5
109	ORD	17:10	JFK	20:10	2
112	ATL	18:00	JFK	20:30	2.5
133	JFK	18:05	ATL	20:35	2.5
136	JFK	18:10	MIA	21:10	3
115	MIA	18:15	JFK	21:15	3
121	IAD	18:30	JFK	19:30	1
124	JFK	19:00	LAX	21:30	5.5
127	JFK	20:00	SFO	22:30	5.5
130	JFK	21:00	ORD	22:00	2
139	JFK	21:30	BOS	23:00	1.5

We will use the above flight schedule as a basis to derive the planning for the fleet assignment as well as aircraft routing in the following chapters.

Table 3.4 Destination in miles, demand means and standard deviations for Ultimate Air network

Flight No.	Origin	Destination	Distance (Miles)	Demand	Standard Deviation
101	LAX	JFK	2475	175	35
102	LAX	JFK	2475	182	36
103	LAX	JFK	2475	145	29
104	SFO	JFK	2586	178	35
105	SFO	JFK	2586	195	39
106	SFO	JFK	2586	162	32
107	ORD	JFK	740	165	33
108	ORD	JFK	740	182	36
109	ORD	JFK	740	170	34
110	ATL	JFK	760	191	38
111	ATL	JFK	760	171	34
112	ATL	JFK	760	165	33
113	MIA	JFK	1090	198	39
114	MIA	JFK	1090	182	36
115	MIA	JFK	1090	168	33
116	BOS	JFK	187	115	23
117	BOS	JFK	187	146	29
118	BOS	JFK	187	120	24
119	IAD	JFK	228	135	27
120	IAD	JFK	228	109	21
121	IAD	JFK	228	98	19
122	JFK	LAX	2475	150	30
123	JFK	LAX	2475	145	29
124	JFK	LAX	2475	125	25
125	JFK	SFO	2586	148	29
126	JFK	SFO	2586	138	27
127	JFK	SFO	2586	121	24
128	JFK	ORD	740	132	26
129	JFK	ORD	740	129	25
130	JFK	ORD	740	117	23
131	JFK	ATL	760	168	33
132	JFK	ATL	760	160	32
133	JFK	ATL	760	191	38
134	JFK	MIA	1090	165	33
135	JFK	MIA	1090	184	36
136	JFK	MIA	1090	192	38
137	JFK	BOS	187	147	29
138	JFK	BOS	187	135	27
139	JFK	BOS	187	146	29
140	JFK	IAD	228	105	21
141	JFK	IAD	228	115	23
142	JFK	IAD	228	118	23

References

Etschamaier, Maximilian, M. and Mathaisel, D. (1985), Airline Scheduling: An Overview, *Transportation Science*, 9(2), pp. 127-138.

Grandeau, S., Clarke, M. and Mathaisel, D. (1998), Operations research in the airline industry – edited by Gang Yu. *Kluwer International Series*, pp. 312-336.

Grosche, T., Heinzl, A. and Rothlauf, F. (2001), A conceptual approach for simultaneous flight schedule construction with genetic algorithms, *EvoWorkshop 2001*, Springer-Verlag, Berlin/Heidelberg.

Janic, M. (2000), Air transport system analysis and modeling capacity, quality of service and economics, Gordon and Breach Science Publishers, Amsterdam.

Kuzminski, P. (1999, September), Air carrier route system and schedule, *MITRE Center for Advanced Aviation System Development*.

Radnoti, G. (2002), Profit Strategies for Air Transportation, *Aviation Week Books*, pp. 297-324, McGraw-Hill, New York.

Yu, G. and Thengvall, B. (2002), Optimization in the Airline Industry, *Handbook of Applied Optimization* – edited by P.M. Pardalos and M.G.C. Resende, Oxford University Press, New York.

Chapter 4

Fleet Assignment

Introduction

Following the construction of a flight schedule and its corresponding network, the next step is to assign the right fleet-type to each flight in the schedule. The task of fleet assignment is to match each aircraft-type in the fleet with a particular route in the schedule. It should be noted that this phase of planning concerns only fleet-type and not a particular aircraft. The goal of fleet assignment is to assign as many flight segments as possible in a schedule to one or more fleet-types, while optimizing some objective function and meeting various operational constraints (Abara 1989). Fleet assignment should not be confused with fleet planning (Clark 2001). Fleet planning is a strategic decision normally undertaken when an airline is conceived, and concerns the number and type of aircraft needed for operation. It entails the process of acquiring the appropriate aircraft-types in order to serve the anticipated markets based on the airline's strategic plan. Fleet planning addresses fleet-size and fleet-mix. In fleet assignment, however, we assume that the airline is operational with the existing aircraft in its fleet, and the problem is to assign a fleet-type to each flight-leg.

Airlines typically operate a number of different fleet-types. Each fleet-type has different characteristics and costs, such as seating capacity, landing weights, crew, maintenance and fuel (Yu and Thengvall 1999). Table 4.1 presents the fleet diversity

Table 4.1 Fleet diversity for select airlines

Airline	B 737	A319/ 320/321	A300	A330	A340	B757	B767	B777	B747	DC10/ MD11	MD 80/90	F-100	Total
Air France	30	115	1	10	22	-	-	25	35	-	-	-	238
America West	44	80	-	-	-	13	-	-	-	-	-	-	137
American Airlines	77	-	31	-	-	150	77	46	-	-	338	53	772
British Airways	42	68	-	-	-	13	19	43	57	-	-	-	242
Delta Air Lines	135	-	-	-	-	108	106	8	-	8	136	-	501
Lufthansa	59	73	12	15	32	64	-	-	30	21	-	-	306
Northwest	-	135	-	2	-	-	-	-	32	-	158	-	327
Southwest	383	-	-	-	-	-	-	-	-	-	-	-	383
United	145	153	-	-	-	91	51	55	26	-	-	-	521
US Airways	116	95	-	10	-	31	10	-	-	-	-	-	262

Source: Air Transport Intelligence, 2003 – http://www.rati.com

for select airlines. Maintenance cost is a major factor that persuades airlines to be less diverse when planning for their fleet. Fleet diversity requires the airlines to have skilled crew and personnel for each fleet-type, plan for different maintenance checks, and have less flexibility in replacing an aircraft when a failure occurs.

Indicator Definitions

Before addressing the mathematical model for the Fleet Assignment problem, some terms commonly used in the airline industry are explained:

ASM (ASK): Available Seat Miles (Kilometers), represents the annual airline capacity, or supply of seats, and refers to the number of seats available for passengers during the year multiplied by the number of miles (kilometers) that those seats are flown.

RPM (RPK): Revenue Passenger Miles (Kilometers), represents the total number of paying passengers flown on all flight segments multiplied by the number of miles (kilometers) that those passengers are flown. RPM (RPK) is considered to be demand. It should be noted that RPM (RPK) is typically less than ASM (ASK). This is because airlines will not have all the seats filled on all flight segments during the entire year.

Yield: Yield is how much an airline makes per revenue passenger mile (kilometer). In other words, yield is how much an airline makes per mile (kilometer) on each seat sold. Yield is obtained by dividing total operating revenue divided by RPM (RPK).

RASM (RASK): Revenue Per Available Seat Mile (Kilometer), or "unit revenue" represents how much an airline made across all the available seats that were supplied. RASM (RASK) is calculated by dividing the total operating revenue by available seat mile (kilometer) or ASM (ASK). Since ASM (ASK) is generally larger than RPM (RPK), yield has a higher value than RASM (RASK).

CASM (CASK): Cost Per Available Seat Mile (Kilometer) or "unit cost" is the average cost of flying one seat for a mile (kilometer). CASM (CASK) is calculated by dividing the total operating cost by ASM (ASK).

Table 4.2 presents the above measures for select US airlines differentiated by market segments.

Table 4.2 US major carriers' unit revenues and expenses, by region

Carrier	ASM 0	RPM 0	RASM (cents)	CASM (cents)	Yield (cents)
Alaska	**17,922,378**	**12,251,858**	**9.24**	**10.18**	**12.25**
Domestic	16,285,702	11,023,424	9.57	10.5	12.81
Latin	1,636,676	1,228,434	6.92	7.95	8.84
America West	**26,545,129**	**19,079,952**	**7.51**	**9.51**	**10.24**
Domestic	25,979,593	18,679,485	7.46	9.5	10.14
Latin	565,536	400,467	9.02	9.63	13.26
ATA	**14,989,548**	**11,000,096**	**6.51**	**6.34**	**6.16**
Domestic	12,152,584	9,158,074	6.32	5.89	7.22
Atlantic	2,836,964	1,842,022	7.23	8.11	1.49
American	**153,009,076**	**106,204,606**	**9.5**	**11.32**	**12.5**
Domestic	103,908,494	71,403,281	9.4	11.53	12.65
Atlantic	20,295,974	14,902,309	8.77	10.43	10.44
Latin	23,649,773	16,159,790	10.34	11.09	13.64
Pacific	5,154,835	3,739,226	10.82	10.08	10.22
Continental	**81,202,692**	**58,763,517**	**9.47**	**10.73**	**11.68**
Domestic	53,840,744	39,055,715	9.82	12.15	12.63
Atlantic	14,162,942	10,527,675	8.49	8.07	8.59
Latin	9,503,884	6,835,194	9.84	8.59	12.11
Pacific	3,695,122	2,344,933	6.54	5.04	7.53
Delta	**141,419,284**	**97,662,652**	**9.25**	**10.54**	**11.66**
Domestic	107,279,363	73,255,141	9.63	10.69	12.41
Atlantic	23,393,438	17,715,403	7.73	10.09	8.62
Latin	7,025,910	4,127,514	8.33	9.73	11.36
Pacific	3,720,573	2,564,594	8.44	10.84	8.53
Northwest	**98,524,030**	**73,253,479**	**9.47**	**10.34**	**10.59**
Domestic	58,856,556	42,024,614	10.46	11.18	12.9
Atlantic	14,121,795	11,146,032	6.94	7.61	7.39
Pacific	25,545,679	20,082,833	8.21	9.6	7.28
Southwest	**65,623,088**	**44,663,524**	**7.59**	**7.29**	**11.41**
Domestic	65,623,088	44,663,524	7.59	7.29	11.41
United	**164,847,910**	**116,635,053**	**9.34**	**11.4**	**10.86**
Domestic	100,837,182	70,632,035	9.93	12.02	12.25
Atlantic	24,008,608	17,805,938	8.14	10.18	8.94
Latin	7,332,441	4,981,730	8.13	10.59	9.93
Pacific	32,669,679	23,215,350	8.55	10.46	8.4
US Airways	**66,720,095**	**45,964,013**	**12.11**	**14.74**	**13.62**
Domestic	55,879,046	37,967,208	12.98	16.05	14.69
Atlantic	9,132,413	6,711,714	6.52	7.15	7.08
Latin	1,708,636	1,285,091	10.25	9.81	12.66

Source: First Equity Aviation & Aerospace Almanac, 2003 – ECLAT Consulting

The above figures are total measures across the various market segments and all fleets. Table 4.3 shows average ASM, RPM and CASM by fleet-type.

Table 4.3 US major carriers' unit revenues and expenses, by fleet-type

Aircraft	ASM	RPM	CASM
A300-600	749,266	483,523	5.50
A319	428,284	278,843	4.50
A320-200	518,301	360,241	4.50
A321	741,194	492,437	3.00
B737-200	266,352	176,271	6.20
B737-300	394,850	248,375	5.70
B737-400	412,051	273,492	7.10
B737-500	295,569	192,774	6.50
B737-700	572,830	394,469	3.10
B737-800/900	509,172	338,763	3.90
B747-200	1,551,265	1,053,479	5.50
B747-400	1,892,889	1,298,440	4.60
B757-200	686,353	463,571	4.40
B767-200	719,460	471,907	5.50
B767-300	1,016,661	648,583	4.20
B777-200	1,451,275	945,293	3.70
DC-10-30	1,224,904	882,189	4.20
DC-10-40	524,910	401,717	5.10
DC-10-10	886,418	727,173	3.70
MD-11	1,254,607	691,432	5.50
MD-80	394,273	257,716	5.90

Source: First Equity Aviation & Aerospace Almanac, 2003 – ECLAT Consulting

Mathematical Model

A major concern in formulating the fleet assignment problem is keeping track of the fleet at different stations (airports) at any given point in time. Fortunately, researchers have developed an ingenious method of adopting a time-space network to formulate this problem. Figure 4.1 shows such a network for five cities.

This approach facilitates the process of modeling the Fleet Assignment problem. The above time-space network presents the airports as columns, and times of the day as rows. In this network, the arcs (arrows) are the flights, and nodes represent the arrival/departure of a flight segment at a specific airport, at a specific time of the day. A wrap around arc is a ground arc which connects the last node to the first node in a given city. These arcs normally represent the aircraft that stay overnight in an airport, and connect the last arrival to the next day's departure flight (see Figure 4.1).

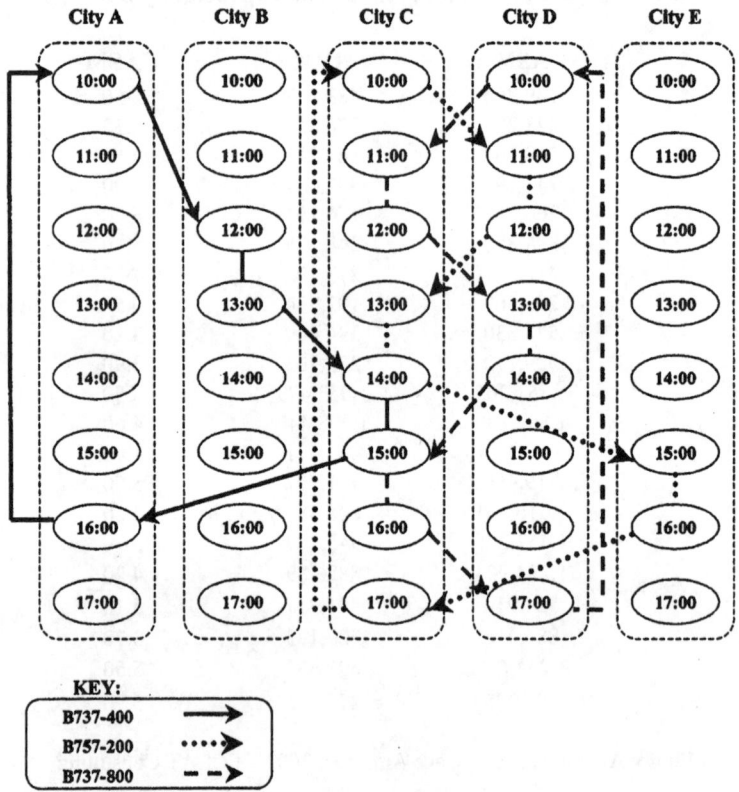

Figure 4.1 An example of a time-space network

The Fleet Assignment problem is basically formulated as a multi-commodity network problem (see Chapter 2). Each node represents supply/demand, which can be satisfied through a diverse fleet. The model seeks to minimize the total cost or maximize the net profit by assigning the most appropriate fleet-type to each flight-leg. The constraints ensure that each flight is assigned to a particular fleet-type, and that the number of aircraft for each fleet does not exceed the number of available aircraft. Other side-constraints may include curfew, range, noise, forced-turns, maintenance and user-specific restrictions.

In the mathematical model presented here, the objective function represents the total cost of the network, which we seek to minimize. These costs include two parts: operating costs and spill costs.

Operating Costs

The operating costs for a flight mainly depend on the type of the fleet assigned to that flight and are determined as follows:

Operating costs of a flight = CASM of the fleet × distance × number of seats on the aircraft

Let us return to the fleet diversity for Ultimate Air, in the case study we introduced in Chapter 3. We have two types of fleet, namely Boeing 738-800 and Boeing 757-200. The seating capacities for these two fleet types are 162 and 200 seats, respectively. Furthermore, we have the following information for this airline:

- Cost per available seat mile (CASM) for B737-800 and B757-200 are $0.042 (4.2 cents) and $0.044 (4.4 cents) respectively;
- Revenue per available seat mile (RASM) is $0.15 (15 cents).

Using the above information we can determine the operating cost for each flight in the Ultimate Air schedule for the two fleet-types. As an example, for flight 122 (JFK-LAX), the distance between JFK and LAX is 2,475 miles (see Table 3.4 Chapter 3). Hence, the operating costs of this flight for the two fleet-types are:

operating cost for B737-800=$.042 × 2475 × 162=$16,839.90

operating cost for B757-200=$.044 × 2475 × 200=$21,780.00

Passenger Spill Costs

An important issue in assigning fleet-types to flights is the passenger demand for each flight segment. Assigning large capacity aircraft to flights with low demand leads to low utilization and consequently low load factor for the airline. On the other hand, assigning small aircraft to flight-legs with high demand leads to passenger spills. Spill is the degree of average demand, which exceeds the capacity offered. The spill cost is therefore the revenue of lost passengers due to insufficient aircraft capacity.

Let us once again consider flight 122 (JFK-LAX) in our Ultimate Air case study. Our historical data for flight 122 shows that the demand for this flight is normally distributed with a mean of 150 and a standard deviation of 30 passengers (see Table 3.4, Chapter 3). Figure 4.2 shows the demand distribution for this flight. The shaded areas show the probability of passenger spills for the two fleet-types. The spill is basically the truncation of the demand distribution beyond the aircraft capacity.

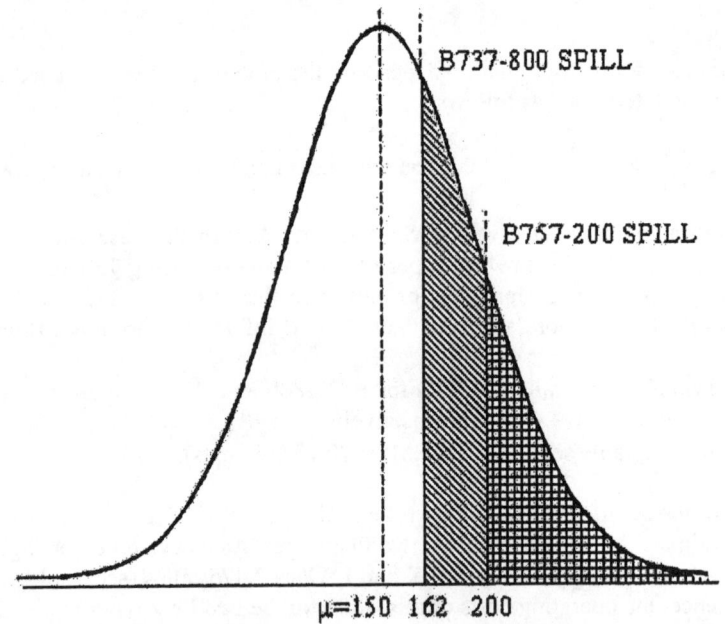

Figure 4.2 Demand distribution and passenger spills

The expected spill costs are determined as follows:

Expected spill cost for a fleet = expected number of passenger spill × RASM × distance

The expected number of passenger spill is calculated as follows:

Expected number of passenger spill = $\int_{c}^{\infty}(x-c)f(x)dx$

In the above equation, c is the fleet capacity and $f(x)$ is the probability distribution function of the demand. The above integral can be obtained using mathematical software (e.g., MAPLE) or some calculators. It is possible and perhaps easier to use a Microsoft Excel spreadsheet to approximate the above expected number of passenger spill using simulation. The following steps show the Excel functions used to determine the expected number of spilled passengers for a B737-800 fleet-type with 162 seats.

- Cell A1: NORMINV (RAND(),150,30)
- Cell B1: IF (A1>162,A1-162,0)

Cell A1 randomly generates a demand from normal distribution with a mean of 150 and a standard deviation of 30. Cell B1 checks to see if the demand in cell

A1 exceeds 162 seats. If it does, then cell B1 is assigned to their difference (i.e., passenger spill), otherwise passenger spill is zero. The above two cells are copied and pasted (downward) many times (we used 10,000 replications). The average of column B, denoted by AVERAGE(B:B), calculates the expected number of spilled passengers.

Using the above approximation method, the expected numbers of passenger spill (rounded to two decimal places) for the two fleet-types are as follows:

- Expected passenger spill for B737-800 with 162 seat capacity = 6.91
- Expected passenger spill for B757-200 with 200 seat capacity = .60

The expected spill costs for the two fleet-types are therefore calculated as:

- Expected spill costs for B737-800 = $6.91 \times .15 \times 2475 = \$2565.33$
- Expected spill costs for B757-200 = $.60 \times .15 \times 2475 = \$222.75$

It may seem that this model attempts to assign larger capacity fleet type to all flights since expected shortages are penalized, but excess capacity or surplus seats are not. It should be noted that the larger capacity fleet type was already penalized when we calculated the operating costs above.

Recapture Rate

A closely related topic to passenger spill is the recapture rate. The recapture rate represents the percentage of passengers that were spilled, but could be accommodated or recaptured on other flights by the same airline. That is, if a passenger cannot get a seat on a specific flight, the airline offers earlier or later flights (in some cases with bonuses) to the passenger for consideration. If the passenger accepts the offer for another flight, then this passenger is considered to be recaptured. The recapture rate among the major airlines is typically very high. This is due to high flight frequencies offered by these airlines as well as other marketing incentives such as frequent-flyer programs.

Returning to our Ultimate Air case study, due to low flight frequencies, the recapture rate is low. Let us assume that this rate is 15% for this airline. This rate means that 85% of passengers who request a reservation for a flight on Ultimate Air and are denied such a request, are lost to other airlines. Therefore the expected spill costs for the two fleet-types for flight 122 are:

- Expected spill costs for B737-800 = $\$2565.33 \% .85 = \$2180.31$
- Expected spill costs for B757-200 = $\$222.75 \% .85 = \$189.34$

Now we can determine the total cost of assigning a fleet-type to a flight-leg by adding the operating and spill costs. The total cost for each fleet when assigned to flight 122 is:

- Total cost of assigning B737-800 to flight 122 = $16,839.90+$2,180.31 = $19,020.21
- Total cost of assigning B757-200 to flight 122 = $21,780.00+$189.34 = $21,969.34

Similarly, we determine the total costs for all other flights.

Objective Function

To setup the objective function for Ultimate Air, we need to first select our decision variables in a way that addresses the assignment of the fleet-type to the flight-leg. The following decision variables are commonly adopted for fleet assignment models.

$$x_{i,j} = \begin{cases} 1 \text{ if flight } i \text{ is assigned to fleet-type } j \\ 0 \text{ otherwise} \end{cases}$$

$G_{k,j}$ = integer decision variable representing number of aircraft of fleet-type j on ground at node k

In the binary decision variable $x_{i,j}$ index i represents the flight-leg (42 flight-legs for Ultimate Air), while index j represents the fleet-type (for our case study we have two fleet-types). For simplicity in our notation, we designate j to take the value 1 for B737-800, and the value 2 for B757-200 fleets. Based on this definition, $x_{101,1}$ represents the binary decision variable for flight 101 assigned to a B737-800 fleet. Similarly, $x_{101,2}$ represents the same flight, but assigned to fleet-type 2 (i.e., B757-200) etc. Decision variable $G_{k,j}$ will be used to address the set of constraints for aircraft balance. This set of decision variables will be discussed later in the constraints section.

The objective function is basically to minimize the total cost by assigning the most appropriate fleet-type to flights as follows:

$$\text{Minimize } 21485.26x_{101,1} + 22556x_{101,2} + 24222.37x_{102,1} + 23556x_{102,2} + \ldots + 1558.42x_{142,1} + 2006x_{142,2}$$

Constraints

There are three main sets of constraints in the fleet assignment model. They are discussed as follows:

Flight Cover

The first set of constraints is what is typically known as flight cover. Flight cover implies that each flight must be flown. To cover a flight, the sum of all the decision variables representing that flight must add up to 1. As an example, to cover flight 101 in our Ultimate Air case study, we write:

$$x_{101,1} + x_{101,2} = 1$$

This constraint ensures that flight 101 is covered. Furthermore, the flight will be covered by only one type of fleet since the sum of binary decision variables adds up to 1. Only one of the two binary decision variables in this constraint will take a value of 1, forcing the other variable to be zero. We write similar constraints for all other 41 flights in our case study.

Aircraft Balance

The next set of constraints concerns the aircraft balance or equipment continuity within the fleets. This set of constraints ensures that an aircraft of the right fleet-type will be available at the right place at the right time. Earlier, we introduced the concept of a time-space network. We adopt this concept to address this set of constraints. Referring to Figure 4.1, each node represents an arrival or departure. Recall that each node represents a specific time at a specific airport. So, the number of aircraft at any node changes with respect to an instant before that node. To clarify this, consider Figure 4.3. In this figure we have an arrival node. Just before this node, there were two aircraft (of the same fleet-type) at the airport. After this arrival, we now have another aircraft (of the same fleet-type again) added to those already at this airport.

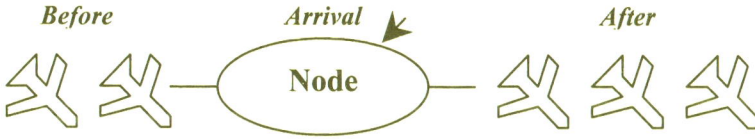

Figure 4.3 Example of aircraft balance

Referring to Figure 4.3, the set of constraints for aircraft balance or equipment continuity states that:

> Number of aircraft of a particular fleet-type on the ground at a node = Number of aircraft in that fleet on the ground an instant before that node + arrival of aircraft of the same fleet type at that node − (minus) departures of aircraft of the same fleet type from that node.

For example, the balance constraint for the node in Figure 4.3 is:

> Number of aircraft at this node = 2 (number of aircraft before this node) + 1 (one arrival) − 0 (no departure from this node) = 3.

Adopting this approach, we can now write the constraints for balance for each airport in our Ultimate Air case study. Let us consider LAX. The flights in and out of LAX (extracted from our flight schedule in Chapter 3) are as shown in Table 4.4.

Table 4.4 Arrival/departure flights for LAX

Flight No.	Origin	Departure Time	Destination	Arrival Time	Duration of Flight (Hrs.)
101	LAX	5:00	JFK	13:30	5.5
102	LAX	9:45	JFK	18:15	5.5
122	JFK	7:35	LAX	10:05	5.5
103	LAX	15:20	JFK	23:50	5.5
123	JFK	16:00	LAX	18:30	5.5
124	JFK	19:00	LAX	21:30	5.5

Figure 4.4 presents this table as a time-space network, similar to Figure 4.3 discussed earlier.

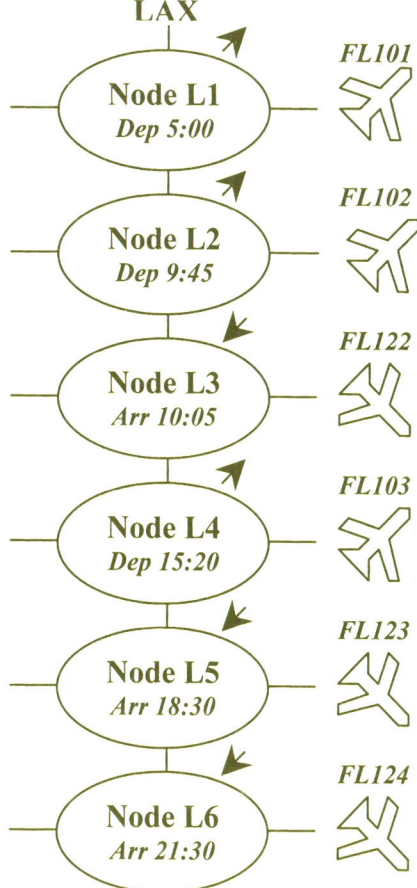

Figure 4.4 Time-space network for LAX

We have two types of fleet. We use the decision variable $G_{k,j}$ to write the constraints for aircraft balance for each fleet type. Let us first consider the B737-800 fleet-type. Based on Figure 4.4 above, the first node at LAX is at L1. The number of B737-800 aircraft at this node, based on the rule for balance, is basically the number of aircraft carried over from the previous day (wrap-around arc from node L6) minus one departure (flight 101), so:

$$G_{L1,1} = G_{L6,1} - x_{101,1}$$

At node L2 (see Figure 4.4), we have another departure (flight 102) so:

$$G_{L2,1} = G_{L2,1} - x_{102,1}$$

At node L3, we have an arrival (flight 122), therefore:

$$G_{L3,1} = G_{L2,1} + x_{122,1}$$

Similarly, we write the other three constraints for this fleet-type as follows:

$$G_{L4,1} = G_{L3,1} - x_{103,1}$$
$$G_{L5,1} = G_{L4,1} + x_{123,1}$$
$$G_{L6,1} = G_{L5,1} + x_{124,1}$$

The constraints for the B757-200 fleet are similar to the B737-800 as follows:

$$G_{L1,2} = G_{L6,2} - x_{101,2}$$
$$G_{L2,2} = G_{L2,2} - x_{102,2}$$
$$G_{L3,2} = G_{L2,2} + x_{122,2}$$
$$G_{L4,2} = G_{L3,2} - x_{103,2}$$
$$G_{L5,2} = G_{L4,2} + x_{123,2}$$
$$G_{L6,2} = G_{L5,2} + x_{124,2}$$

Similarly, we write the balance constraints for all other airports in the schedule. There are 42 flights in our Ultimate Air case study. Each flight has a departure and an arrival. We have two fleet types. Therefore, the total number of constraints for aircraft balance is 168 (42×2×2).

Fleet Size

This set of constraints is adopted to ensure that the number of aircraft within each fleet does not exceed the available fleet-size. To address this, we must count the number of aircraft that are grounded overnight for that fleet-type at different airports. Referring to Figure 4.4, the last node, L6 (originating node for wrap-around arc) represents the total number of aircraft in LAX at the end of the day. For this airport, $G_{L6,1}$ represents the total number of grounded B737-800 aircraft in LAX overnight. Similarly, the number of grounded B757-200 aircraft at the last node in LAX is $G_{L6,2}$.

The total number of B737-800 aircraft in our network is therefore:

$$G_{L6,1} + G_{S6,1} + G_{B6,1} + G_{O6,1} + G_{A6,1} + G_{I6,1} + G_{M6,1} + G_{J42,1}$$

In the above expression, the integer variables represent the number of aircraft at the last nodes at LAX, SFO, BOS, ORD, ATL, IAD, MIA and JFK, respectively. Note that at JFK, we have 42 daily flights arriving or departing from this airport. Therefore, the last node is represented as $J42$.

Similarly, the total number of B757-200 aircraft in our network is:

$$G_{L6,2} + G_{S6,2} + G_{B6,2} + G_{O6,2} + G_{A6,2} + G_{I6,2} + G_{M6,2} + G_{J42,2}$$

In our case study, Ultimate Air, assume that we have 9 and 6 aircraft in our B737-800 and B757-200 fleets, respectively. We can now incorporate these constraints into our model as follows:

$$G_{L6,1} + G_{S6,1} + G_{B6,1} + G_{O6,1} + G_{A6,1} + G_{I6,1} + G_{M6,1} + G_{J42,1} \leq 9$$
$$G_{L6,2} + G_{S6,2} + G_{B6,2} + G_{O6,2} + G_{A6,2} + G_{I6,2} + G_{M6,2} + G_{J42,2} \leq 6$$

Since there are only two fleet-types, there are only two constraints in this set.

Solution to Fleet Assignment Problem

The linear integer program for fleet assignment for Ultimate Air has 252 (84 binary and 168 integer) variables and 212 constraints. Using an optimization software, the solution to this problem generates a minimum daily cost of fleet assignment of $410,612.57. The following table shows the number of aircraft for each fleet-type staying overnight at each airport. These numbers represent the right number of aircraft for each fleet-type at the right airport at the right time.

Table 4.5 Optimal number of aircraft grounded overnight at each airport

Airports	737-800 Fleet	757-200 Fleet
Los Angeles (LAX)	2 aircraft	1 aircraft
San Francisco (SFO)	2 aircraft	-
Boston (BOS)	1 aircraft	-
New York (JFK)	3 aircraft	2 aircraft
Chicago (ORD)	1 aircraft	-
Atlanta (ATL)	-	1 aircraft
Washington D.C. (IAD)	-	-
Miami (MIA)	-	2 aircraft

The following table presents the assignment of each flight to either one of the two fleet-types.

Table 4.6 Fleet assignment for Ultimate Air

Flight No.	Origin	Destination	Fleet Type
101	LAX	JFK	737-800
104	SFO	JFK	737-800
116	BOS	JFK	737-800
140	JFK	IAD	737-800
125	JFK	SFO	757-200
107	ORD	JFK	737-800
122	JFK	LAX	737-800
137	JFK	BOS	737-800
110	ATL	JFK	757-200
119	IAD	JFK	737-800
113	MIA	JFK	757-200
131	JFK	ATL	757-200
102	LAX	JFK	737-800
105	SFO	JFK	757-200
117	BOS	JFK	737-800
128	JFK	ORD	737-800
134	JFK	MIA	737-800
141	JFK	IAD	737-800
108	ORD	JFK	737-800
138	JFK	BOS	757-200
111	ATL	JFK	757-200
120	IAD	JFK	737-800
114	MIA	JFK	757-200
132	JFK	ATL	737-800
118	BOS	JFK	757-200
129	JFK	ORD	737-800
135	JFK	MIA	757-200
142	JFK	IAD	737-800
103	LAX	JFK	737-800
106	SFO	JFK	737-800
126	JFK	SFO	737-800
123	JFK	LAX	737-800
109	ORD	JFK	737-800
112	ATL	JFK	737-800
133	JFK	ATL	757-200
136	JFK	MIA	757-200
115	MIA	JFK	737-800
121	IAD	JFK	737-800
124	JFK	LAX	737-800
127	JFK	SFO	737-800
130	JFK	ORD	737-800
139	JFK	BOS	737-800

Note that the above solution only shows the assignment of flights to fleet-type. It does not show the assignment of flights to any specific aircraft within each fleet.

Fleet Assignment

This type of assignment is called aircraft routing, which will be discussed in the next chapter.

Scenario Analysis

In this section we address some questions pertaining to the number of aircraft and different fleet combinations.

Case 1

It may be of interest to us to see what is the minimum number of aircraft to cover all flights. In this case, the objective function is modified to minimize the total number of aircraft. Therefore, the fleet size constraints are deleted from the set of constraints and become the objective function as follows:

$$Min\ G_{L6,1} + G_{S6,1} + G_{B6,1} + G_{O6,1} + G_{A6,1} + G_{I6,1} + G_{M6,1} + G_{J42,1} + \\ G_{L6,2} + G_{S6,2} + G_{B6,2} + G_{O6,2} + G_{A6,2} + G_{I6,2} + G_{M6,2} + G_{J42,2}$$

Running this integer/linear program results in 13 aircraft of which nine are 737-800 and four are 757-200. According to this result, the minimum number of aircraft that are needed to fly the published Ultimate Air flights is 13. However, as we will discuss in Chapter 5, the number of aircraft needed are more than 13.

Case 2

In this case, we evaluate various combinations of the two fleets. In our Ultimate Air example, we assumed that we have nine 737 and six 757 aircraft. We now change this combination to see its impact on total daily cost. Table 4.7 shows different costs associated with different number of aircraft combinations between the two fleet-types.

Table 4.7 Total daily cost for various aircraft combinations

Number of B737-800 aircraft	Number of B757-200 aircraft	Total daily cost
8	7	$411,890
6	9	$416,116
11	4	$409,362
15	0	$413,970
0	15	$446,364

Fleet Assignment Model (FAM)

We now formally present the general mathematical model for the Fleet Assignment problem. The following model, referred to as the basic Fleet Assignment Model (FAM), is a simplified version of FAM proposed by Hane et al., 1995.

Sets

F = Set of flights
K = Set of fleet-types
C = Set of last-nodes, representing all nodes with aircraft grounded overnight at an airport in the network
M = Number of nodes in the network

Index

i = Flight Index
j = Index for fleet
k = Index for nodes

Parameters

$C_{i,k}$ = Cost of assigning fleet-type k to flight i

N_j = Number of available aircraft in fleet-type j.

$S_{i,k} = \begin{cases} +1 \text{ if flight i is an arrival at node k} \\ -1 \text{ if flight i is a departure from node k} \end{cases}$

Decision Variables

$x_{i,j} = \begin{cases} 1 \text{ if flight } i \text{ is assigned to fleet-type } j \\ 0 \text{ otherwise} \end{cases}$

$G_{k,j}$ = integer decision variable representing number of aircraft of fleet-type j on ground at node k

The integer linear programming model is as follows:

$$\text{Min} \sum_{j \in J} \sum_{i \in F} c_{i,j} x_{i,j} \qquad (4.1)$$

Subject to

$$\sum_{j \in J} x_{i,j} = 1 \qquad \text{for all } i \in F \qquad (4.2)$$

$$G_{k^-,j} + \sum_{i \in F} S_{i,k} x_{i,j} = G_{k,j} \qquad \text{for all } k \in M \text{ and } j \in J \qquad (4.3)$$

$$\sum_{k \in C} G_{k,j} \leq N_j \qquad \text{for all } j \in J \qquad (4.4)$$

$$x_{i,j} \in \{0,1\} \qquad \text{for all } i \in F \text{ and } j \in J \qquad (4.5)$$

$$G_{k,j} \in Z^+ \qquad \text{for all } k \in M \text{ and } j \in J \qquad (4.6)$$

In the above model, the objective function in (4.1) seeks to minimize the total cost of assigning the various fleet-types to all the flights in the schedule.

Constraints (4.2) are the flight cover constraints to ensure that each flight is flown by one type of fleet.

Constraints (4.3) are the aircraft balance constraints. The number of aircraft for any fleet-type at any node is the number of aircraft of that fleet-type just before that node (represented in the model by $G_{k^-,j}$) plus the arrivals (represented by $S_{i,k}$ taking a value +1) minus the departures (represented by $S_{i,k}$ taking a value of -1).

Set of constraint (4.4) represents the fleet-size. The number of aircraft in fleet type j, should not exceed the available number of aircraft in that fleet (N_j).

Constraints (4.5) and (4.6) represent the binary and integer status of the decision variables. Z^+ is the set of positive integer numbers.

For other mathematical approaches to fleet assignment models see, for example, Jarrah, et al. (2000), Ioachim, et al. (1999), Barnhart, et al. (1998), and Subramanian et. al. (1994).

References

Abara, J. (1989), Applying integer linear programming to the fleet assignment problem. *INTERFACES* 19(4), 20-28.

Barnhart, C., Boland, N., Clarke, L.W., Johnson, E.L., Nemhauser, G.L. and Shenoi, R. (1998), Flight string modeling for aircraft fleeting and routing. *Transportation Science* 32(3), 208-220.

Clarke, P. (2001), *Buying the Big Jets*, Ashgate Publishing.

Hane, C.A., Barnhart, C., Johnson, E.L., Marsten, R.E., Nemhauser, G.L. and Sigismondi, G. (1995), The fleet assignment problem: solving a large-scale integer program. *Mathematical Programming* 70, 211-232.

Ioachim, I., Desrosiers, J., Soumis, F. and Belanger, N. (1999), Fleet assignments and routing with schedule synchronization. *European Journal of Operations Research* 119, 75-90.

Jarrah, A., Goodstein, J. and Narasimhan, R. (2000), An efficient airline re-fleeting model for the incremental modification of planned fleet assignments. *Transportation Science* 34(4), 349-363.

Subramanian, R., Schrr, R.P. Jr., Quillinan, J.D., Wiper, D.S. and Marsten, R.E. (1994), Coldstart: fleet assignments at Delta Air Lines. *INTERFACES* 24(1), 104-120.

Talluri, K.T. (1996), Swapping applications in a daily airline fleet assignment. *Transportation Science* 30(3), 237-248.

Yu, G. and Thengvall, B.G. (1999), Airline Optimization. *Applied Optimization*, Pardalos, P.M. and Resende, M.G.C. (eds.) Oxford University Press.

Chapter 5

Aircraft Routing

Introduction

The solution obtained from the fleet assignment in the previous chapter identifies the flow of fleet through the network. However, it does not identify which specific aircraft from that fleet is assigned to each flight leg. Aircraft routing is the process of assigning each individual aircraft (referred to as tail number) within each fleet to flight legs. The aircraft routing is also referred to as aircraft rotation, aircraft assignment or tail assignment. The major goal of this assignment problem is to maximize the revenue or minimize operating cost with the following considerations (Clarke et al. 1997, Gopalan and Talluri 1998):

- Flight coverage: Each flight leg must be covered by only one aircraft.
- Aircraft load balance: The aircrafts must have balanced utilization loads.
- Maintenance requirements: Not all the airports that an airline flies to have the capability to perform maintenance checks on all fleet types. The airlines normally have maintenance bases, typically at their hubs, for different fleet types. The maintenance consideration is to ensure that the aircrafts are flown through the network in a manner that allows them to receive the required maintenance checks at the right time and at the right base.

Aircraft Tail Number

Aircraft are normally distinguished by their tail registration numbers. A tail number is a unique serial number assigned to each aircraft for each airline in each country. The airlines choose to organize their tail suffix numbering system according to their convenience. In the US, aircraft tail numbers consist of a prefix 'N' and five alpha/numeric characters. These characters normally represent the fleet type, the sequence of aircraft in the fleet and the airline. As an example, in N723TZ, N is the country code for USA, 723 is used to designate the particular aircraft, and TZ is the airline code for ATA. For other countries, the tail number typically consists of two characters designating the country, followed by three alpha/numeric characters. For example, a Boeing 747-4H6 for Malaysia Airlines, may be assigned the tail number 9M-MPK, where 9M is the country code designator for Malaysia (Airliners.Net, 2004).

Maintenance Requirements

Maintenance activities are the backbone of a successful and profitable airline company. In the airline industry, the role of maintenance is to provide safe, airworthy, on-time aircraft every day. An airline generally has a diverse fleet of aircraft. Each fleet type has a predetermined maintenance program established by the aircraft manufacturer and the Federal Aviation Administration (FAA). Aircraft maintenance must be planned and performed according to the prescribed procedures and standards.

The FAA mandates that the airlines perform four types of aircraft maintenance, commonly referred to as A-, B-, C- and D-checks. These checks vary in scope, duration and frequency. The most common maintenance check is the A-check, which involves a visual inspection of major systems. The FAA mandates that airlines perform the A-checks approximately every 60 flight hours. This is equivalent to five or six operating days. If an aircraft does not receive the A-check within this period, it is grounded until such maintenance is performed. B-checks involve a thorough visual inspection and lubricating all moving parts. This type of maintenance is performed every 300 to 600 hours of flight. C- and D-checks involve taking the aircraft out of service, and are performed every one to four years.

The airline maintenance practices, however, are generally more stringent. They perform A-checks every three to four days. The time required to perform an A-check on an aircraft is about 3 to 10 hours. The A-checks are normally performed between 10pm and 8am while the aircraft is on the ground. Therefore, the aircraft routing problem must ensure that the aircraft is at the right base at the right time for this maintenance. Most aircraft routing models incorporate these A-checks in their formulations since they are routine.

Mathematical Approach

The fleet assignment problem for Ultimate Air, solved in Chapter 4, assigned various flight legs to our 737 and 757 fleet-types. These flight legs are presented in Tables 5.1 and 5.2 for the 737-800 and 757-200 aircraft types, respectively. This section develops a mathematical model so as to assign specific aircraft within the two fleet-types to each of the flight legs.

There are several approaches to modeling aircraft routing (see Talluri 1998, Arguello et al. 1997, Bard et al. 2001, Paoletti 1998, Desaulniers 1997, Bartholomew et al. 2003).

Table 5.1 B737-800 Fleet Assignment

Flight No.	Origin	Departure Time	Destination	Arrival Time	(Hrs.)	Fleet Type
101	LAX	5:00	JFK	13:30	5.5	737-800
104	SFO	5:05	JFK	13:35	5.5	737-800
116	BOS	6:15	JFK	7:45	1.5	737-800
140	JFK	6:20	IAD	7:20	1	737-800
107	ORD	7:30	JFK	10:30	2	737-800
122	JFK	7:35	LAX	10:05	5.5	737-800
137	JFK	7:40	BOS	9:10	1.5	737-800
119	IAD	8:15	JFK	9:15	1	737-800
102	LAX	9:45	JFK	18:15	5.5	737-800
117	BOS	10:00	JFK	11:30	1.5	737-800
128	JFK	10:05	ORD	11:05	2	737-800
134	JFK	10:35	MIA	13:35	3	737-800
141	JFK	12:00	IAD	13:00	1	737-800
108	ORD	12:20	JFK	15:20	2	737-800
120	IAD	14:25	JFK	15:25	1	737-800
132	JFK	14:35	ATL	17:35	2.5	737-800
129	JFK	15:05	ORD	16:05	2	737-800
142	JFK	15:15	IAD	16:15	1	737-800
103	LAX	15:20	JFK	23:50	5.5	737-800
106	SFO	15:25	JFK	23:55	5.5	737-800
126	JFK	15:30	SFO	18:00	5.5	737-800
123	JFK	16:00	LAX	18:30	5.5	737-800
109	ORD	17:10	JFK	20:10	2	737-800
112	ATL	18:00	JFK	20:30	2.5	737-800
115	MIA	18:15	JFK	21:15	3	737-800
121	IAD	18:30	JFK	19:30	1	737-800
124	JFK	19:00	LAX	21:30	5.5	737-800
127	JFK	20:00	SFO	22:30	5.5	737-800
130	JFK	21:00	ORD	22:00	2	737-800
139	JFK	21:30	BOS	23:00	1.5	737-800

Table 5.2 B757-200 Fleet Assignment

Flight No.	Origin	Departure Time	Destination	Arrival Time	(hrs.)	Fleet type
125	JFK	7:25	SFO	9:55	5.5	757-200
110	ATL	8:10	JFK	10:40	2.5	757-200
113	MIA	9:10	JFK	12:10	3	757-200
131	JFK	9:30	ATL	12:00	2.5	757-200
105	SFO	9:50	JFK	18:20	5.5	757-200
138	JFK	12:30	BOS	14:00	1.5	757-200
111	ATL	13:10	JFK	15:40	2.5	757-200
114	MIA	14:30	JFK	17:30	3	757-200
118	BOS	15:00	JFK	16:30	1.5	757-200
135	JFK	15:10	MIA	18:10	3	757-200
133	JFK	18:05	ATL	20:35	2.5	757-200
136	JFK	18:10	MIA	21:10	3	757-200

The mathematical approach adopted in this chapter is a modified model proposed by Kabbani and Patty (1992) as they applied it to American Airlines. This approach uses a set partitioning formulation (see Chapter 2 for definition) to determine the daily routing for each aircraft. In this approach, all possible valid aircraft routings are generated. These routings are represented as rows, and the flights as columns in the set-partition matrix. We then seek to identify the best routes that cover all flights while meeting maintenance opportunities, turn around-time, routing cycles, etc.

Maintenance Routing

The mathematical approaches to the aircraft routing problem typically assume that the same schedule is repeated daily over a period of time. A similar approach is adopted for the weekends, when the frequency of flights is lower.

In our Ultimate Air example, we assume that we have the maintenance facilities for the two fleet-types only at our hub, i.e., JFK. Each aircraft must be routed so that it stays overnight at JFK, at most after three days of operation.

Valid Routings

For a routing to be valid, it needs to incorporate the turn-around time. Turn-around time is the minimum time needed for an aircraft from the time it lands until it is ready to depart again. This time includes the taxi into the gate, unloading passengers and baggage, cleaning, inspections, boarding new passengers, loading new baggage, etc. The turn around time varies from 20 minutes to 1 hour among airlines.

Aircraft Routing

In the Ultimate Air example, we assume that the turn-around time is 45 minutes. According to this turn-around time, a valid routing cannot include flight 113 followed by flight 138 in our 757 fleet. As we see in Table 5.2, flight 113 arrives at JFK at 12:10, while flight 138 departs JFK at 12:30. The turn-around time is 20 minutes, which is less than our minimum of 45 minutes.

Routing Cycles

For Ultimate Air, we assume that only routes with three-day closed cycles are valid. A closed cycle is when an aircraft starts from a city, and at the end of the three-day cycle, ends up at that same city to start another cycle. This requirement is included to better present the process of aircraft routing by reducing the number of potential routings. It should be noted that closed cycles are not typically a requirement for airlines. The airlines usually develop monthly aircraft routing with no closed cycles. That is, an aircraft has the potential to have a totally different routing every day with no pattern or cycles as long as it receives the required maintenance checks.

Figure 5.1 presents a valid sample of a one-day routing. The aircraft stays at JFK every night and repeats the cycle every day. This routing provides a maintenance opportunity for the aircraft every night. It should be noted that each time an aircraft is at a maintenance station, it does not necessarily mean that maintenance is performed on the aircraft.

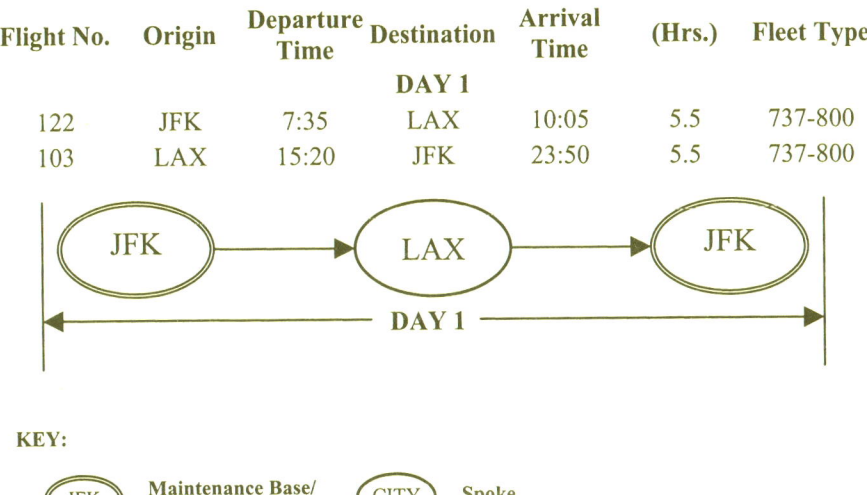

Figure 5.1 B737-800 one-day routing

Figure 5.2 presents a valid sample of a two-day routing. The aircraft starts-off at LAX, spends the first night at JFK, and on the second night is routed back to LAX.

Flight No.	Origin	Departure Time	Destination	Arrival Time	Flight Hrs	Fleet Type
			DAY 1			
101	LAX	5:00	JFK	13:30	5.5	737-800
129	JFK	15:05	ORD	16:05	2	737-800
109	ORD	17:10	JFK	20:10	2	737-800
			DAY 2			
140	JFK	6:20	IAD	7:20	1	737-800
120	IAD	14:25	JFK	15:25	1	737-800
127	JFK	19:00	LAX	21:30	5.5	737-800

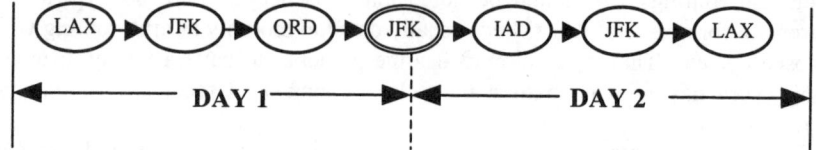

Figure 5.2 B737-800 two-day routing

Similarly, Figure 5.3 presents a valid sample of a three-day routing, where the aircraft is routed to JFK at the end of the second day for maintenance.

Figure 5.4 shows an invalid routing, as it does not provide a maintenance opportunity at JFK after three days of operations.

Note that in our Ultimate Air example, we only selected one, two and three-day routing cycles. The airlines may extend these routings to weekly routings, etc. with a maintenance opportunity every three days.

Route Generators

For the proposed set portioning mathematical model, we begin by generating all possible valid aircraft routings. It may seem that generating these routes is a very difficult and tedious task. This is certainly the case if we want to enumerate all possible routes manually. Automated systems are used extensively to generate and filter these routes for the airlines in a relatively short time.

Recall that in our Ultimate Air example, we are only interested in three-day cycle aircraft routings. That is, after three days the aircraft ends up at the same airport from which it started-out on the first day of its cycle, only to repeat another cycle. To provide the maintenance opportunity for the aircraft, the routing must include at least one overnight stay at JFK.

A computer program was developed to generate three-day-cycle aircraft routes. These aircraft are routed through a series of feasible flights. This route then selects at least one overnight stay in JFK at the end of the first and/or second

Aircraft Routing 65

Flight No.	Origin	Departure Time	Destination	Arrival Time	Flight Hrs	Fleet Type
			DAY 1			
107	ORD	7:30	JFK	10:30	2	737-800
141	JFK	12:00	IAD	13:00	1	737-800
120	IAD	14:25	JFK	15:25	1	737-800
124	JFK	19:00	LAX	21:30	5.5	737-800
			DAY 2			
101	LAX	5:00	JFK	13:30	5.5	737-800
129	JFK	15:05	ORD	16:05	2	737-800
109	ORD	17:10	JFK	20:10	2	737-800
			DAY 3			
140	JFK	6:20	IAD	7:20	1	737-800
119	IAD	8:15	JFK	9:15	1	737-800
141	JFK	12:00	IAD	13:00	1	737-800
120	IAD	14:25	JFK	15:25	1	737-800
130	JFK	21:00	ORD	22:00	2	737-800

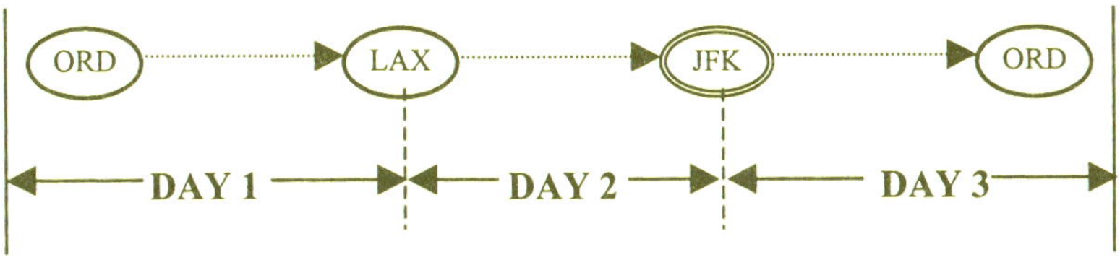

ORD ········▶ LAX ········▶ JFK ········▶ ORD

◀──── DAY 1 ────▶◀──── DAY 2 ────▶◀──── DAY 3 ────▶

Figure 5.3   B737-800 three-day routing

day for maintenance. At the end of the third day, the aircraft is routed back to the airport where it started its three-day cycle. The steps or pseudo-code for this program are as follows:

- Read the flight numbers, departure and arrival cities, as well as departure and arrival times for a set of flights assigned to a specific fleet (identified by fleet routing);
- Create all possible valid one-day routings incorporating turn-around times – place in a file;
- Attach each feasible one day routing of this file to all other one-day routings in this file. Do this step twice to create three-day routings – place in a file;
- Examine each element of this three-day file according to the following criteria:
  It starts and ends at the same city;
  Each day, flights start at the city where the aircraft ended the day before;
  An overnight stay at JFK occurs at least once.
- Add each element that satisfies all the above conditions to a file of potential valid three-day routing candidates.

Flight No.	Origin	Departure Time	Destination	Arrival Time	Flight Hrs	Fleet Type
			DAY 1			
116	BOS	6:15	JFK	7:45	1.5	757-200
131	JFK	9:30	ATL	12:00	2.5	757-200
111	ATL	13:10	JFK	15:40	2.5	757-200
133	JFK	18:05	ATL	20:35	2.5	757-200
			DAY 2			
110	ATL	8:10	JFK	10:40	2.5	757-200
138	JFK	12:30	BOS	14:00	1.5	757-200
118	BOS	15:00	JFK	16:30	1.5	757-200
139	JFK	21:30	BOS	23:00	1.5	757-200
			DAY 3			
116	BOS	6:15	JFK	7:45	1.5	757-200
131	JFK	9:30	ATL	12:00	2.5	757-200
111	ATL	13:10	JFK	15:40	2.5	757-200
139	JFK	21:30	BOS	23:00	1.5	757-200
			DAY 4			
117	BOS	10:00	JFK	11:30	1.5	757-200
138	JFK	12:30	BOS	14:00	1.5	757-200
118	BOS	15:00	JFK	16:30	1.5	757-200
133	JFK	18:05	ATL	20:35	2.5	757-200
			DAY 5			
110	ATL	8:10	JFK	10:40	2.5	757-200
138	JFK	12:30	BOS	14:00	1.5	757-200
118	BOS	15:00	JFK	16:30	1.5	757-200
136	JFK	21:30	BOS	23:00	1.5	757-200

BOS → ATL → BOS → BOS → ATL → BOS

← DAY 1 →|← DAY 2 →|← DAY 3 →|← DAY 4 →|← DAY 5 →

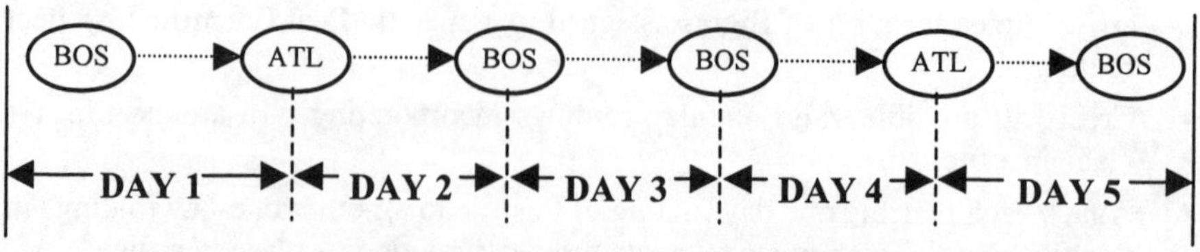

Figure 5.4 B757-200 five-day routing with no opportunity for overnight maintenance at the JFK hub

This program also generates the mathematical model suitable for linear programming software. Running this program generated a total of 6221 and 455 valid three-day routings for the 737-800 and 757-200 fleet-types, respectively! Tables 5.3 and 5.4 show samples of five valid three-day routings for each fleet-type, respectively.

Table 5.3 Sample three-day routing for B757-200 fleet

SAMPLE	DAY 1	DAY 2	DAY 3	Utilization (Hrs.)
High Utilization					
Routing sample #1 City Pair Routing	FLT 131 JFK-ATL	FLT 111 ATL-JFK	FLT 133 JFK-ATL	FLT 110 ATL-JFK	FLT 138 JFK-BOS	FLT 118 BOS-JFK	FLT 133 JFK-ATL	FLT 110 ATL-JFK	FLT 138 JFK-BOS	FLT 118 BOS-JFK	21
Routing sample #2 City Pair Routing	FLT 110 ATL-JFK	FLT 138 JFK-BOS	FLT 118 BOS-JFK	FLT 136 JFK-MIA	FLT 113 MIA-JFK	FLT 138 JFK-BOS	FLT 118 BOS-JFK	FLT 133 JFK-ATL	17
Medium Utilization					
Routing sample #3 City Pair Routing	FLT 136 JFK-MIA	FLT 113 MIA-JFK	FLT 133 JFK-ATL	FLT 110 ATL-JFK	FLT 138 JFK-BOS	FLT 118 BOS-JFK	14
Routing sample #4 City Pair Routing	FLT 133 JFK-ATL	FLT 111 ATL-JFK	FLT 131 JFK-ATL	FLT 111 ATL-JFK	10
Low Utilization					
Routing sample #5 City Pair Routing	FLT 138 JFK-BOS	FLT 118 BOS-JFK	FLT 138 JFK-BOS	FLT 118 BOS-JFK	6

Table 5.4 Sample three-day routing for B737-800 fleet

SAMPLE	DAY 1				DAY 2				DAY 3				(Hrs.)
	High Utilization												
Routing sample #1	FLT 122	FLT 103			FLT 122	FLT 103			FLT 122	FLT 103			33
City Pair Routing	JFK-LAX	LAX-JFK			JFK-LAX	LAX-JFK			JFK-LAX	LAX-JFK			
Routing sample #2	FLT 137	FLT 117	FLT 123		FLT 101	FLT 129	FLT 109	FLT 139	FLT 116	FT 134	FLT 115		27
City Pair Routing	JFK-BOS	BOS-JFK	JFK-LAX		LAX-JFK	JFK-ORD	ORD-JFK	JFK-BOS	BOS-JFK	JFK-MIA	MIA-JFK		
	Medium Utilization												
Routing sample #3	FLT 109				FLT 137	FLT 127			FLT 104	FLT 129	FLT 109	FLT 130	20.5
City Pair Routing	ORD-JFK				JFK-BOS	JFK-SFO			SFO-JFK	JFK-ORD	ORD-JFK	JFK-ORD	
Routing sample #4	FLT 101	FLT 139			FLT 116				FLT 122				14
City Pair Routing	LAX-JFK	JFK-BOS			BOS-JFK				JFK-LAX				
	Low Utilization												
Routing sample #5	FLT 116	FLT 141	FLT 120	FLT 139	FLT 116				FL 137				8
City Pair Routing	BOS-JFK	JFK-IAD	IAD-JFK	JFK-BOS	BOS-JFK				JFK-BOS				

Mathematical Model for 757-200 Fleet

Since the 757-200 fleet has a lower number of flights and routing candidates, we start by developing the mathematical model for this fleet. The mathematical model for the 737-700 fleet will follow later on in this chapter.

Decision Variable

The goal of the aircraft routing problem is to assign routes to individual aircraft within a specific fleet-type. In the previous section, we generated all possible valid routings. Each of these routings qualifies as a candidate to be assigned to an aircraft. Among all these candidates, we need to identify those routings that optimize the objective function and satisfy the constraints.

We define the following binary decision variable to find such routings for the 757-200 fleet.
Let:

$$x_j = \begin{cases} 1 \text{ if route } j \text{ is selected}, \quad j=1,2,..,455 \\ 0 \text{ otherwise} \end{cases}$$

Objective Function

The available mathematical models use different measures for the objective function (see list of references). Some of these measures include:

- *Maximizing through values* Non-stop flights are the first choice for passengers. In the absence of such point-to-point flights, passengers must take connecting flights. A through flight is a type of connection that uses the same aircraft for the flights involved. This enables the passengers to remain onboard rather than deplaning, searching for and walking to their connecting flight gate. Through flights are especially attractive in very busy airports. Accordingly, the airlines place higher values on those routes with favorable through flights (Jarrah and Strehler 2000, Clarke et al. 1997).

- *Minimizing cost* Airlines may assign pseudo-costs to penalize routings which they consider to be unfavorable. These unfavorable routes may include bad connection times and circular routings where aircraft are isolated by flying between a small number of spokes, etc. (Armacost 2002).

- *Maximizing maintenance opportunities* Those routings that provide multiple maintenance opportunities for the aircraft are given higher weights.

Assume that in our Ultimate Air case, the objective is to select those routings that maximize maintenance opportunities. To clarify this, let us return to the five sample routings for the 757-200 fleet presented in Table 5.3. The first three samples have only one overnight stay at JFK in their three-day cycles. Accordingly, the coefficients of these variables in the objective function are one. For sample routings four and five, this coefficient is two since they have two overnight stays at JFK in their three-day cycles. We determine these coefficients for every routing candidate for this fleet. Again, a simple computer program can easily generate these coefficients. Thus, the objective function for our 757-200 fleet is as follows:

$$\text{Maximize} \sum_{j=1}^{455} m_j x_j$$

where m_j is the number of maintenance opportunities for route j. The values that m_j can take are 1, 2 and 3. Note that as we discussed earlier, we have 455 valid routings for the flights assigned to 757-200 fleet.

Constraints for 757-200 Fleet

There are two sets of constraints for our aircraft routing problem: Flight coverage and the number of available aircraft.

Flight Coverage

Each routing candidate covers a certain number of flights in its three-day cycle. each flight must be covered everyday. For example, sample 1 routing candidate for the 757-200 fleet in Table 5.3 covers flights 131,111 and 133 in day one. In day two it covers flights 110,138, 118 and 133. This routing covers flight 131 in its first day but does not fly this flight in the other two days of its cycle. Accordingly, other routings with flight 131 in their second and third day of cycles must be selected to cover flight 131 in all three days. To cover all flights, we need one constraint for each flight for each day of the three-day cycle.

As an example, searching through all the 454 routing candidates, only six candidates actually cover flight 125 in different days as shown in Table 5.5.

Table 5.5 Routing candidates for flight 125

Routing Candidate Variable	Day 1	Day 2	Day 3
x_1	125	105	131-111
x_2	125	105	138-118
x_3	131-111	125	105
x_4	138-118	125	105
x_5	105	131-111	125
x_6	105	138-118	125

According to the above variable notations, to cover flight 125 in day one, we write the following constraint:

$$x_1 + x_2 = 1$$

This is because flight 125 in day one only appears in x_1 and x_2. Similarly, to cover this flight in the second and third day of the cycle we write the following constraints:

$$x_3 + x_4 = 1 \quad \text{flight 125 in the second day of the cycle}$$
$$x_5 + x_6 = 1 \quad \text{flight 125 in the third day of the cycle}$$

Similarly, we write the constraints for the other 11 flights. The total number of constraints required to cover all daily flights for the 757-200 fleet is 36 (12 flights × three-day cycles).

Number of Available Aircraft

Each routing candidate is a three-day cycle assigned to one aircraft. Accordingly, the number of selected routes should not exceed the available number of aircraft in the fleet. In Chapter 4, we assumed that we have six 757-200 aircraft. The following constraint ensures that the number of selected routes is limited to the number of aircraft.

$$x_1 + x_2 + \ldots + x_{455} \leq 6$$

Solution for 757-200 Fleet

We used an optimization software to solve this problem. The program reported that there is no feasible solution to this problem! That is, with six aircraft, it is not possible to cover all the flights assigned to the 757-200 fleet. However, our fleet routing in Chapter 4 showed that these six aircraft are capable of flying all our 757-200 flights through the network. So, why do we not get a feasible solution to our aircraft routing problem? The answer is that the fleet routing problem does not consider the following constraints that we have imposed on our aircraft routings.

- A 45-minute turn-around time;
- Three-day closed cycles, starting and ending at the same city. This requirement eliminates a large number of potential routes that are perfectly acceptable to the airlines. Note that we introduced this arbitrary requirement to reduce the problem size.
- At least one overnight stay at JFK for maintenance in a three-day period.

These additional constraints in the aircraft routing problem result in an infeasible solution for our problem.

To search for solutions, we eliminated the constraint on the number of available aircraft to see how many aircraft would be needed to fly the proposed daily schedule of flights assigned to the 757-200 fleet. We ran this model, and the feasible solution now required eight aircraft. The solution for this model with eight aircraft is presented in Table 5.6.

It should be noted that the airlines frequently face this problem where the existing aircraft are not enough to fly the proposed schedule. The main reason is that the arriving and departing flights in the proposed schedule are not synchronized.

Let us look at our Ultimate Air schedule and set of constraints. We see that the two flights, 125 and 105, have only two routing candidates each day while other flights have many possibilities (see the constraints for flight 125 in the previous section). Table 5.7 examines these two flights more closely.

Table 5.6 Feasible eight aircraft solution for the 757-200 fleet

Routing	DAY 1	DAY 2	DAY 3
1	125	105	138-118
2	110	131-111	131-111-133
3	113-135	114	136
4	131-111-136	113-136	114
5	105	138-118	125
6	114	135	113-135
7	138-118	125	105
8	133	110-133	110

Table 5.7 Flights 105 and 125

Flight No.	Origin	Departure Time	Destination	Arrival Time	(Hrs.)	Fleet Type
125	JFK	7:25	SFO	9:55	5.5	757-200
105	SFO	9:50	JFK	18:20	5.5	757-200

Looking at Table 5.7, we see that flight 125 arrives at SFO at 9:55. The aircraft flying this flight cannot fly flight 105 because it departs at 9:50. Therefore, the aircraft flying flight 125 to SFO is stranded for the entire day, as there are no other flights from SFO for it to connect with. So, one possibility that the operations team at Ultimate Air may consider is to synchronize these two flights. To do this, we need to delay the departure time for flight 105 (or fly flight 125 earlier). If we delay flight 105 by one hour to incorporate our 45-minute turn-around time, then these two flights can be paired. The revised schedule for these two flights is shown in Table 5.8.

Table 5.8 Revised schedule for flight 105

Flight No.	Origin	Departure Time	Destination	Arrival Time	(Hrs.)	Fleet Type
125	JFK	7:25	SFO	9:55	5.5	757-200
105	SFO	10:50	JFK	19:20	5.5	757-200

With this revised schedule, the two flights, 125 and 105, can be paired. This change is incorporated into the route generator program and the revised three-day valid routes are generated. The process for developing the linear integer model is repeated, as described earlier. Solving the new model generates multiple optimal solutions with six available aircraft. Table 5.9 presents one of these solutions. As

Aircraft Routing

we see, the same routings are repeated every day of the three-day cycle, but in different sequences, which result in multiple optimum solutions.

Table 5.9 One of the optimal solutions with six aircraft

Routing	DAY 1	DAY 2	DAY 3
1	125-105	135	114
2	110-138-118-136	113	131-111-133
3	113	131-111-133	110-138-118-136
4	131-111-133	110-138-118-136	113
5	114	125-105	135
6	135	114	125-105

As this process has shown, changing the departure time for one flight results in a solution with two less aircraft. Furthermore, examining this solution more closely, we notice that the aircraft flying flights 113, 114 and 135 are also stranded at their respective destinations, away from the JFK hub, at the end of the day. Despite the fact that we are covering all our flights with the available six aircraft of the 757-200 fleet-type, it is possible to add more flights without needing more aircraft. Further synchronizing the arrival and departure times for these flights will further reduce number of aircraft needed.

The value of the objective function for this solution is nine. This represents the total number of aircraft grounded overnight at JFK over the three-day cycle. The check mark (✔) in Table 5.10 shows the overnight aircraft stays at JFK for the above solution.

Table 5.10 Overnight stays at JFK for the optimal solution

Routing	Night 1	Night 2	Night 3
1	✔		✔
2		✔	
3	✔		
4			✔
5	✔	✔	
6		✔	✔
Total	3	3	3

According to this solution, each night, three 757-200 aircraft stay at JFK for maintenance. Routes 1, 5 and 6 provide two maintenance opportunities each during their three-day cycles.

This process of changing arrival/departure times is very common among airlines. The initial schedule proposed by the marketing department and schedule-

74   *Airline Operations and Scheduling*

builders (Chapter 3) is submitted to the operations team for feasibility. The operations team provides feedback to the schedule-builders on operational feasibility and possible changes to the schedule. This feedback process continues until all parties are satisfied with the schedule.

Once the airline finds its routings to be feasible and satisfactory, it then assigns each route to a particular aircraft tail number. Note that in the above aircraft routing process, we are indifferent to the method used for assigning tail numbers to the selected routes. If, however, there are such influencing factors as aircraft age within the fleet, then the airline may use some rule/criteria for assigning specific tail numbers to routes.

Solution for 737-800 Fleet

The same mathematical model approach as described earlier for the 757-200 fleet is adopted for aircraft routing of the 737-800 fleet. Recall that we have nine aircraft in this fleet. Again, there are no feasible solutions to this aircraft routing problem with only nine aircraft. Relaxing this constraint, results in the solution presented in Table 5.11, which requires 12 aircraft.

Table 5.11   Solution for aircraft routing of 737-800 fleet with 12 aircraft

Routing	Day 1	Day 2	Day 3
1	101-142-121-139	116-134-115	140-119-128-108-124
2	116-134-115	126	104-142-121-139
3	104-126	106	126
4	140-119-128-108-127	104-132	112
5	102	122-103	123
6	107-141-120-124	102	137-117-129-109-130
7	132	112	122-103
8	106	137-117-142-121-130	107-141-120-127
9	122-103	123	102
10	123	101-129-109-139	116-134-115
11	137-117-129-109-130	107-141-120-127	106
12	112	140-119-128-108-124	101-132

Similarly, examining this solution, we notice that flights 102, 106, 126, 112 and 123 are all stranded at their respective destinations at the end of the day. We need one aircraft each day just to fly these flights. Table 5.12 shows the detailed schedule for these five flights.

Aircraft Routing

Table 5.12   Flight schedule for B737-800 stranded flights

Flight No.	Origin	Departure Time	Destination	Arrival Time	(Hrs.)
102	LAX	9:45	JFK	18:15	5.5
106	SFO	15:25	JFK	23:55	5.5
126	JFK	15:30	SFO	18:00	5.5
123	JFK	16:00	LAX	18:30	5.5
112	ATL	18:00	JFK	20:30	2.5

In an effort to pair the above flights, considering our 45-minute turn-around time, the revised schedule is presented in Table 5.13.

Table 5.13   Revised flight schedule for B737-800 stranded flights

Flight No.	Origin	Departure Time	Destination	Arrival Time	(Hrs.)
102	LAX	7:45	JFK	16:15	5.5
106	SFO	10:25	JFK	18:55	5.5
126	JFK	18:30	SFO	21:00	5.5
123	JFK	19:00	LAX	21:30	5.5
112	ATL	19:00	JFK	21:30	2.5

Incorporating these changes, and running the program with this revised schedule, still results in no feasible solution. That is, even with these changes, it is still not possible to fly all flights with nine aircraft in a three-day cyclic routing. By relaxing the constraint on the number of aircraft, we see that the minimum number of aircraft required to fly the daily schedule of 737-800 flights is 10. The changes made to the flight schedule for the stranded flights (Table 5.13) reduced the number of aircraft needed from 12 to 10. Table 5.14 shows the routings for this 10-aircraft solution.

Table 5.14 Aircraft routing solution for B737-800 with revised schedule

Routing	Day 1	Day 2	Day 3
1	101-126	104-142-121	141-120-123
2	104-132-112	140-119-128-108-124	102-126
3	116-134-115	129-109-130	107-129-109-139
4	140-119-128-108-127	106-139	116-134-115
5	107-142-121	137-117-127	104-142-121-130
6	122-103	122-103	122-103
7	137-117-129-109-130	107-141-120-126	106
8	102-123	101-132-112	140-119-128-108-124
9	141-120-124,	102-123	101-132-112
10	106-139	116-134-115	137-117-127

Other minor changes to the flight schedule also failed to generate a solution that flies all the above flights with nine aircraft. Again, our routing problem here is more restricted than a typical airline routing problem because of our closed-cycle requirement.

It is of course possible to manually make major changes to the schedule by pairing the flights such that a feasible solution is obtained with nine aircraft. Tables 5.15 (schedule) and 5.16 (routings) represent such a solution with a totally modified schedule. However, it is not clear if this operationally feasible solution is also attractive to the marketing department and passengers.

Aircraft Routing

Table 5.15 B737-800 fleet schedule with major modifications

Flight No.	Origin	Departure Time	Destination	Arrival Time	(hrs.)
101	LAX	11:00	JFK	19:30	5.5
104	SFO	12:30	JFK	21:00	5.5
116	BOS	9:30	JFK	11:00	1.5
140	JFK	6:20	IAD	7:20	1
107	ORD	10:00	JFK	12:00	2
122	JFK	7:35	LAX	10:05	5.5
137	JFK	7:00	BOS	8:30	1.5
119	IAD	8:15	JFK	9:15	1
102	LAX	12:30	JFK	21:00	5.5
117	BOS	17:00	JFK	18:30	1.5
128	JFK	7:00	ORD	9:00	2
134	JFK	9:00	MIA	12:00	3
141	JFK	12:00	IAD	13:00	1
108	ORD	16:00	JFK	18:00	2
120	IAD	14:25	JFK	15:25	1
132	JFK	17:00	ATL	19:30	2.5
129	JFK	13:00	ORD	15:00	2
142	JFK	16:25	IAD	17:25	1
103	LAX	13:00	JFK	21:30	5.5
106	SFO	13:30	JFK	22:00	5.5
126	JFK	8:30	SFO	11:00	5.5
123	JFK	8:00	LAX	10:30	5.5
109	ORD	21:45	JFK	23:45	2
112	ATL	20:30	JFK	23:00	2.5
115	MIA	13:00	JFK	16:00	3
121	IAD	18:30	JFK	19:30	1
124	JFK	9:00	LAX	11:30	5.5
127	JFK	10:00	SFO	12:30	5.5
130	JFK	19:00	ORD	21:00	2
139	JFK	14:00	BOS	15:30	1.5

Table 5.16   Aircraft routing for B737-800 with nine aircraft

Routing	Day 1	Day 2	Day 3
1	122-101	126-104	123-102
2	126-104	123-102	124-103
3	123-102	124-103	127-106
4	124-103	127-106	122-101
5	127-106	122-101	126-104
6	140-119-141-120-142-121	137-116-139-117	128-107-129-108-130-109
7	137-116-139-117	128-107-129-108-130-109	134-115-132-112
8	128-107-129-108-130-109	134-115-132-112	140-119-141-120-142-121
9	134-115-132-112	140-119-141-120-142-121	137-116-139-117

Mathematical Models

In this section, the above mathematical model as proposed by Kabbani and Patty (1992) is formally presented.

Sets
F   =   Set of flights
R   =   Set of feasible routings

Indices
j =   Route index
i =   Flight index

Parameters
c_j =   Cost of route j
$a_{i,j}$ =   1 if flight i is covered by route j, and 0 otherwise
N   =   Total number of aircraft in the fleet

Decision variable
$$x_j = \begin{cases} 1 \text{ if route } j \text{ is selected} \\ 0 \text{ otherwise} \end{cases}$$

$$\text{Minimize} \quad \sum_{j \in R} c_j x_j$$

Subject to:

$$\sum_{j \in R} a_{i,j} x_j = 1 \qquad \text{for all } i \in F \qquad (5.1)$$

$$\sum_{j \in R} x_j \leq N \qquad\qquad\qquad (5.2)$$

$$x_j \in \{0,1\} \qquad \text{for all } j \in R$$

In the above integer linear program, the objective function seeks to minimize the total cost of selected routes. If other objectives, such as the ones presented in this chapter are sought, then the above objective function can accordingly be modified. Constraint (5.1) ensures that each flight is covered by one and only one route. Constraint (5.2) restricts the number of selected routes to the available number of aircraft within a particular fleet-type.

Recent work attempts to solve the fleet assignment and aircraft routing problems simultaneously (Barnhart et al. 1996, Ioachim et al. 1999). Barnhart et al. (1996), propose a model based on strings of flights as decision variables. These strings start and end at a maintenance station, with maintenance being performed after the last flight. The departure time of the string is the departure time of the first flight, and arrival time is the arrival time of the last flight in the sequence. Cordeau et al. 2001, propose a simultaneous approach to aircraft routing and crew scheduling. These methods result in a large number of decision variables.

References

Airliners.Net (2004), Manchester - International (Ringway) (MAN / EGCC) UK – England, February 8, 2004. http://www.airliners.net/search/photo.search?regsearch=9M-MPK& distinct_entry=true.

Arguelo, M.F., Bard, J.F. and Yu, G. (1997), A GRASP for aircraft routing in response to groundings and delays. *Journal of Combinatorial Optimization* 5, 211-228.

Armacost, A., Barnhart, C. and Ware, K. (2002), Composite Variable Formulations for Express Shipment Service Network Design. *Transportation Science* 36(1), 1-20.

Bard, J., Yu, G. and Arguelo, M.F. (2001), Optimizing aircraft routings in response to groundings and delays. *IIE Transactions* 33, 931-947.

Barnhart, C., Boland, N.L., Clarke, L.W., Johnson, E.L., Nemhauser, G.L. and Shenoi, G. (1996), Flight string models for aircraft fleeting and routing. *Transportation Science* 32(3), 208-220.

Bartholomew-Biggs, M., Parkhurst, S. and Wilson, S. (2003), Global optimization approaches to an aircraft routing problem. *European Journal of Operational Research* 146(2003) 417-431.

Clarke, L., Hane, C., Johnson, E. and Nemhauser, G. (1997), Maintenance and Crew Considerations in Fleet Assignment. *Transportation Science* 30(3), 249-260.

Clarke, L., Johnson, E., Nemhauser, G. and Zhu, Z. (1997), The aircraft rotation problem. *Annals of Operations Research* 69(1997) 33-46.

Cordeau, J.F., Stojkovic, G., Soumis, F. and Desrosiers, J. (2001), Benders Decomposition for Simultaneous Aircraft Routing and Crew Scheduling. *Transportation Science* 35(4), 375-388.

Desaulniers, G., Desrosiers, J., Dumas, Y., Solomon, M.M. and Soumis, F. (1997), Daily aircraft routing and scheduling. *Management Science* 43(6), 841-855.

Gopalan, R. and Talluri, K. (1998), The Aircraft Routing Problem. *Operations Research* 46(2), 260-271.

Ioachim, I., Desrosiers, J., Soumis, F. and Belanger, N. (1999), Fleet Assignment and Routing with Schedule Synchronization Constraints. *European Journal of Operational Research* 119(1999) 75-90.

Jarrah, A.I. and Strehler, J.C. (2000), An optimization model for assigning through flights. *IIE Transaction* 32, 237-244.

Kabbani, N. (1992), Aircraft routing at American Airlines. *Presented at AGIFORS* October 4-9, 1992.

Paoletti, B., Cappelletti, S., Cinfrignini, L. and Lenner, C. (1998), AGIFORS Proceedings, 235-246.

Talluri, K. (1998), The four-day aircraft maintenance routing problem. *Transportation Science* 32(1), 43-53.

Chapter 6

Crew Scheduling

Introduction

Crew scheduling involves the process of identifying sequences of flight legs and assigning both the cockpit and cabin crews to these sequences. Crew scheduling, like aircraft routing (Chapter 5), is normally performed after the fleet assignment process.

Total crew cost, including salaries, benefits, and expenses, is the second largest cost figure, after the cost of fuel, for airlines. Table 6.1 presents the total number of crew, annual crew salaries and benefits, and flight crew expenses for select US airlines.

Table 6.1 Crew cost for US major carriers

Carrier	Number of Flight Crew	Flight Crew Salaries & Benefits (000)	Flight Crew Expenses (000)	Expenses Salaries & Benefits (%)
Alaska	1,329	$259,953	$103,736	39.91%
America West	1,675	$215,470	$48,722	22.61%
ATA	783	$130,209	$51,223	39.34%
American	12,297	$2,458,453	$1,484,596	60.39%
Continental	4,209	$866,526	$493,458	56.95%
Delta	8,074	$2,084,427	$1,039,582	49.87%
Northwest	5,534	$1,164,550	$613,037	52.64%
Southwest	3,966	$664,415	$320,153	48.19%
United	7,992	$2,300,091	$1,423,988	61.91%
US Airways	3,743	$851,466	$471,672	55.40%

Source: Form 41 (version 5.6) [CD-ROM], 2002 – Database Products, Inc.

The third column in this table represents regular flight crew salaries & benefits. The fourth column, flight crew expenses, includes per diems and other expenses incurred for hotels, parking, meals, taxi-cabs, among others, in order for an airline to maintain its crew at a city other than their home base. Note that this cost is in addition to the salaries and benefits that the airlines pay to their flight crew. The last column shows flight crew expenses as a percentage of salaries and benefits (column 4 divided by column 3).

Unlike the fuel cost, a large portion of flight crew expenses are controllable (Anbil, 1991). As Table 6.1 suggests, even a small percentage of savings in flight crew expenses through better scheduling translates into millions of dollars, which ultimately can determine the survival or demise of an airline. Because of such large anticipated savings, the crew scheduling problem has received considerable attention from both academia and industry.

Crew scheduling is one of the most computationally intensive combinatorial problems (see Ryan 1992, Bixby et al. 1992, Gamache et al. 1998, Klabjan 2001). Computational complexity will be discussed in detail in Chapter 11. The crew scheduling problem is typically solved in two phases, crew pairing and crew rostering. This is mainly because the two problems are too large to address simultaneously.

Crew Pairing

The first phase in the crew scheduling is to develop crew pairing. Crew pairing is a sequence of flight legs, within the same fleet, that starts and ends at the same crew base. A crew base is the home station or city in which the crew actually lives. Large airlines typically have several crew bases. The sequence of crew pairing must satisfy many constraints such as union, government and contractual regulations. A crew pairing sequence may typically span from one to five days, depending on the airline. The objective of crew pairing is to find a set of pairings that covers all flights and minimizes the total crew cost. The final crew pairing includes dates and times for each day. A typical assumption in crew pairing is that flight schedules are repeated daily. This assumption may be true for the week-day schedules, but for the weekends, the airlines normally have a lower frequency of flights. The adopted approach is normally to solve the crew pairing problem for a typical weekday, and then make modifications and adjustments for the weekends.

Note that in this phase of crew pairing, we generate pairings of flight legs that are feasible and satisfy the regulations. In this phase, we do not address individual crew members. This phase is also referred to as an impersonal phase. The assignment of each specific crew member to these pairings will be discussed in the second phase, i.e., crew rostering, later in this chapter.

The following definitions are used in addressing the crew pairing problem:

- *Duty*: A working day of a crew may consist of several flight segments. The length of a duty is determined by Federal Aviation Regulations (FAR) in the United States, as well as by individual airline rules. Under the Federal law, airline pilots cannot fly more than eight hours in a 24-hour period. They also must be able to rest for eight hours in that same time span.

Sit connection: A connection during duty is called a sit connection. This involves the waiting times, on the part of the crew, for changing planes onto their next leg of duty. Normally, airlines impose minimum and maximum sit connection times, typically between 10 minutes and three hours.

- *Rest*: A connection between two duties is referred to as rest, overnight connection or layover.

Figure 6.1 illustrates a sample from Ultimate Air's B757-200 fleet's two-day crew pairing, showing duty periods, sits within duty periods, overnight rests, and sign-in and sign-out times, assuming the crew home base is at JFK. Based on this figure, a crew pairing is a sequence of duties separated by rest periods.

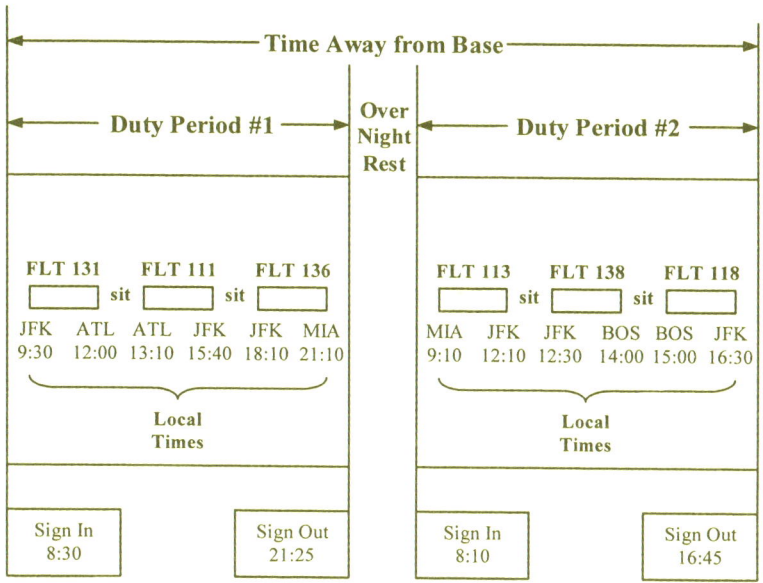

Figure 6.1 A typical pairing with duty periods, sits within duty periods, overnight rests and sign-in and sign-out times

As Figure 6.1 for our two-day pairing suggests, the crew is staying overnight, away from their home base, and therefore, the airline has to pay for their per diems, accommodation, food, etc.

The objective of the crew pairing problem is to minimize the total cost of assigning crews to flight legs, such that every flight is covered, and making sure that union, government, and airline rules are satisfied. Furthermore, the constraints should also consider the number of available crews at each base. This problem usually seeks pairings that translate into a high utilization of crew flying time, and minimum sit connection times.

The airlines normally attempt to keep the crew with the same aircraft (tail number) on multiple flight legs as much as possible. This way, crew-related problems, such as delays and cancelled connecting flights, will be reduced. Delayed, cancelled connecting flights, or other difficulties in flight pairings result in deadheading. Deadheading happens when the crew is transported as non-revenue passengers.

It should be noted that the solutions for the aircraft routing (Chapter 5) and crew pairing cannot be the same. First, crew members need more rest. An aircraft can be utilized for 14 hours in one day, but the crew can stay with the aircraft only 8 hours. Second, crew pairing identifies flight legs that start and end at the same crew base (i.e., only JFK to JFK in our case). This is not a constraint for the aircraft routing problem (where, for example SFO to SFO is possible) as long as it stays at a maintenance station overnight every 3-5 days. Third, the crew pairing problem does not consider turn-around times as they may just land with one aircraft and takeoff with another in a very short time.

Similar to aircraft routing discussed in Chapter 5, the crew pairing problem is typically formulated as a set-partitioning problem (see Chapters 2 and 5) with some side constraints. In this set-partitioning problem, the rows of the matrix represent feasible crew pairings and the columns are scheduled daily flights.

Pairings Generators

The pairings are generated based on rules and regulations. Note that at this stage, these pairings just show the sequence of flights assigned to crew members. It starts with a crew-base and adds all the feasible flight legs according to the specified rules. It finally ends up at the same crew base from which it started. A pairing satisfying all the rules and regulations is called a legal pairing. The length of a pairing depends on the airline and union regulations. A pairing may span from one to five days. Some of the rules in generating the feasible pairings include the total daily flight time, and minimum and maximum sit-connection times. All possible feasible pairings are generated during this phase. For large airlines with many daily flights, the number of pairings generated becomes very large (billions of legal pairings!). This is especially very applicable to airlines with large hubs. Each flight leg at this hub can be potentially paired with many departing flights. This combination is compounded if the aircraft is re-routed to the hub several times in a day. In such cases, the generators are normally equipped with some extra rules and filters to identify and select good potential pairings. Klabjan (2003) provides an overview of these rules and filters to reduce the number of pairings.

The following represents the crew pairing requirements for Ultimate Air:

- Each duty should not exceed 8 hours of flight time;
- A maximum length of two days is allowed for a routing (i.e., two-day pairings);
- The home base for the crew is JFK;

- The minimum and maximum sit connection times are 10 minutes and three hours, respectively.

A similar program to route generators, in Chapter 5, was developed to generate the potential crew pairings. The steps for this program are as follows:

- Read the flight numbers, along with their departure and arrival cities and times, for a set of flights assigned to a specific fleet-type (as identified by fleet routing module);
- Create all possible one and two-day pairings - place in a file;
- Examine each pairing in this file for:
    - The pairing ends up at JFK over the routing cycle;
    - For two-day pairing, the first flight of the second day starts out at the city where it ended up the night before;
    - The duty does not exceed 8 hours of flight time in any given day;
    - The sit-connection times are between the allowable minimum and maximum times;
- If a pairing satisfies all of the above conditions, it is added to a file of potential valid pairing candidates.

This program generated a total of 28 and 314 legal pairings for the 757-200 and 737-800 fleet-types, respectively. Note that the number of crew pairing candidates is much lower than potential aircraft routings (Chapter 5) for both fleet types. The main reason is that for crew pairing we generated only one and two-day pairings as opposed to three-day routings in Chapter 5. Furthermore, other factors such as a maximum of eight hour flight blocks per day, and a maximum three hour sit-connection times, contribute to the lower numbers of possible combinations. Table 6.2 presents all 28 legal pairings for the 757-200 fleet. In this table, if the pairings are one-day, then no flights appear in the day two column.

Table 6.2   All legal crew pairings for B757-200 fleet

Crew Pairing Index	Day-one Flights	Day-two Flights	Flight Hours
1	125	105	11
2	131	110	5
3	131	111	5
4	131	110-138-118	8
5	133	110	5
6	133	111	5
7	133	110-138-118	8
8	135	113	6
9	135	114	6
10	135	113-138-118	9
11	136	113	6
12	136	114	6
13	136	113-138-118	9
14	138	118	3
15	131-111		5
16	131-111-133	110	10
17	131-111-133	111	10
18	131-111-133	110-138-118	13
19	131-111-136	113	11
20	131-111-136	114	11
21	131-111-136	113-138-118	14
22	138-118		3
23	138-118-133	110	8
24	138-118-133	111	8
25	138-118-133	110-138-118	11
26	138-118-136	113	9
27	138-118-136	114	9
28	138-118-136	113-138-118	12

Since the number of combinations for the 737-800 fleet is large, five one-day and two-day pairing samples are presented in Tables 6.3 and 6.4.

Table 6.3 Sample one-day crew pairing for B737-800 fleet

SAMPLE	DAY 1				Crew Utilization (Hrs.)
High Utilization					
Pairing #1	FLT 140	FLT 119	FLT 128	FLT 108	6
City Pairs	JFK-IAD	IAD-JFK	JFK-ORD	ORD-JFK	
Dept-Arr Times	6:20-7:20	8:15-9:15	10:05-11:05	12:20-15:20	
Low Utilization					
Pairing #2	FLT 140	FLT 119			2
City Pairs	JFK-IAD	IAD-JFK			
Dept-Arr Times	6:20-7:20	8:15-9:15			

Table 6.4 Sample two-day crew pairing for B737-800 fleet

SAMPLE	DAY 1			DAY 2			Crew Utilization (Hrs.)
High Utilization							
Pairing #3	FLT 142	FLT 121	FLT 127	FLT 104	FLT 142	FLT 121	15
City Pairs	JFK-IAD	IAD-JFK	JFK-SFO	SFO-JFK	JKF-IAD	IAD-JFK	
Dept-Arr Times	15:15-16:15	18:30-19:30	20:00-22:30	5:05-13:35	15:15-16:15	18:30-19:30	
Medium Utilization							
Pairing #4	FLT 132	FLT 112	FLT 130	FLT 107	FLT 141	FLT 120	11
City Pairs	JFK-ATL	ATL-JFK	JFK-ORD	ORD-JFK	JFK-IAD	IAD-JFK	
Dept-Arr Times	14:35-17:35	18:00-20:30	21:00-22:00	7:30-10:30	12:00-13:00	14:25-15:25	
Low Utilization							
Pairing #5	FLT 140			FLT 119			2
City Pairs	JFK-IAD			IAD-JFK			
Dept-Arr Times	6:20-7:20			8:15-9:15			

Mathematical Model for B757-200 Fleet

Similar to Chapter 5, since the 757-200 fleet has a lower number of crew pairings, we first start developing the mathematical model for this fleet. The mathematical model for the 737-800 will follow later on in this chapter.

Decision Variable

Having generated potential valid crew pairings, the task of the mathematical model is to identify which candidates should be selected. We define the following binary decision variable:

$$x_j = \begin{cases} 1 \text{ if pairing } j \text{ is selected}, \quad j=1,2,..,28 \\ 0 \text{ otherwise} \end{cases}$$

Objective Function

The determination of cost for crew pairings is a complex process (Barnhart, 1997). It is based on the sum of all duty cost in the pairing, cost of time away from the base, and minimum guaranteed pay multiplied by the number of duties. The maximum of these three costs determines the above cost function for each pairing.

In our Ultimate Air example, we assume two-day pairings to be three times as costly as one-day pairings. This is because, in two-day pairings, the crew stays away from home base for one night, and hence the airline is responsible for the incurring costs. Therefore, according to Table 6.2, the cost coefficient is one for pairings 15 and 22, and three for all other pairings.

The objective functions for our 757-200 fleet, therefore, is as follows.

$$\text{Minimize } \sum_{j=1}^{28} c_j x_j$$

where c_j is the cost of pairing j. For our Ultimate Air, c_j is designated the value 1 for one-day, and 3 for two-day pairings.

Flight Coverage Constraints for B757 Fleet

Each pairing candidate covers a certain number of flights. We must ensure that the crew covers each flight exactly once. To write the coverage constraint for flight 125, according to Table 6.2, we write:

$$x_1 = 1$$

This is because flight 125 only appears in crew pairing 1. Referring to Table 6.2 again, flight 114 appears in crew pairings 9, 12, 20 and 27. Therefore to cover this flight we have:

$$x_9 + x_{12} + x_{20} + x_{27} = 1$$

Crew Scheduling 89

Similarly, referring to Table 6.2, we can write the flight coverage constraints for the other 10 flights with this fleet-type.

Note that unlike the three-day aircraft routing in which we had a constraint for each flight for each day, in crew pairing we address each flight only once. This is because we are interested in knowing which flights should be paired rather than the actual assignment of flights to days. A two-day pairing requires two sets of crews with a one-day lag. Each set of crew covers one duty of the pairing. Thus all flights are covered. We will discuss the assignment of pairings to days in the second phase, crew rostering.

Crew Pairing Solution for B757-200 Fleet

We used an optimization software to solve the above integer linear program model. Four two-day pairings were selected. The objective function is therefore 12. Table 6.5 presents the solution, showing pairings and flights, as well as departure and arrival times.

Table 6.5   Solution to crew pairing for B757-200 fleet

Solution	DAY 1			DAY 2		
Pairing #1	FLT 125			FLT 105		
City Pairs	JFK-SFO			SFO-JFK		
Dept-Arr Times	7:25-9:55			9:50-18:20		
Pairing #21	FLT 131	FLT 111	FLT 136	FLT 113	FLT 138	FLT 118
City Pairs	JFK-ATL	ATL-JFK	JFK-MIA	MIA-JFK	JFK-BOS	BOS-JFK
Dept-Arr Times	9:30-12:00	13:10-15:40	18:10-21:10	9:10-12:10	12:30-14:00	15:00-16:30
Pairing #9	FLT 135			FLT 114		
City Pairs	JFK-MIA			MIA-JFK		
Dept-Arr Times	15:10-18:10			14:30-17:30		
Pairing #5	FLT 133			FLT 110		
City Pairs	JFK-ATL			ATL-JFK		
Dept-Arr Times	18:05-20:35			8:10-10:40		

Crew Pairing Solution for B737-800 Fleet

Similarly, we develop the mathematical model for crew pairing of the 737-800 fleet. Solving this mathematical model generates the following solution, presented in Table 6.6, for this fleet.

Table 6.6 Solution to crew pairing for B737-800 fleet

Solution	DAY 1			DAY 2		
Pairing #1	FLT 140	FLT 119	FLT 134	FLT 115		
City Pairs	JFK-IAD	IAD-JFK	JFK-MI	MIA-JFK		
Dept-Arr Times	6:20-7:20	8:15-9:15	10:35-13:35	18:25-21:25		
Pairing #2	FLT 122			FLT 103		
City Pairs	JFK-LAX			LAX-JFK		
Dept-Arr Times	7:35-10:05			15:20-23:50		
Pairing #3	FLT 137	FLT 117				
City Pairs	JFK-BOS	BOS-JFK				
Dept-Arr Times	7:40-9:10	10:00-11:30				
Pairing #4	FLT 141	FLT 120	FLT 125	FLT 104	FLT 142	FLT 121
City Pairs	JFK-IAD	IAD-JFK	JFK-SFO	SFO-JFK	JFK-IAD	IAD-JFK
Dept-Arr Times	12:00-13:00	14:25-15:25	7:25-9:55	5:05-13:35	15:15-16:15	18:30-19:30
Pairing #5	FLT 132	FLT 112	FLT 130	FLT 107		
City Pairs	JFK-ATL	ATL-JFK	JFK-ORD	ORD-JFK		
Dept-Arr Times	14:35-17:35	18:00-20:30	21:00-22:00	7:30-10:30		
Pairing #6	FLT 129	FLT 109	FLT 139	FLT 116	FLT 128	FLT 108
City Pairs	JFK-ORD	ORD-JFK	JFK-BOS	BOS-JFK	JFK-ORD	ORD-JFK
Dept-Arr Times	15:05-16:05	17:10-20:10	21:30-23:00	6:15-7:45	10:05-11:05	12:20-15:20
Pairing #7	FLT 123			FLT 102		
City Pairs	JFK-LAX			LAX-JFK		
Dept-Arr Times	16:00-18:30			9:45-18:15		
Pairing #8	FLT 124			FLT 101		
City Pairs	JFK-LAX			LAX-JFK		
Dept-Arr Times	19:00-21:30			5:00-13:30		
Pairing #9	FLT 127			FLT 106		
City Pairs	JFK-SFO			SFO-JFK		
Dept-Arr Times	20:00-22:30			15:25-23:55		

Crew Pairing Mathematical Model

In this section, the crew pairing model, as was adopted above, is formally presented.

Sets
- F = Set of flights
- P = Set of feasible pairings
- K = Set of crew home base cities

Indices
- j = Pairing index
- i = Flight index
- k = Crew home base index

Parameters

c_j = Cost of crew paring j

$a_{i,j} = \begin{cases} 1 & \text{if flight } i \text{ is covered by pairing } j \\ 0 & \text{otherwise} \end{cases}$

$h_{k,j} = \begin{cases} 1 & \text{if home base city (starting and ending flight) for pairing } j \text{ is city } k \\ 0 & \text{otherwise} \end{cases}$

b_{lower_k} ≡ minimum number of crew to be used at home base city k

b_{upper_k} ≡ maximum number of crew to be used at home base city k

Decision Variable

$x_j = \begin{cases} 1 & \text{if pairing } j \text{ is part of the solution} \\ 0 & \text{otherwise} \end{cases}$

The mathematical model is formulated as:

$$\text{Min} \sum_{j \in P} c_j x_j \qquad (6.1)$$

Subject to:

$$\sum_{j \in P} a_{i,j} x_j = 1 \qquad \text{for all flight legs } i \in F \qquad (6.2)$$

$$b_{lower_k} \leq \sum_{j \in P} h_{k,j} x_j \leq b_{upper_k} \qquad \text{for all home bases } k \in K \qquad (6.3)$$

In this model, the objective function (6.1) attempts to minimize the total cost of flight pairings. Constraint (6.2) guarantees that each flight leg is covered only once. The side constraints (6.3) ensure that the selected flight pairings stay within the available number of crew members at each home base.

Some recent works (see Klabjan 2003) have attempted to integrate the two problems of crew pairing and aircraft routing. It should be noted that the difficulty in dealing with larger problems than those presented here will be compounded by integrating both these problems.

Crew Rostering

Once the crew pairing problem is solved, the second phase is crew rostering. Crew rostering is the process of assigning individual crew members to crew pairings, usually on a monthly basis.

Some airlines, mainly Europeans, allow their crews to select a number of pairings as identified in the first phase, together with rest periods on specific days to construct their monthly personalized schedule (see Sarra 1998, Giafferri et al. 1982, Hjorring 2000, Konig and Strass 2000). The airline then attempts to grant these schedules if possible. Crew training days, seniority, and other internal regulations are some of the factors that influence the assignment of these schedules to crews.

US Airlines, however, develop their monthly crew schedules based on the solutions generated in the crew pairing phase, independent of crew desires. This approach is then used to construct the monthly schedule by incorporating employee time off, training, union rules, and other contractual obligations. The airlines then assign crews to these schedules based on their in-house priority system. This method, where the employees bid for pre-constructed rosters is referred to as a *bid line procedure*. In both rostering systems, the objective is to maximize crew utilization, evenly distributing individual crew workload and rest times.

Since the rules and regulations vary among the airlines, the crew rostering process, and the available literature on this topic, is also diverse. Some of these methods include (Gamache et al. 1999):

- Assigning high priority employees to high priority pairings;
- Developing monthly rosters for individual crew members based on their requests;
- Developing monthly rosters for each day of the month without considering the crew requests.

It should be noted that the processes of assigning cockpit aircrew members (captain, and first officer) and cabin aircrew members (flight attendants) are typically different. The cockpit aircrew members usually have the required licenses/type-ratings to fly only a specific fleet of aircraft, while cabin aircrew members can be assigned to multiple fleet-types.

Ultimate Air Rosters

As explained earlier, a roster is a series of crew pairings separated by rest periods and days off. For Ultimate Air, we attempt to develop anonymous rosters on which its employees can bid.

For presentation purposes, and in an effort to keep the rostering problem to a manageable size, we will develop the rosters on a weekly basis, instead of monthly rosters which are more common among airlines. The process of developing monthly rosters is basically the same as that of one done weekly.

The assumptions for the Ultimate Air crew rosters are as follows:

- At least one day off between pairings;
- Two pairings per week;
- Balanced workload among all rosters. A work week of 20 flight hours is desirable.

Table 6.7 presents all possible combinations on the allocation of pairings to days of the week. This table incorporates the above rules on two pairings per week and at least one day off between pairings. Each (✔) symbol represents a pairing. Note that each pairing spans a two-day period. Therefore, if a crew is assigned to a pairing on Monday, then this crew member will be flying both on Monday and Tuesday. Since we require at least one day rest between pairings, this crew member cannot fly on Wednesday, but can fly on Thursday, Friday, Saturday or Sunday.

Table 6.7 Possible weekly crew roster combinations for Ultimate Air

Monday	Tuesday	Wednesday	Thursday	Friday	Saturday	Sunday
✔			✔			
✔				✔		
✔					✔	
✔						✔
	✔			✔		
	✔				✔	
	✔					✔
		✔			✔	
		✔				✔
			✔			✔

We assume that the assignment of crew to rosters, in each week, takes into consideration their previous weeks' rosters. That is to say, if a crew member is assigned to a pairing which starts on Saturday of this week, this crew member cannot be assigned to a roster which starts on Monday, etc.

Similar to the crew pairing mathematical model in the previous section, a series of set partitioning approaches are adopted to assign rosters to individual crew members. We use a set-partitioning approach first to identify the anonymous rosters. In this approach, the rows of the set-partitioning matrix represent the valid roster combinations, and the columns are the daily pairings, which span the entire week.

Again, since the 757-200 fleet has a smaller problem size, we develop the crew rosters for this fleet first.

Crew Rosters for B757-200 Fleet

Table 6.5 presented the solution to our crew pairing phase for the 757-200 fleet. Four pairings were identified, which covered all the scheduled 757-200 flights in a day. Let us call these four pairings P1, P2, P3 and P4. Considering these pairing combinations, and assigning these pairings to days in Table 6.7, we get 160 possible valid rosters. Table 6.8 presents three sample valid rosters with corresponding total weekly flight hours.

Table 6.8 Three sample rosters for B757-200 fleet

Sample Rosters	Mon	Tue	Wed	Thu	Fri	Sat	Sun	Flight Hrs.
1	P1			P2				25
2			P3			P1		17
3		P4			P2			19

Decision Variable

Similar to crew pairing, the task of this mathematical model is to identify which rosters, among the 160 potential candidates, should be selected. We define the following decision variable:

$$x_j = \begin{cases} 1 \text{ if roster } j \text{ is selected}, \ j=1,2,..,160 \\ 0 \text{ otherwise} \end{cases}$$

Objective Function

As explained earlier, a major goal of Ultimate Air is to create balanced rosters around 20 weekly flights hours. The objective function is therefore constructed in an attempt to minimize the total deviations of the rosters' weekly flight hours from the target of 20 flight hours. The objective function is therefore represented as:

$$\text{Minimize} \sum_{j=1}^{160} \left| h_j - 20 \right| \cdot x_j$$

where h_j is the total weekly flight hours for roster j. We use absolute values because the term $h_j - 20$ may be positive, zero, or negative depending on the

Crew Scheduling 95

roster. In this manner, a negative deviation (low weekly flight hours) is treated as bad as a positive deviation (high weekly flight hours). Referring to our sample rosters in Table 6.8, the coefficient for the variable representing sample 1 is |25-20|=5. Similarly, the objective function coefficients for the other two samples are |17-20|=3 and |19-20|=1, respectively.

Pairing Coverage Constraints for B757-200 Fleet

Each roster candidate covers a certain number of pairings in each day. We must ensure that the rosters cover each pairing every day, exactly once. As an example, sample 1 in table 6.8 covers pairings 1 and 2 on Monday and Thursday, respectively. So this sample is a candidate to cover P1 on Monday and P2 on Thursday.

A simple program similar to Chapter 5 can search through our 160 candidates to identify which ones cover which pairings, and on what days. We have four pairings that need to fly every day of the week, which makes a total of (4×7) 28 constraints as follows:

$$\sum_{j=1}^{160} a_{i,j} x_j = 1 \quad \text{For all } i = 1, 2, .., 28$$

In this set of constraints, index i represents a specific pairing in a given day. As an example, the number 1 represents P1 on Monday, while 2 stands for P2 on Monday,..., and 28 is P4 on Sunday. The parameter $a_{i,j}$ is defined as follows:

$$a_{i,j} = \begin{cases} 1 \text{ if roster } j \text{ covers pairing } i \\ 0 \text{ otherwise} \end{cases}$$

Rostering Solution for B757-200 Fleet

The above integer linear program with 160 binary decision variables and 28 constraints was solved using optimization software. The solution for the objective function is 28 hours, which represents the sum of deviations of all rosters from our target of 20 flight hours. Table 6.9 presents the solution to these weekly rosters. There are 14 disjointed (non-overlapping) rosters, each covering two pairings per day. As we can see from the solution, each pairing is covered exactly once every day. In order to keep the flight hours more balanced, one approach is to rotate the rosters every week among the crew members. This rotation of weekly rosters not only provides a fair and balanced number of flight hours over the whole month for a particular crew member, but is also very desirable for the airlines and crew to stay current with their network of airports.

Table 6.9 Solution to crew rosters for B757-200 fleet

Rosters	Mon	Tue	Wed	Thu	Fri	Sat	Sun	Flight Hours
1	P1	0	0	P4	0	0	0	16
2	0	P1	0	0	P4	0	0	16
3	0	0	P1	0	0	P4	0	16
4	0	0	0	P1	0	0	P4	16
5	P2	0	0	0	0	0	P3	20
6	0	P2	0	0	P3	0	0	20
7	0	0	P2	0	0	P3	0	20
8	0	P3	0	0	P1	0	0	17
9	0	0	P3	0	0	P1	0	17
10	0	0	0	P3	0	0	P1	17
11	P3	0	0	0	0	0	P2	20
12	P4	0	0	P2	0	0	0	19
13	0	P4	0	0	P2	0	0	19
14	0	0	P4	0	0	P2	0	19

According to Table 6.9, we need at least 14 captains and 14 first officers for our 757-200 fleet. The airlines normally have a number of reserve captains and first officers to accommodate unforeseen circumstances. As explained earlier, these are anonymous rosters and can be assigned to any crew member. Once these rosters are constructed, the airline, based on its rules and regulations, assigns them to each individual crew member.

Rostering Solution for B737-800 Fleet

A similar approach is adopted for deriving the solution for the 737-800 fleet. We have nine pairings for this fleet. There are a total of 810 roster candidates and 63 (9 pairings × 7 days/week) constraints. Table 6.10 presents the solution for crew rostering for this fleet. This solution generates a total of 35 hours deviation for 28 rosters.

Table 6.10 Solution to crew rosters for B737-800 fleet

Rosters	Mon	Tue	Wed	Thu	Fri	Sat	Sun	Flight Hours
1	0	P1	0	0	P8	0	0	19
2	0	0	P1	0	0	P8	0	19
3	P1	0	0	0	P9	0	0	19
4	0	0	P2	0	0	0	P5	20
5	P2	0	0	0	0	P7	0	22
6	0	P2	0	0	P7	0	0	22
7	P3	0	0	P4	0	0	0	18
8	0	P3	0	0	P4	0	0	18
9	0	0	P3	0	0	P4	0	18
10	0	0	0	P3	0	0	P4	18
11	P4	0	0	0	0	0	P3	18
12	0	P4	0	0	P3	0	0	18
13	0	0	P4	0	0	P3	0	18
14	P5	0	0	P2	0	0	0	20
15	0	P5	0	0	0	0	P6	20
16	0	0	P5	0	0	P6	0	20
17	0	P6	0	0	0	0	P2	22
18	0	0	P6	0	0	P2	0	22
19	P6	0	0	0	0	P5	0	20
20	0	0	0	P6	0	0	P9	22
21	0	0	P7	0	0	0	P1	19
22	0	P7	0	0	P2	0	0	22
23	P7	0	0	0	P6	0	0	22
24	0	0	0	P7	0	0	P8	22
25	P8	0	0	P1	0	0	0	19
26	0	P8	0	0	P1	0	0	19
27	0	0	P8	0	0	P1	0	19
28	0	0	0	P8	0	0	P8	22
29	P9	0	0	P5	0	0	0	20
30	0	P9	0	0	P5	0	0	20
31	0	0	0	P9	0	0	P7	22
32	0	0	P9	0	0	P9	0	22

Crew Rostering Mathematical Model

The mathematical model for crew rostering depends on how we choose to construct the rosters, i.e., either individualized or anonymous rosters. The approach that was presented in this chapter was based on developing anonymous rosters. Klabjan (2003) provides a review of various rostering problems.

Sets:
P = Set of all pairings over all days of the roster period
R = Set of valid rosters

Indices:
j = Roster index
i = Pairing index

Parameters:

c_j = Deviation of roster j flight time from a target value

$$a_{i,j} = \begin{cases} 1 & \text{if pairing } i \text{ is covered by roster } j \\ 0 & \text{otherwise} \end{cases}$$

Decision Variable:

$$x_j = \begin{cases} 1 & \text{if roster } j \text{ is part of the solution} \\ 0 & \text{otherwise} \end{cases}$$

The mathematical model is formulated as:

$$\text{Minimize} \sum_{j \in R} c_j x_j \qquad (6.4)$$

Subject to:

$$\sum_{j \in R} a_{i,j} x_j = 1 \qquad \text{For all pairings } i \in P \qquad (6.5)$$

In this model, the objective function (6.4) attempts to minimize the total sum of deviations. Constraint (6.5) guarantees that each flight pairing in each day is covered only once.

References

Anbil, R., Gelman, E., Patty, B. and Tanga, R. (1991), Recent advances in crew-pairing optimization at American Airlines. *Interfaces* 21(1), 62-74.

Barnhart, C., Johnson, E., Nemhauser, G.L. and Vance, P.H. (1997), Airline crew scheduling: a new formulation and decomposition algorithm. *Operations Research* 45(2), 188-200.

Bixby, R.E., Gregory, J.W., Lustig, I.J., Arsten, R.E. and Shanno, D.F. (1992), Very large scale linear programming: a case study in combining interior point and simplex methods. *Operations Research* 40(5), 885-897.

Desaulniers, G., Desrosiers, J., Dumas, Y., Marc, S., Rioux, B., Solomon, M.M. and Soumis, F. (1997), Crew pairing at Air France. *European Journal of Operational Research* 97, 245-259.

Donmaz, A. (1991), Turkish Airlines crew management system. *Presented at 31st Annual AGIFORS Symposium.* October 13-18, 1991. Brainerd, Minnesota.

Emden-Weinert, T. and Proksch, M. (1999), Best practice simulated annealing for the airline crew scheduling problem. *Journal of Heuristics* 5, 419-436.

Gamache, M., Soumis, F., Marquis, G. and Desrosiers, J. (1999), A column generation approach for large-scale aircrew rostering problems. *Operations Research* 47(2), 247-263.

Gelman, E., Gulsen, M., Narayanan, A. and Nguyen, T. (2000), Flight crew manpower planning – forecasting and modeling. *Presented at AGIFORS.* August, 2000.

Gelman, E., Krishna, A. and Ramaswamy, S. (1996), Large scale crew scheduling at United Airlines. *Present at AGIFORS Symposium* November 6, 1996. Atlanta, Georgia.

Giafferri, C., Hamon, J. and Lengline, J. Automatic Monthly Assignment of Medium-Haul Cabin Crew – Air France. *Presented at 22nd Annual AGIFORS Symposium.* October 3-8, 1982. Lagonissi, Greece.

Hjorring, C.A, Karisch, S.E. and Kohl, N. (2000), Carmen Systems' recent advances in crew scheduling. *Carmen Systems AB.*

Klabjan, D. (2003), Large-scale Models in the Airline Industry. *Dept. of Mechanical and Industrial Engr., Univ. of Illinois, Urbana-Champaign, IL*. December 8, 2003, 1-20.

Klabjan, D., Johnson, E.L., Nemhauser, G.L., Gelman, E. and Ramaswamy, S. (2002), Airline crew scheduling with time windows and plane-count constraints. *Transportation Science* 36(3), 337-348.

Klabjan, D., Johnson, E.L., Nemhauser, G.L., Gelman, E. and Ramaswamy, S. (2001), Solving large airline crew scheduling problems: random pairing generation and strong branching. *Computational Optimization and Applications* 20,73-91.

Konig, J. and Strauss, C. (n.d.), Rostering-integrated Services and Crew Efficiency. ATIC Aviation-Information-Technology-Consulting, Kaltenleutgebnerstr. 9a/2/8, A – 1230 Vienna, Austria.

Konig, J. and Strauss, C. (n.d.), Supplements in airline Cabin service. ATIC Aviation-Information-Technology-Consulting, Kaltenleutgebnerstr. 9a/2/8, A – 1230 Vienna, Austria.

Ryan, D.M. (1992), The solution of massive generalized set partitioning problems in aircrew rostering. *Journal of Operational Research Society* 43(5), 459-467.

Sarra, D. (1988), SATURN – The Automatic Assignment Model – Alitalia. *Presented at XXVII Annual AGIFORS Symposium.* October 16-21, 1988. New Seabury, Cape Cod, Massachusetts.

Tingley, G. (1979), Still Another Solution Method for the Monthly Aircrew Assignment Problem – Swissair. *Presented at 19th Annual AGIFORS Symposium.* September 1979. Pugnochiuso, Italy.

Yu, G. and Thengvall, B. (1999), "Airline Optimization". Chapter in Handbook of Applied Optimization, P.M. Pardalos and M.G.C. Resende eds., Oxford University Press, 1999.

Chapter 7

Manpower Planning

Introduction

An airline's product is measured by its timeliness, accuracy, functionality, quality and price (Yu 1998). The airline employees and equipment are the factors that determine such measures. Manpower planning for airlines represents one of the most important and challenging tasks, which covers a wide range spanning from hiring, training, to scheduling of human resources (Yu and Thengvall 2002). The concepts of hiring and training are normally very much dependant on the airline strategic plans (Verbeek 1991). Manpower scheduling refers to the actual work plan including working, non-working days, times, shifts, locations and leave periods. Scheduling the employees for an airline is an enormous task. There are pilots, flight attendants, ground crew, baggage handlers, reservationists, cooks, janitors, mechanics, administrators etc.

The main purpose of manpower scheduling is to derive a cyclic (normally weekly) plan for each employee so that the total manpower costs are minimized, efficiency and utilization are maximized, subject to meeting the requirements and regulations (Brusco and Jacobs 1998).

Chapter 6, on crew scheduling presented the process of assigning flight crews to flight legs while this chapter introduces mathematical models on manpower planning for ground crews. Simulation models (Chapter 13) are also used to plan for manpower planning.

Mathematical Modeling Case Study

We begin the introduction to the mathematical model by applying it to our case study. Table 7.1 presents the weekly manpower requirements for ground operations (check-in counters and baggage handlers) at JFK for our Ultimate Air airline example.

The weekly manpower requirements are normally different at different times of the day and different days of the week. The daily operations are divided into four time blocks with duration of four hours each. According to this table, for example, on Mondays from 6am-10 am, we need 8 employees, etc. The following contractual issues and airline policies apply:

- Each employee works for 8 hours consequently in a day.

- There are currently three working shifts, shift 1 (6am-2pm), shift 2 (10am-4pm) and shift 3 (2pm-10pm).
- Each employee works for five days consecutively followed by two days off.

Table 7.1   Check-in counter agents requirement at JFK for Ultimate Air

Shift/day	Mon	Tue	Wed	Thu	Fri	Sat	Sun
6am-10 am	8	8	8	8	10	10	6
10am-2pm	12	10	12	10	16	16	8
2pm-6pm	16	12	16	12	20	20	8
6pm-10pm	9	8	9	8	12	12	4

The objective is to determine the minimum size for the workforce and their working schedules so that the above manpower requirements and regulations are met.

The mathematical approach discussed in this section is a modified version of the Personnel Scheduling model by Brusco et al. (1995). This method has been used in the development of the automated manpower planning system at United Airlines. For other mathematical approaches to manpower planning see Brusco and Jacobs (1998).

We adopt the following decision variable:

$x_{i,j}$ = number of employees who begin work in day i adopting shift j

In this decision variable, index i, represents the day that an employee starts his/her five-day work week. Index j, represents the shift that the employee is assigned to. Tables 7.2 and 7.3 show the indices used to represent shifts and days of the week respectively.

Table 7.2   Index for shifts (j)

8-hour shift	Index (j) for Shift
6am-2pm	1
10am-6pm	2
2pm-10pm	3

Table 7.3 Index for days of the week (i)

Starting Day of the Working Week	Index (i) for Day
Mon	1
Tues	2
Wed	3
Thur	4
Fri	5
Sat	6
Sun	7

According to these tables, $x_{1,1}$ represents the number of employees who should start their work week on Monday from 6am-2pm shift, and so on.

The objective function is to minimize the total workforce (headcount) as follows:

$$\text{Minimize } x_{1,1} + x_{1,2} + x_{1,3} + \ldots x_{7,1} + x_{7,2} + x_{7,3}$$

Note that the employees in decision variables are disjoint, meaning no employee appears in two decision variables. As an example, those employees who start their working week on Monday from 6am-2pm, represented by decision variable $x_{1,1}$, are different from those who start on Monday from 10am-6pm represented by $x_{1,2}$. So adding all the decision variables represents the total workforce for this case study, which we wish to minimize.

For the constraints, we should satisfy the manpower requirements for each time block of the day. We have seven days with four time blocks in each day, resulting in a total of 28 constraints. We classify these constraints in their four respective time blocks.

Constraints

The constraints must cover the manpower requirements for every shift of every day. The following presents the constraints for each time block.

Time Block 6am-10am

The employees working in this time block includes only those who start their shift at 6am (first shift). Those who start their shifts at 10am or 2pm (second or third shifts) will not be present during this time block. To express this constraint for say, Monday, 6am-10pm, we have the following constraint:

$$x_{1,1} + x_{4,1} + x_{5,1} + x_{6,1} + x_{7,1} \geq 8$$

The above constraint specifies that the total number of employees available for work on Monday from 6am to 10am includes those who start their working week on Monday ($x_{1,1}$), plus those who start on Thursday ($x_{4,1}$), Friday ($x_{5,1}$), Saturday ($x_{6,1}$), and Sunday ($x_{7,1}$). We require 8 employees on Monday in the first time block. This number appears as the right hand side for the constraint. Note that since each employee works five days consequently followed by two days off, those who start their working week on Tuesday or Wednesday will not be present for work on Monday.

Similarly we write six more constraints for the first time block of other days within the week.

Constraints for Time Block 10am-2pm

Since each employee works for eight hours, then the employees working in this time block include those who start their shifts at 6am (first shift) and 10am (second shift). The constraint for this time block for Monday is as follows:

$$x_{1,1} + x_{4,1} + x_{5,1} + x_{6,1} + x_{7,1} + x_{1,2} + x_{4,2} + x_{5,2} + x_{6,2} + x_{7,2} \geq 12$$

The first five terms are the same as the constraint for Monday 6am-10am time block. The second five terms represent those employees who start their shifts at 10am on different days. The right hand side represents the number of required employees for Monday's second time block. Similarly six more constraints are added for other days of the week representing this second time block.

Constraints for Time Block 2pm-6pm

The employees working in this time block include those who start their shifts at 10am (second shift) and 2pm (third shift). The constraint for this time block for Monday is as follows:

$$x_{1,2} + x_{4,2} + x_{5,2} + x_{6,2} + x_{7,2} + x_{1,3} + x_{4,3} + x_{5,3} + x_{6,3} + x_{7,3} \geq 16$$

The first five terms are the same as the constraint for Monday 10am-2pm time block. The second five terms represent those employees who started their shifts at 2pm on different days. The right hand side represents the number of required employees for Monday's third time block. Similarly six more constraints are added for other days of the week.

Constraints for Time Block 6pm-10pm

The employees working in this time block includes only those who start their shifts at 2pm (third shift). Those who have started at 6am (first shift) or 10am (second shift) have already finished their 8-hour working day and are not present during this time block. The constraint for Monday's time block is as follows:

$$x_{1,3} + x_{4,3} + x_{5,3} + x_{6,3} + x_{7,3} \geq 9$$

We see that only those employees with third shift appear in this constraint. Similarly six more constraints are added for other days of the week.

Solution

The above linear integer programming model has 21 integer decision variables and 28 constraints. Solving this model using a software generates the solution presented in Table 7.4. This table shows the required number of employees who start their working week in different shifts of the day. A total of 36 employees are required to meet the manpower requirement for this case study.

Table 7.4   Solution to manpower planning

Day/Shift	Shift 1 (6am-2pm)	Shift 2 (10am-6pm)	Shift 3 (2pm-10pm)
Mon	2	1	3
Tue	4	0	7
Wed	0	1	0
Thur	2	4	4
Fri	2	0	0
Sat	2	2	2
Sun	0	0	0

Mathematical Model

The mathematical model proposed by Brusco et al. (1995) addresses both part-time and full-time employees, their limits, numerous combinations of shifts, working days, and weekly rotations. This method has been used in the development of the automated manpower planning system at the United Airlines called Pegasys. This automated system aides the airline in determining the optimal manpower planning system in their 119 domestic airports as well as many international locations. Pegasys uses flight schedules, passenger forecasts, baggage and cargo loads to compute labor requirements. The mathematical model for this automated system utilizes personnel tour scheduling which involves the determination of work and non-work days during the week as well as the associated daily shift starting and finishing times for each employee. The mathematical model is as follows:

Sets
$D =$ Set of days in the weekly planning
$S =$ Set of allowable shifts
$T =$ Set of all time-blocks in the weekly planning

Index
$i =$ Index for day in the weekly planning
$J =$ Index for shift
$k =$ Index for time block

Parameters

$a_{i,j,k} = \begin{cases} 1 \text{ if time block } k \text{ is work period in shift type } j \text{ which begins in day } i \\ 0 \text{ otherwise} \end{cases}$

R_k Number of employees required to be present in time block k

Decision Variable

$x_{i,j} =$ Number of employees who begin work in day i adopting shift j

The integer linear program is as follows:

Minimize $\sum_{i \in D} \sum_{j \in S} x_{i,j}$

Subject to

$$\sum_{i \in D} \sum_{j \in S} a_{i,j,k} \cdot x_{i,j} \geq R_k \quad \forall k \in T$$

$$x_{i,j} \in Z^+ \quad \forall i \in D, \forall j \in S$$

In this model, the objective function attempts to minimize the total work force subject to availability of manpower for each time block of the day. Z^+ represents the set of positive integer numbers.

References

Brusco, M.J. and Jacobs, L.W. (1998), Personnel tour scheduling when starting-time restrictions are present. Management Science 44(4), 534-547.

Brusco, M.J., Jacobs, L.W., Bongiorno, R.J., Lyons, D.V. and Tang, B. (1995), Improving personnel scheduling at airline stations. Operations Research 43(5), 741-751.

Verbeek, P.J. (1991), Decision support system – an application in strategic manpower planning of airline pilots, European Journal of Operational Research, 55, 368-381.

Yu, G. (1998), Industrial applications of combinatorial optimization, Kluwer Academics Publishers. Yu, G. and Thengvall, B. "Optimization in the Airline Industry." Handbook of Applied Optimization, edited by P.M. Pardalos and M.G.C. Resende, Oxford University Press, New York, 2002.

PART II
OPERATIONS AND DISPATCH OPTIMIZATION

Chapter 8

Revenue Management

Introduction

Revenue or yield management represents an important part of daily airline operations. It is concerned with maximizing the revenue or yield. However, yield or revenue management is somewhat misleading. The concept is not to manage yield or revenue, but rather to optimize it through the use of tools and techniques that maximize total revenue.

The concept of yield management is appropriate for business environments offering products (goods or services) with the following characteristics:

- It is expensive or impossible to store excess inventory;
- Future demand is uncertain;
- The firm can differentiate among customer segments (i.e., customers are willing to pay different prices for the same product);
- The fixed cost for offering the product is high, while the marginal cost is low;
- The capacity to offer the product is fixed.

The following industries are examples of business environments that have the above five characteristics:

- Car rentals;
- Broadcasting;
- Hotels;
- Cruise lines;
- Airlines;
- Trains, buses.

In all these industries, if the product is not sold or rented today, the revenue is lost forever. In the airline industry, the product is the airline seat. If the seat is not sold, and the plane departs, the revenue that could have been generated by selling that seat is lost.

Thus, the main challenge in revenue management is to set the price based on current market conditions, with the question becoming: 'do we turn down an existing customer in anticipation of other more profitable customers?'

A variety of analytical tools that addresses this question falls under the revenue management topic. Since these tools are used by firms offering perishable products (i.e., either expensive or impossible to store), they are also called *perishable asset revenue management tools*. See McGill and Van Ryzen (1999) for a review of revenue management models for non-airline service sectors.

Airline Revenue Management

The techniques of revenue management are relatively new. After deregulation in 1978, airlines were free to set the price for their seats. This led to heavy competition and new opportunities for revenue management. American and Delta Air Lines credit revenue management techniques for an increase in revenue amounting to $500 million and $300 million per year respectively.

An airline typically offers seats for several origin-destination (OD) itineraries in various fare classes. The seat fares not only differ among the traditional first, business and economy classes, but are also differentiated within the same class as well.

Considering that the seats offered, and their availability, is the source of revenue for the airline, the concept of revenue management thus primarily translates into a seat inventory control problem. Accordingly, the airline seat inventory control system has received a lot of attention from both the airline industry and academia.

Seat Inventory Control Problem

The seat inventory control problem is to decide if a seat should be sold at a current booking request, or if it should be saved for a more profitable customer. The mathematical models described in this chapter attempt to determine seat allocations according to the demand pattern at the beginning of the booking periods, and are referred to as *static* seat inventory control problems. See the list of references at the end of this chapter for an overview of *dynamic* seat inventory control systems.

Nested and Non-Nested Allocations

Basically, there have been two approaches to the airline seat allocation problem: Nested and non-nested. In non-nested approaches, distinct numbers of seats called buckets are exclusively assigned to each fare class. The sum of these buckets adds up to the total aircraft seat capacity. In nested allocations, each fare class is assigned a booking limit, which is the total number of seats assigned to that fare class plus the sum of all seat allocations to its lower fare classes. To clarify this further, consider an Airbus 320 with 150 seats. The following table shows the seats allocated to each fare class under nested and non-nested assignments:

As an example, for fare class B, under the non-nested approach, 50 seats are allocated, while under the nested approach there are 120 or (30+20+20+50) seats allocated to this class.

Revenue Management 111

Table 8.1   Example of non-nested and nested airline seat allocations

Fare Class	Non-Nested Allocation	Nested Allocation
Y	30	150
B	50	120
M	20	70
H	20	50
Q	30	30

Earlier revenue management approaches considered non-nested allocations. However, a major difficulty with non-nested approaches is that if the limit for a fare class is reached, a booking request for that class is denied, while a lower fare bucket remains open. In a nested seat allocation, this booking denial does not happen as the inventories are shared among each fare class and its lower classes. Figure 8.1 shows a depiction of both non-nested and nested approaches for the airline seat allocations example described in Table 8.1.

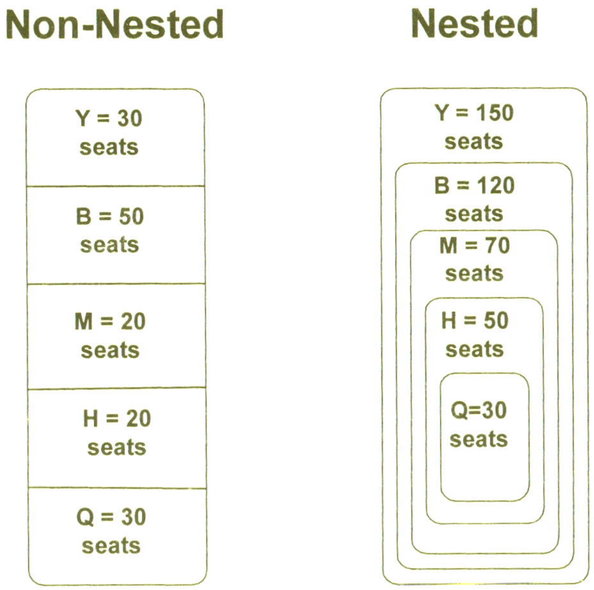

Non-Nested

- Y = 30 seats
- B = 50 seats
- M = 20 seats
- H = 20 seats
- Q = 30 seats

Nested

- Y = 150 seats
  - B = 120 seats
    - M = 70 seats
      - H = 50 seats
        - Q = 30 seats

Figure 8.1   Nested and non-nested airline seat allocations

Within both the nested and non nested approaches, a further problem concerns the allocation of seats by either single or networked flight-legs, referred to as the *single-leg seat inventory control problem* and the *network (multi-leg) seat inventory control problem,* respectively. In the following sections, both the nested and non-nested single-leg, and the nested and non-nested networked-legs are discussed. Before addressing these problems, however, we should understand the concept of expected marginal revenue.

Expected Marginal Revenue

At the core of the seat inventory control system is the expected marginal revenue (EMR). The EMR of potentially selling a seat in a fare class is the probability of being able to fill that seat multiplied by the average fare of that class. The concept of probability is introduced here since the demands for different flight legs and fare classes vary (stochastic demand).

In order to sell S seats for fare class i, we should have at least S requests for this fare class. We present this number of seats in fare class i as S_i.

Let r_i be the random variable representing the number of requests, and $p_i(r_i)$ be the probability distribution for r_i for fare class i. Assuming a continuous probability distribution for r_i, the probability of selling S_i seats in fare class i is:

$$P_i\left[r_i \geq S_i\right] = \int_{S_i}^{\infty} p_i\left(r_i \geq S_i\right) dr_i \quad (8.1)$$

As an example, if the probability distribution function is normal, then the above probability is represented by the shaded area in Figure 8.2.

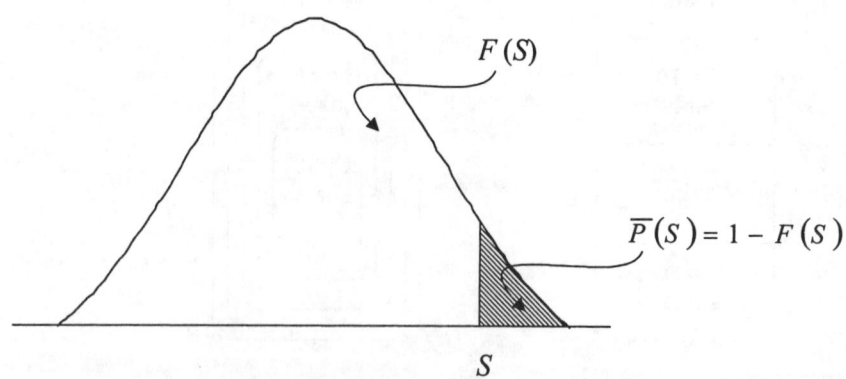

Figure 8.2 Normal probability distribution for demand with shaded area representing demand exceeding a certain level

Referring to Figure 8.2, the above probability (equation 8.1) can be rewritten as:

$$P_i\left[r_i \geq S_i\right] = \int_{S_i}^{\infty} p_i\left(r_i \geq S_i\right) dr_i = 1 - F_i\left(S_i\right) \quad (8.2)$$

where $F_i(S_i)$ is the cumulative distribution function of having S_i or lower requests for fare class i. The literature on revenue management adopts the notation $\overline{P}_i(S_i)$ to represent the above probability (see Figure 8.2).

Therefore:

$$P_i\left[r_i \geq S_i\right] = \int_{S_i}^{\infty} p_i\left(r_i \geq S_i\right) dr_i = 1 - F_i\left(S_i\right) = \overline{P}_i\left(S_i\right) \quad (8.3)$$

Going back to the definition of expected marginal revenue, the EMR for the Sth seat in fare class i, is simply the above probability multiplied by the average fare level in the respective fare class, or:

$$EMR\left(S_i\right) = f_i \cdot \overline{P}_i\left(S_i\right) \quad (8.4)$$

where $EMR(S_i)$ is the expected marginal revenue for the Sth seat in fare class i, f_i is the average fare level for class i, and $\overline{P}_i(S_i)$ is the probability of selling S or more seats in fare class i, as defined above.

To clarify this, let us consider the following example. Assume that the demand for class Y for a specific flight is normally distributed with a mean of 10 and a standard deviation of 2. The fare for this class is $400. The following table shows the EMR for each seat. According to this table, the EMR of selling the first seat in this fare class is $400. This is because for a normal probability distribution function, with a mean of 10 and a standard deviation of 2, the probability that a first seat is sold is almost 1. This probability reduces to 0.8413 for the 8th seat in this class, and so on. Note that the above table can be easily set up using Microsoft EXCEL's *NORMDIST* function.

Table 8.2   **Probability and expected marginal revenue for each seat in the fare class**

Seat (S)	$\overline{P}_i(S_i)$	$EMR(S_i)$
1	1.0000	$400.00
2	1.0000	$400.00
3	0.9998	$399.91
4	0.9987	$399.46
5	0.9938	$397.52
6	0.9772	$390.90
7	0.9332	$373.28
8	0.8413	$336.54
9	0.6915	$276.58
10	0.5000	$200.00

Note: The probabilities are rounded to 4 decimal places.

Single-Leg Seat Inventory Control Problem

In this problem, every flight-leg is independent of other legs and is optimized separately. The problem is to determine how many seats should be allocated to each fare class in an attempt to maximize the total revenue.

Non-Nested Model

Littlewood (1972) was the first to introduce a two fare non-nested seat inventory system. He proposed that as long as the expected marginal revenue from a seat for a higher fare passenger is larger than that of a lower fare passenger, then that seat should not be sold at a lower fare. In this model we have two fare levels: *Full fare* and *discount fare*. To express this mathematically, let:

f_1 = Full fare level

f_2 = Discount fare level

$P(r_1 \geq S_1)$ = Probability that the demand for full fare seat (r_1) is equal or exceeds S_1

We want to determine S_i, the number of seats protected for full fare paying passengers. Of course, subtracting this number from the total seat capacity determines the number of seats available for discount fare paying passengers. According to Littlewood, low fare passengers should be accepted as long as:

$$f_2 \geq f_1 \Pr(r_1 \geq S_1) \qquad (8.5)$$

The smallest value of S_i that satisfies the above condition is the protected number of seats for full fare paying passengers.

The following example explains how seat protections are determined using Littlewood's model:

> We want to determine the number of protected seats for full fare paying passengers on an Airbus 320 with 150 seats. The full and discount fares on a specific flight are $250 ($f_1$) and $100 ($f_2$) respectively. Historical data shows that the demand for a full fare class is normally distributed with a mean of 100 and a standard deviation of 15 passengers.

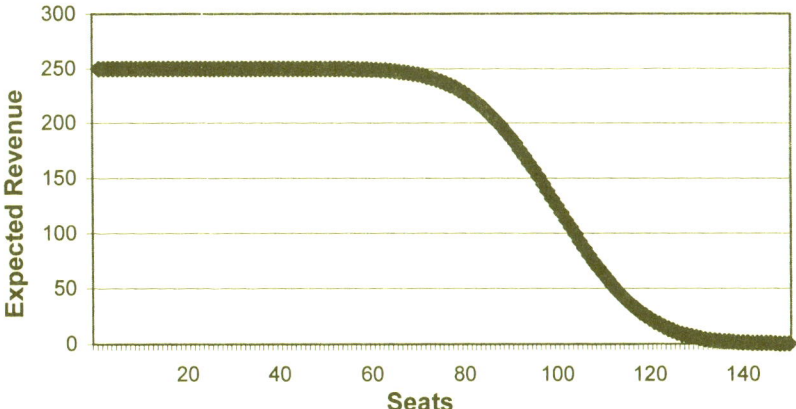

Figure 8.3 Expected marginal revenue for full-fare paying passengers

Figure 8.3 presents the EMR values for the full fare level ($250). The EMR values are determined similarly to the process described in table 8.2. This figure shows EMR for different numbers of seats. According to this figure, the EMR starts declining from the 70th seat until it reaches around the 140th seat, which has almost zero value for EMR.

According to the inequality in (equation 8.5), the requests for discount fares are accepted if this fare exceeds the EMR for the full fare level. The EMR for a full fare paying passenger for the 103rd seat is $105.19, and for the 104th seat is $98.72. Therefore the smallest value for S_l is 103. Thus, the airline should protect 103 seats for full fare paying passengers, and the remaining 47 (150-103) seats for the discount fare paying passengers.

Nested Model

Belobaba (1987) extended the above two-fare-class rule to multiple nested fare classes by introducing the term *expected marginal seat revenue* (EMSR). This method generates the nested protection level for different class fares. He proposed that in a nested seat allocation, the number of seats which should be protected for fare class i over fare class j is:

$$EMSR\left(S^i_j\right) = f_i \cdot \overline{P}_i\left(S^i_j\right) = f_j \qquad (8.6)$$

In this model, S^i_j is the number of seats that should be protected for higher class i over class j, while f_i and f_j are the average fare levels for the two classes of i and j respectively.

Based on this model, the number of seats protected for the highest fare class (Π_1) is S^1_2 satisfying:

$$EMSR\left(S^1_2\right) = f_1 \cdot \overline{P}_1\left(S^1_2\right) = f_2 \qquad (8.7)$$

To capture the nested seat allocation characteristic, the total protection level for the two highest fare classes (Π_2) is the sum of the individual protection levels S^1_3 and S^2_3 satisfying:

$$EMSR\left(S^1_3\right) = f_1 \cdot \overline{P}_1\left(S^1_3\right) = f_3 \qquad (8.8)$$

and

$$EMSR\left(S^2_3\right) = f_2 \cdot \overline{P}_2\left(S^2_3\right) = f_3 \qquad (8.9)$$

The total protection level for the highest two fares is therefore:

$$\Pi_2 = S^1_3 + S^2_3 \qquad (8.10)$$

Applying the same principle, the protected number of seats for the (n-1) fare class is determined by:

$$\Pi_{n-1} = \sum_{i=1}^{n-1} S^i_n \qquad (8.11)$$

The booking limit or the number of seats available for each class i, represented by BL_i, is determined by subtracting the number of seats protected for the higher fare class, Π_{i-1}, from the total aircraft seat capacity, C. Therefore:

$$BL_i = C - \Pi_{i-1} \qquad (8.12)$$

It should be noted, that based on our definition for nested seat allocation, the booking limit for the highest fare class is:

$$BL_1 = C \qquad (8.13)$$

BL_i may also be negative (especially for lower fare classes), in which case the above booking limit becomes:

$$BL_i = Max(0, C - \Pi_{i-1}) \qquad (8.14)$$

The nested protection for fare class i is therefore the difference between the booking limits for that fare and its lower fare class as follows:

$$NP_i = BL_i - BL_{i+1} \qquad (8.15)$$

where NP_i is the nested seat protection level for fare class i. Figure 8.4 shows the booking levels and seat protections as described by this model.

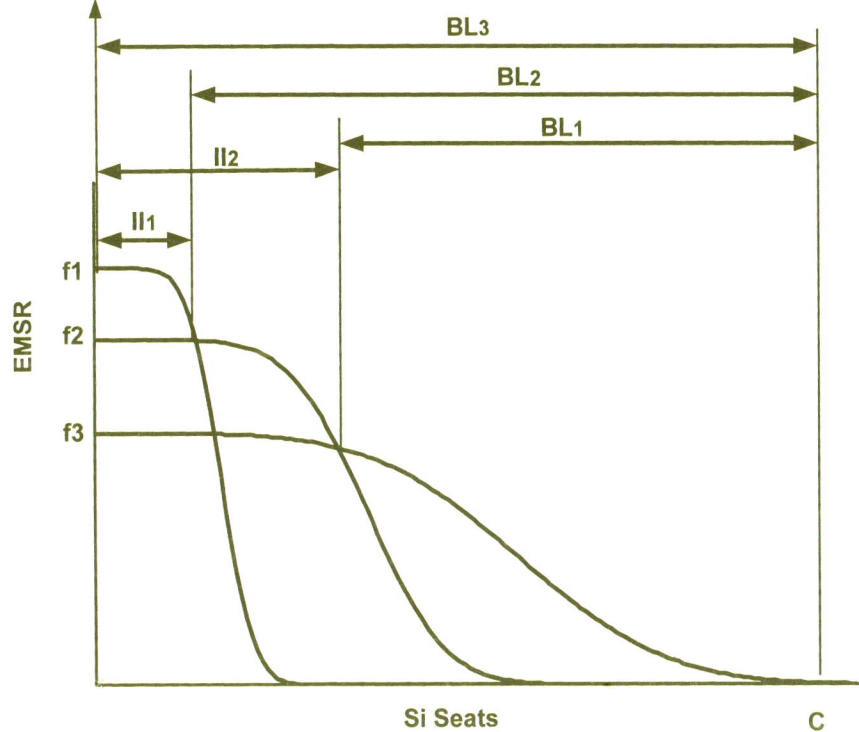

Figure 8.4 Seat protections and booking levels for three fare classes under the nested seat allocation model

To clarify the above nested seat allocation model, consider an Airbus 320 with 150 seats. The following table shows the distribution of demand for four classes, with the fare levels for each class on a specific flight. All demand for different fare classes follow normal distributions with indicated means and standard deviations. We want to adopt the above nested EMSR approach to determine the seat allocation and booking level for each fare class.

Table 8.3   Fare classes, demand distributions and fare levels for a flight

Fare Class	Demand distribution	Fare level
Y	Mean = 25 SD=5	$580
B	Mean = 54 SD=12	$480
M	Mean = 84 SD= 23	$350
Q	Mean = 130 SD=20	$250

To determine the booking limits, an EXCEL spreadsheet may be useful. A table similar to Table 8.2 is constructed for every fare class. Figure 8.5 shows the EMSR for the four classes.

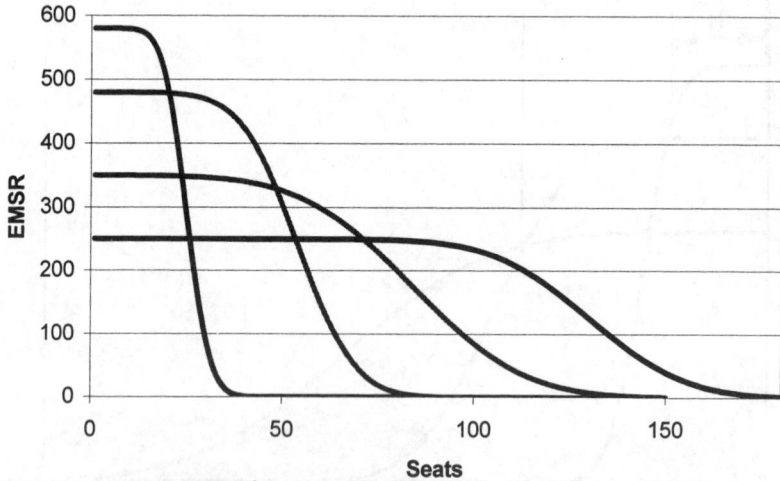

Figure 8.5   EMSR for the four-fare-class example

By comparing different EMSR within different fare classes, we can determine S^i_j. Table 8.4 shows the values of S^i_j or the protected number of seats for each fare class over each of its lower classes. As an example, S^1_2 in this table is 20 seats, which represents the number of protected seats for Y over the M fare class, etc.

Table 8.4 Protected number of seats for each fare class over lower classes

Fare class/Fare class	M (fare class 2)	B (fare class 3)	Q (fare class 4)
Y (fare class 1)	20	23	25
M (fare class 2)	-	46	53
B (fare class 3)	-	-	71

Using the above definitions, the protection level for each fare class and booking limit is as follows:

$$\Pi_1 = S_2^1 = 20$$

$$\Pi_2 = S_3^1 + S_3^2 = 23 + 46 = 69$$

$$\Pi_3 = S_4^1 + S_4^2 + S_4^3 = 25 + 53 + 71 = 149$$

Therefore 20 seats should be protected for class Y; 69 seats for classes Y and M; and 149 seats for classes Y, M and B. We can therefore determine the booking limits as follows:

$$BL_1 = C = 150$$
$$BL_2 = C - \Pi_1 = 150 - 20 = 130$$
$$BL_3 = C - \Pi_2 = 150 - 69 = 81$$
$$BL_4 = C - \Pi_3 = 150 - 149 = 1$$
$$NP_1 = BL_1 - BL_2 = 150 - 130 = 20$$
$$NP_2 = BL_2 - BL_3 = 130 - 81 = 49$$
$$NP_3 = BL_3 - BL_4 = 81 - 1 = 80$$
$$NP_4 = C - NP_1 - NP_2 - NP_3 = 150 - 20 - 49 - 80 = 1$$

Based on the above values for booking limits, 20 seats should be protected for fare class Y, 49 for class M, 80 for class B, and finally only 1 seat should be allocated to fare class Q. For a nested allocation, these protections result in 1 seat for fare class Q, 81 seats for class B, 130 seats for class M, and finally all 150 seats to class Y.

The above method is very popular due to its simplicity and ease of implementation. It finds the optimal booking limits between each pair of fare classes. It does not, however, consider the fact that the fare classes are sequentially nested within each other and hence interrelated. In other words, this method does not consider the joint probability distribution among the fare classes. Other researchers (see McGill and Van Ryzin, 1999 for a list of references) have developed optimal booking levels by considering multiple (more than 2) nested fare classes.

Network (Multi-Leg) Seat Inventory Control Problem

The seat inventory policy that was described in the previous section considered the revenue generated only on one flight-leg. It is very common, however, to see passengers on the same flight having different itineraries due to the airline hub and spoke systems. We use the term *Origin-Destination* (OD) to represent the starting and ending points of an itinerary. Figure 8.6 shows a simplified network. Passengers flying from Orlando to Chicago or Los Angeles will be on the same flight (F1) departing Orlando for the Atlanta hub. At Atlanta these passengers change flights to their respective destinations.

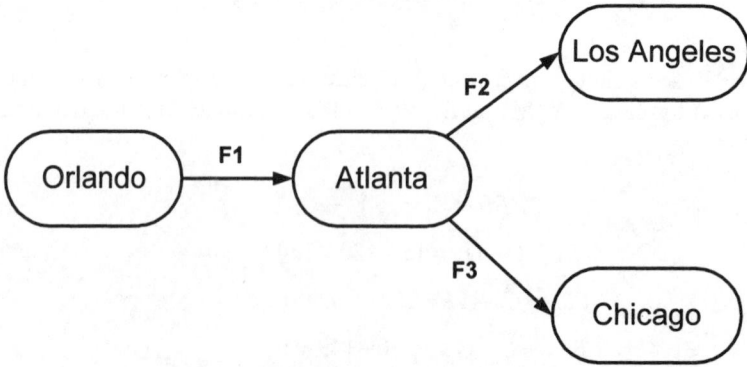

Figure 8.6 A simple network representing passengers with different origin-destination itineraries

In this simplified network, we have passengers with ODs: (Orlando-Atlanta), (Orlando-Los Angeles), (Orlando-Chicago), (Atlanta-Los Angeles) and (Atlanta-Chicago). The network seat inventory control system attempts to assign seats with different fare classes on each flight-leg to different OD passengers so that the total revenue over the entire network is maximized. The following sections study this network revenue management under *deterministic* and *stochastic* demand models.

Network Seat Inventory Control Model with Deterministic Demand (Non-nested)

In this model we consider that the demand for each fare class and each OD is deterministic, and hence known in advance.
Let us define:

x_{ODF} = Number of protected seats on flight-leg OD (origin-destination) for fare class F.
f_{ODF} = Fare for class F on flight-leg OD.

C_j = Aircraft capacity on flight-leg j.

D_{ODF} = Deterministic demand for OD for fare class F.

The deterministic approach seeks to determine x_{ODF} so that the total revenue generated, from allocating seats to fare classes on every flight-leg, is maximized. The following mathematical model attempts to find these seat allocations:

$$\text{Max} \sum_{ODF} f_{ODF} \cdot x_{ODF}$$

Subject to:

$$\sum_{ODF} x_{ODF} \leq C_j \quad \text{for all ODFs on flight-leg j, for all flight-legs j}$$

$$x_{ODF} \leq D_{ODF} \quad \text{for all ODFs} \tag{8.16}$$

$$x_{ODF} \quad \text{integer for all ODFs}$$

The first set of constraints limits the total number of bookings to aircraft capacity on each leg. The second set ensures that the allocated seats on each OD, and for each fare class F, do not exceed the demand. The solution to this integer linear programming model determines the number of each origin-destination, and each fare class, so that the total revenue over the entire network is maximized.

To demonstrate how this model works, let us consider the network presented in Figure 8.7. Node H represents the hub, and the other nodes are spokes. As the network suggests, passengers wishing to go from A to C will have one stop in H. Therefore, origin-destination A to C consists of two flight-legs, A to H and H to C.

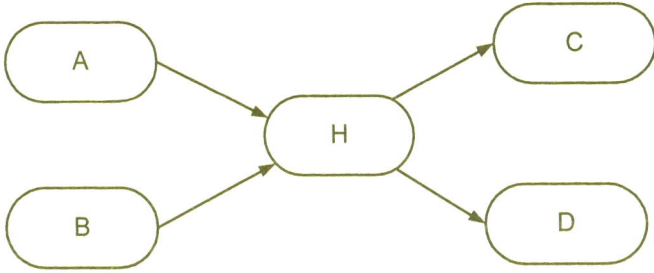

Figure 8.7 Network diagram for the multi-leg example

Table 8.5 presents the deterministic demand and fare level for all ODs in this network. For each flight, we have two fare classes namely, Y and B. All aircraft flying from A and B to H have a capacity of 90 seats, and all aircraft flying from H to C and D have a 142-seat capacity.

Table 8.5   Demand and fare levels for the multi-leg example

Flight-leg	Fare Class Y	Fare Class B
AH	Demand: 38	Demand: 52
	Fare: 354	Fare: 181
AC	Demand: 26	Demand: 43
	Fare: 376	Fare: 286
AD	Demand: 24	Demand: 40
	Fare: 283	Fare: 200
BH	Demand: 25	Demand: 35
	Fare: 236	Fare: 133
BC	Demand: 28	Demand: 38
	Fare: 511	Fare: 281
BD	Demand: 22	Demand: 45
	Fare: 500	Fare: 365
HC	Demand: 35	Demand: 43
	Fare: 354	Fare: 191
HD	Demand: 28	Demand: 40
	Fare: 367	Fare: 195

To formulate this mathematical model, we adopt the following decision variable:

X_{ODF} = Number of seats allocated to origin O, destination D, and fare class F.

The objective function is to maximize the total revenue generated in the network. Thus,

$$\text{Maximize } 354x_{AHY} + 181x_{AHB} + \ldots + 367x_{HDY} + 195x_{HDB}$$

The first set of constraints concerns the aircraft capacity on each leg.

$$x_{AHY} + x_{AHB} + x_{ACY} + x_{ACB} + x_{ADY} + x_{ADB} \leq 90$$
$$x_{BHY} + x_{BHB} + x_{BCY} + x_{BCB} + x_{BDY} + x_{BDB} \leq 90$$
$$x_{HCY} + x_{HCB} + x_{ACY} + x_{ACB} + x_{BCY} + x_{BCB} \leq 142$$
$$x_{HDY} + x_{HDB} + x_{ADY} + x_{ADB} + x_{BDY} + x_{BDB} \leq 142$$

As an example, in the first constraint we specify that the total number of passengers on flight-leg AH, which includes passengers flying from A to H plus

Revenue Management

those who are flying from A to C plus passengers flying from A to D (in both fare classes), should not exceed the aircraft capacity.

The following set of constraints restricts the number of passengers on each origin-destination and fare class to the corresponding demand:

$$x_{AHY} \leq 38$$
$$x_{AHB} \leq 52$$
$$\ldots\ldots$$
$$x_{HDY} \leq 28$$
$$x_{HDB} \leq 40$$

This linear integer program has 16 variables and 20 constraints. Solving this model using an optimization software results in a total network revenue of $89,096. The solution to the seat allocations for each ODF is presented in table 8.6. According to this solution, no seat should be allocated to origin-destination BH. However, 28 seats are allocated to BC. This is because allocating the seat to a passenger with a multiple-leg itinerary (BH+HC), generates more revenue for the airline than a single-leg itinerary from B to H. This is one reason behind the familiar case of a reservations system showing no seats available on a specific flight, while another passenger with a multi-leg OD is successful in making a reservation on the same flight.

Table 8.6   Solution to the deterministic network seat allocation example

Flight-leg	Protected Seats for Y Class	Protected Seats for B Class
AH	Demand: 38	Demand: 52
	Allocation: 38	Allocation: 0
AC	Demand: 26	Demand: 43
	Allocation: 26	Allocation: 14
AD	Demand: 24	Demand: 40
	Allocation: 12	Allocation: 0
BH	Demand: 25	Demand: 35
	Allocation: 0	Allocation: 0
BC	Demand: 28	Demand: 38
	Allocation: 28	Allocation: 0
BD	Demand: 22	Demand: 45
	Allocation: 22	Allocation: 40
HC	Demand: 35	Demand: 43
	Allocation: 35	Allocation: 0
HD	Demand: 28	Demand: 40
	Allocation: 28	Allocation: 40

Network Seat Inventory Control Model with Probabilistic Demand (Non-Nested)

A major difficulty with the previous deterministic network model is that the solution is based on certainty of demand. In many real world cases, the demand is stochastic, and hence varies over time. To capture the variability of demand, the mathematical model in (equation 8.16) is revised to accommodate the probability distribution of demand for different ODFs. In this model, we seek to maximize the expected revenue over the entire network.

Based on expected marginal revenue discussed earlier in this chapter, we have:

$$EMR_{ODF}(S_{ODF}) = f_{ODF} \cdot \overline{P}_{ODF}(S_{ODF}) \qquad (8.17)$$

where:

$EMR_{ODF}(S_{ODF})$ = Expected marginal revenue from the Sth seat in fare class F on OD.

f_{ODF} = Average fare for class F on OD.

$\overline{P}_{ODF}(S_{ODF})$ = Probability of selling the Sth seat (i.e. demand $\geq$ S) in fare class F on OD.

To formulate this mathematical model, we define binary decision variables as follows:

$$x_{S,ODF} = \begin{cases} 1 \text{ if the } S^{th} \text{ aircraft seat is assigned to fare class } F \text{ on origin-destination } OD \\ 0 \text{ otherwise} \end{cases}$$

The objective function is to maximize the total expected revenue through the network.

$$\text{Maximize } \sum_{ODF} \sum_{S=1}^{C_j} EMR_{ODF}(S_{ODF}) \cdot x_{S,ODF}$$

subject to:

$$\sum_{ODF} \sum_{S=1}^{C_j} x_{S,ODF} \leq C_j \qquad \text{for all flight-legs j}$$

The above constraint states that the total number of allocated seats should not exceed the aircraft capacity on each flight-leg.

Let us return to our example for deterministic demand. We assume that all the demand distributions are normal, with the same means as in the deterministic case.

Table 8.7 provides the means and standard deviations of demand for each fare class and OD.

To construct a mathematical model, we need to compute the EMR for each seat on each ODF. An EXCEL spreadsheet is helpful in generating these EMRs. As an example, Table 8.8 shows the EMR for the first ten seats for origin-destination AH for class Y.

Table 8.7   Probabilistic demand for the network seat allocation example

Flight-leg	Fare Class Y	Fare Class B
AH	Demand: 38 SD: 14 Fare: 354	Demand: 52 SD: 11 Fare: 181
AC	Demand: 26 SD: 6 Fare: 376	Demand: 43 SD: 9 Fare: 286
AD	Demand: 24 SD: 4 Fare: 283	Demand: 40 SD: 8 Fare: 200
BH	Demand: 25 SD: 8 Fare: 236	Demand: 35 SD: 4 Fare: 133
BC	Demand: 28 SD: 6 Fare: 511	Demand: 38 SD: 9 Fare: 281
BD	Demand: 22 SD: 4 Fare: 500	Demand: 45 SD: 8 Fare: 365
HC	Demand: 35 SD: 6 Fare: 354	Demand: 43 SD: 12 Fare: 191
HD	Demand: 28 SD: 6 Fare: 367	Demand: 40 SD: 8 Fare: 195

Table 8.8 Expected marginal revenue for the probabilistic network seat allocation example

Seat Number	Probability	Fare	EMR
1	0.995889	$354.00	$352.54
2	0.994936	$354.00	$352.21
3	0.99379	$354.00	$351.80
4	0.992421	$354.00	$351.32
5	0.990792	$354.00	$350.74
6	0.988865	$354.00	$350.06
7	0.986595	$354.00	$349.25
8	0.983938	$354.00	$348.31
9	0.980841	$354.00	$347.22
10	0.97725	$354.00	$345.95

The mathematical model for this case will be to:

$$\text{Maximize } 352.54 x_{1,AHY} + 352.21 x_{2,AHY} + \ldots$$

subject to:

$$x_{1,AHY} + x_{2,AHY} + \ldots + x_{90,ADB} \le 90$$

$$x_{1,BHY} + x_{2,BHY} + \ldots + x_{90,BDB} \le 90$$

$$x_{1,HCY} + x_{2,HCY} + \ldots + x_{90,BCB} \le 142$$

$$x_{1,HDY} + x_{2,HDy} + \ldots + x_{90,BDB} \le 142$$

This mathematical model has more than 1200 binary decision variables and 4 constraints. The four constraints represent the capacity on four flight-legs. The airlines have automated systems that generate the linear programming model, which it then solves either optimally or using heuristics (see chapter 12).

Solving the above binary integer programming model results in a total network expected revenue of $100,298. The solution to the seat allocations for each ODF is presented in Table 8.9.

Revenue Management 127

Table 8.9 Solution to the probabilistic network seat allocation example

Flight-leg	Protected for Class Y	Protected for Class B
AH	Demand: 38	Demand: 52
	Allocations: 37	Allocations: 0
AC	Demand: 26	Demand: 43
	Allocations: 21	Allocations: 16
AD	Demand: 24	Demand: 40
	Allocations: 16	Allocations: 0
BH	Demand: 25	Demand: 35
	Allocations: 10	Allocations: 0
BC	Demand: 28	Demand: 38
	Allocations: 25	Allocations: 0
BD	Demand: 22	Demand: 45
	Allocations: 20	Allocations: 35
HC	Demand: 35	Demand: 43
	Allocations: 38	Allocations: 42
HD	Demand: 28	Demand: 40
	Allocations: 31	Allocations: 40

As we see in this table, for some ODs such as HC and HD, the number of allocated seats for the Y fare class is actually larger than the expected demand. This is due to the higher EMR generated from these seats.

Network Seat Inventory Control Models (Nested)

There are several different methods for nested network seat inventory control systems. The common approach for these methods is to cluster the seat allocations derived from non-nested into *virtual nested* allocations. There are many heuristics for such clustering. In this section, we briefly discuss one of these clustering methods namely, *nesting by fare class*. See McGill and Van Ryzin (1999) for an overview of other clustering methods.

Nesting by Fare Class

In this method, for each fare class on a flight-leg, the respective solutions for non-nested ODF allocations from either deterministic or probabilistic networks are summed together (Williamson 1992). These total allocations are then used as the protection levels for each fare class. The booking limits for each fare class are determined by subtracting these protection levels from the capacity of the flight-leg.

To clarify this, let us return to our non-nested example for the deterministic demand network. Consider the flight-leg AH. We want to determine the booking limits for the two fare classes, Y and B. Returning to Figure 8.7, the passengers on flight-leg AH include those with origin-destinations: AH, AC and AD. The solutions obtained from the non-nested network for these three OD passengers are shown in Table 8.10.

Table 8.10   Seat allocations on flight-leg AH

ODF	Non-Nested Seat Allocations
AHY	38
ACY	26
ADY	24

According to the virtual nesting method described above, we assign the total aircraft capacity to the highest fare class, in this case, fare class Y. The aircraft capacity is 90 seats. Therefore, the booking limit for class Y on flight-leg AH is also 90 seats. For the lower fare class B, the booking limit is simply the booking limit for fare class Y minus the number of seats assigned to fare class Y for all passengers with AH as part of their itinerary. So, the booking limit on flight-leg AH for fare class B is 14 seats (90-38-26-24).

Overbooking

Airlines regularly face passengers who cancel their flight reservations at the last minute, or fail to show-up for flights (called *no-shows*). Certainly the seats allocated to such passengers will remain empty. To generate revenue from these anticipated empty seats, the airlines normally overbook their flights by selling more seats than the capacity on a given flight. This process of overbooking has been studied under revenue management techniques. A major issue in overbooking is to balance the anticipated revenue from selling extra seats versus the anticipated cost of not having enough capacity to accommodate all the passengers.

A common approach to addressing this problem is the *single-period inventory control model*.

Let us define the following parameters:

C_o = Cost of overestimating the number of no-shows. It is the cost of accommodating a passenger with a confirmed reservation when there are no seats available on the flight. This cost is normally referred to as *spillage* cost, and it occurs when the airline sells too many seats, and one or more passengers are denied boarding (referred to as *bumped passengers*). This cost includes finding other arrangements, ticket upgrading, accommodation costs, goodwill costs etc.

C_u = Cost of underestimating the number of no-shows. It represents the lost revenue due to an empty seat. This cost, which is also referred to as cost of *spoilage*, occurs when the airline makes very few seat overbookings, and one or more seats end-up being empty for the flight.

r = Number of overbooked seats.

$P(no\text{-}shows)$ = Probability distribution for the number of no-shows. This is the probability distribution for the number of passengers who cancel their reservations at the last minute, or fail to show-up on a given flight. The airlines typically have historical data on no-shows for every flight, from which such probability distributions can be derived.

The optimum level for r, the number of overbooked seats, is when we have a balance between the expected *spoilage* and *spillage* costs as follows:

$$C_o \cdot P(no-shows \leq r) = C_u \cdot P(no-shows > r) \quad (8.18)$$

We have:

$$P(no-shows \leq r) + P(no-shows > r) = 1$$

Therefore equation (8.18) can be rewritten as:

$$C_o \cdot P(no-shows \leq r) = C_u \cdot [1 - P(no-shows \leq r)]$$

Rearranging this equation, results in:

$$P(no-shows \leq r) = \frac{C_u}{C_u + C_o} \quad (8.19)$$

The solution to this problem is similar to the well-known *newsvendor problem* in operations research. According to this solution, the cumulative probability distribution that meets this threshold determines the optimal value of seats to be overbooked.

Let us consider the following example. According to past data, the number of no-shows on a 150-seat aircraft follows a normal distribution with a mean of 20 and a standard deviation of 10 passengers. The cost of bumping a passenger (C_o) is $300, which includes provisions for accommodation on an alternate flight, board and lodging for an overnight stay, and gift vouchers usable for future flights. On the other hand, the cost of an empty seat (C_u) is $185. According to equation (8.19) we have:

$$P(no-shows \le r) = \frac{185}{300+185} = .3814$$

Using EXCEL's *Norminv* function, or a normal distribution table, we find r =16.98. Rounding this number, results in an optimal number of overbooking of 17 seats. We notice that the optimal number of overbooking (r) is actually less than the expected number of no-shows (20). This is because the cost of *spillage* is larger than the cost of *spoilage*.

References

Belobaba, P.P. (1987), Airline Yield Management: An Overview of Seat Inventory Control, Transportation Science, 21, 63-73.

Belobaba, P.P. and Botimer, T.C. (1992), Airline yield management research issues. *Presented to Optimization Days 1992*, May 4, 1992, Montreal, Canada.

Coulter, K. (1999), The application of airline yield management techniques to a holiday retail shopping setting. *Journal of Product & Brand Management*, 8(1), 61-72.

Elkins, S. and Hormby, S. (1993), Fundamentals of yield management. *Presented at 4th Multi-Industry Yield Management Conference* March 24, 1993, San Antonio, TX.

Hopperstad, C.A. and Belobaba, P.P. (1997), PODS Update: simulation of O-D revenue management schemes. *AGIFORS Symposium* September 1997, Bali.

Jacobs, T.L., Hunt, E. and Korol, M. (2001), Operations research and decision support at American Airlines. *AGIFORS Symposium* August, 2001. Sydney, Australia. 320-331.

Jung, N. and Weber, K. (2001), Integration of pricing and revenue management for a future without booking classes. *AGIFORS 41st Annual Symposium.* August 27 – September 1, 2001. Sydney, Australia. 182-198.

Li, M.Z.F. (2001), Pricing non-storable perishable goods by using a purchase restriction with an application to airline fare pricing. *European Journal of Operations Research* 134, 631-647.

Littlewood, K. (1972), Forecasting and Control of Passenger Bookings, in AGIFORS Symposium Proc. 12, Nathanya, Israel.

McGill, J.I. and Van Ryzin, G.J. (1999, May), Revenue Management: Research Overview and Prospects. *Transportation Science*, 33(12), 233-256.

Netessine, S. and Shumsky, R. (2002), Introduction to the Theory and Practice of Yield Management. *INFORMS Transactions on Education* Vol. 3:1, September 2002, pp. 34-44.

Polt, S. (1998), Forecasting is difficult – especially if it refers to the future. *Presented at 38th AGIFORS Symposium* September 6-11, 1998, Prague.

Realtime: The Ultimate O&D (1998), with no reference information.

Simon, J.L. (1968, May), An almost practical solution to airline overbooking. *Journal of Transport Economics and Policy* 201-202.

Travers, J., Denman, R., Dalziel, N. and Blackburn, R. (1996), Optimising multi-leg flights at British Airways. *Presented at AGIFORS* November 1996.

Wang, K. (1995), Revenue management – an integrated approach. P*resented at AGIFORS 35th Annual Symposium* September 20, 1995, Tel Aviv, Israel.

Williamson, E.L. (1992, June), Airline Network Seat Inventory Control: Methodologies and Revenue Impacts. *Flight Transportation Laboratory Report R 92-3*, Cambridge, Mass.

Chapter 9

Gate Assignment

Introduction

The hub-and-spoke system has resulted in a large volume of baggage and passengers transferring between flights. Assigning arriving flights to airport gates is therefore an important issue in daily operations of an airline. Although the costs of these activities are generally small portions of the overall airline operation costs, they have a major impact on maintaining the efficiency of flight schedules and passenger satisfaction. Some of the factors that impact the assignment of gates to arriving flights include aircraft size, passenger walking distances, baggage transfer, ramp congestion, aircraft rotation and aircraft service requirements (Gu and Chung 1999).

The problem of finding a suitable gate assignment is usually handled in three levels. In the first level, the ground controllers use the flight schedule to examine the capacity of gates to accommodate these flights. The second level involves the development of daily plans before the actual day of operation. In the third level, because of irregular conditions such as delays, bad weather, mechanical failure and maintenance requirements these daily plans are updated and revised on the same hour/day of the operation (Bolat 2000).

The problem of gate assignment is well studied in operations research. A common approach in formulating this problem is from the passenger's perspective in a way that the total passenger walking distance is minimized. The gate assignment problem (GAP) is defined as follows:

Given a set of available gates and flights, the distance matrix between the gates, the passenger transfer matrix between the flights, we seek to assign these flights to the gates so that the total passengers walking distances are minimized.

The researchers have adopted a variety of problem formulation and solution methods to address the various issues in GAP (see Bolat 2000, Haghani 1998, Gu and Chung 1999, Jo, et al. 1997 and Paelink 1991). The model described in this chapter is an integer linear programming model proposed by Bihr 1990.

Mathematical Model for a Case Study

The following case study (not related to Ultimate Air!) involves the assignment of flights to gates. Figure 9.1 shows the C Concourse at San Francisco (SFO) Airport, which has 19 gates (C1-C19). There are already 12 aircraft at the gates (as shown) getting ready for their departures. Within the next 15 minutes seven flights will be

Gate Assignment 133

arriving in this concourse that should be assigned to the remaining gates. These flights are referred to as F1, F2, F3, F4, F5, F6 and F7. In these seven flights, there are passengers who will connect to other departing flights. Without loss of generality, we assume that any of these arriving flights can be accommodated in any of the seven available gates.

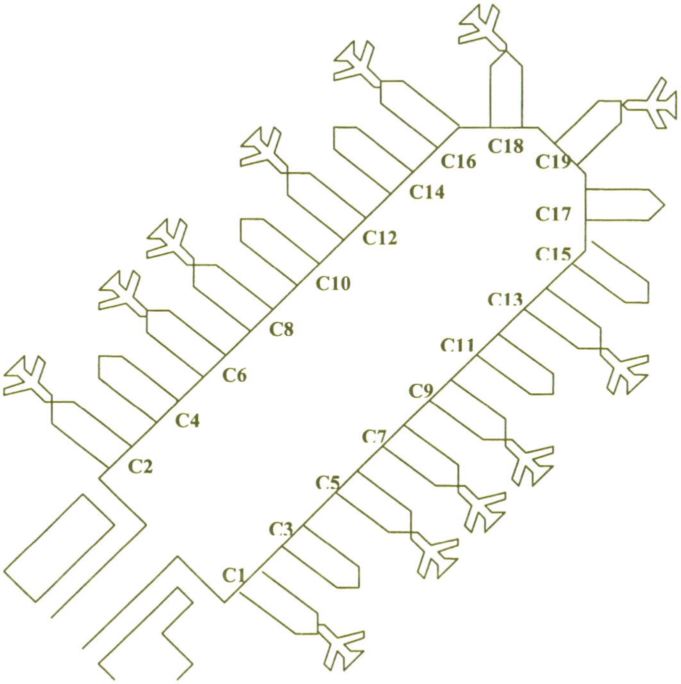

Figure 9.1 C Concourse at SFO

Table 9.1 shows the number of passengers in these flights who will connect to other departing gates. As an example, five passengers from flight F1 should walk to gate 1, etc. Note that in this model it is assumed that the departing flights are initially or tentatively have been designated to gates (Bihr 1990).

Table 9.1   Passenger flow

Departing Gates

Flight/Gate	1	2	3	4	5	6	7	8	9	10	11	12	13	14	15	16	17	18	19
F1	5	5	10	8	15	8	2	10	8	20	5	4	0	9	3	4	1	2	1
F2	5	2	1	4	19	9	4	2	3	2	27	3	8	4	0	2	1	7	2
F3	10	0	4	9	13	4	4	4	3	5	5	8	4	9	11	7	9	4	4
F4	4	8	5	4	10	4	1	0	0	2	4	19	1	2	4	5	5	8	2
F5	4	11	9	9	6	3	1	4	4	2	1	0	3	5	1	2	2	3	4
F6	1	2	42	5	2	7	6	2	4	7	2	3	6	4	10	2	1	0	0
F7	3	3	2	5	9	13	11	2	2	3	7	22	4	0	1	1	2	2	9

The distances in yards between the gates are presented in Table 9.2. Note that in this matrix, only the distances between the candidate arrival gates and other gates are shown.

Table 9.2   Distance matrix

Departing Gates

G/G	1	2	3	4	5	6	7	8	9	10	11	12	13	14	15	16	17	18	19
3	10	40	-	30	10	40	20	50	30	60	40	70	50	80	60	90	70	90	80
4	40	10	30	-	40	10	50	20	60	30	70	40	80	50	90	60	90	70	80
10	70	40	60	30	50	20	40	10	30	-	40	10	50	40	60	30	70	40	50
11	50	80	40	70	30	60	20	50	10	40	-	30	10	40	20	50	30	50	40
14	90	60	80	50	70	40	60	30	50	20	40	10	30	-	40	10	50	20	30
15	70	100	60	90	50	80	40	70	30	60	20	50	10	40	-	30	10	30	20
17	80	100	70	90	60	80	50	70	40	60	30	50	20	40	10	30	-	20	10

Through this model we seek to assign the arriving flights to candidate gates so that the total passengers' walking distance is minimized.

Using the above two tables (Tables 9.1 and 9.2) we can find the total walking distances of passengers on flight i if this flight is assigned to arrival gate j. The walking distance is calculated as follows:

Walking distance = $\sum$ number of passengers × distance

For example, if flight F1 is assigned to the candidate arrival gate 3, then the total walking distances for all passengers on this flight assigned to this gate is calculated as follows:

Total walking distance = 5%10+5%40+10%0+8%30+15%10+8%40+2%20+10%50+8%30+20%60+5%40+4%70+0%50+9%80+3%60+4%90+1%70+2%90+1%80
= 5010 Yards

In other words, by assigning flight F1 to gate 3, five passengers on this flight must walk a distance of 10 yards each, to gate 1, five passengers must walk 40 yards each, to gate 2; and 10 passengers will depart from the same gate as they arrived and therefore not having to walk. We repeat the above calculations for every flight assigned to every candidate gate. The following table shows the total walking distances for passengers aboard each flight by assigning them to every possible gate:

Table 9.3 Traveling distances

Flight/gate	3	4	10	11	14	15	17
F1	5010	4390	3820	4870	5060	6650	7090
F2	4240	5290	4190	3020	4650	4400	4970
F3	5610	5950	4930	4270	4910	4950	5320
F4	4500	3990	3280	3580	3460	4320	4460
F5	2950	2720	3060	3490	3620	4330	4530
F6	3060	4310	4740	3900	5760	5300	6020
F7	4680	4380	3290	3620	3970	4960	5220

We define the following binary decision variable:

$$x_{i,j} = \begin{cases} 1 \text{ if flight } i \text{ is assigned to candidate gate } j \\ 0 \text{ otherwise} \end{cases}$$

The objective function is therefore:

$$\text{Minimize } 5010x_{F1,3} + 4390x_{F1,4} + \ldots + 5220x_{F7,17}$$

For constraints, we should ensure that every flight is assigned to a gate. We have seven gates (3,4,10,11,14,15 and 17) available. The constraint for flight F1 is:

$$x_{F1,3} + x_{F1,4} + x_{F1,10} + x_{F1,11} + x_{F1,14} + x_{F1,15} + x_{F1,17} = 1$$

The above constraints ensure that flight F1 is assigned to one and only one gate among the 7 available gates. Similarly we write the other six constraints for other flights.

If we run this integer linear program with the above constraints we see that one gate is assigned to two or more flights at the same time; rendering it not feasible. So we must ensure that each gate is also assigned to one flight (aircraft) only. The following additional set of constraints imposes this restriction for gate 3.

$$x_{F1,3} + x_{F2,3} + x_{F3,3} + x_{F4,3} + x_{F5,3} + x_{F6,3} + x_{F7,3} = 1$$

Similarly we write the constraints for other six gates.

The above integer linear programming model has 49 binary decision variables and 14 constraints.

136 *Airline Operations and Scheduling*

Solving this problem using an optimization software generates the following matching flights to gates solution. The total walking distances for this optimal solution among all passengers is 26,000 yards.

Table 9.4   Solution to gate assignment

Flight	Gate assigned to
F1	10
F2	11
F3	15
F4	17
F5	4
F6	3
F7	14

Figure 9.2 shows the allocation of these gates to flights.

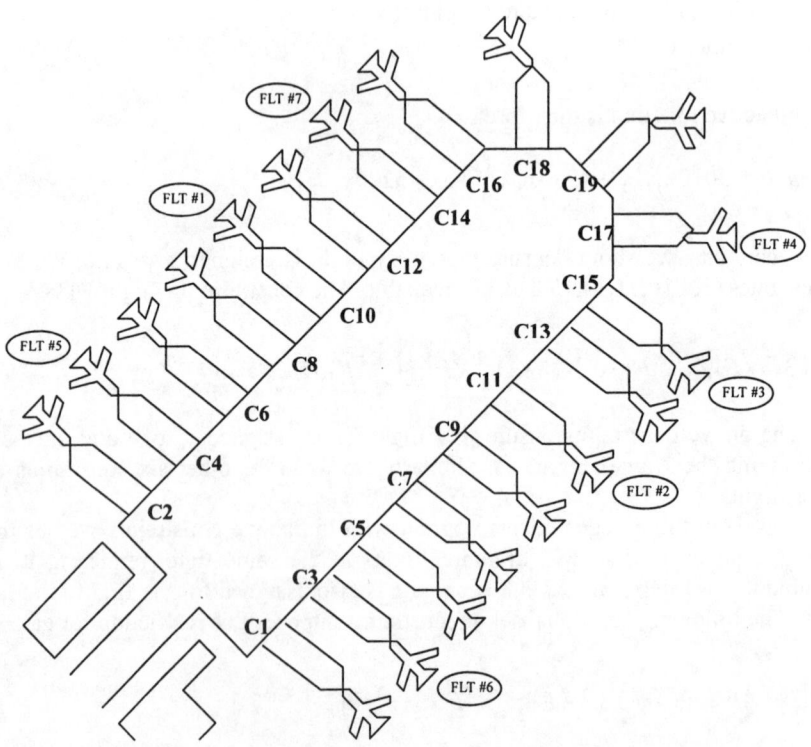

Figure 9.2   Assignment of gates to flights

Now, we can relax the assumption that any gate can accommodate any aircraft. Let us assume that gates 10 and 14 cannot be used for the aircraft in flight F1. To address this, simply add the following constraints to restrict the assignment of gates 10 and 14 to flight F1.

$x_{F1,10} = 0$

$x_{F1,14} = 0$

Running the model with these new constraints generates the following solution with a total walking distances of 26,700 yards.

Table 9.5   Revised assignments of gates to flights

Flight	Gate assigned to
F1	4
F2	11
F3	15
F4	14
F5	17
F6	3
F7	10

Mathematical Model

The mathematical model for the above case study proposed by Bihr (1990) can formally be presented as:

Indices
i index for arriving flights
j,k index for gates

Sets
F set of arriving flights
G set of available gates for arriving flights
K set of departing gates

Parameters

$p_{i,k}$ number of passengers arriving on flight i and departing from gate k

$d_{k,j}$ distance units (in yards, meters, feet, etc) from departing gate k to arriving gate j.

$c_{i,j}$ Total walking distance for all passengers on flight i assigned to arrival gate j. This value is determined by multiplying the above two matrices as follows:

$$c_{i,j} = \sum_{k \in K} p_{i,k} \cdot d_{k,j} \qquad \text{for all } i \text{ and } j$$

Decision Variable

$$x_{i,j} = \begin{cases} 1 & \text{if flight } i \text{ is assigned to gate } j \\ 0 & \text{otherwise} \end{cases}$$

Minimize $\sum_{i \in F} \sum_{j \in G} c_{i,j} x_{i,j}$

Subject to

$$\sum_{j \in G} x_{i,j} = 1 \qquad \text{for all } i \qquad (9.1)$$

$$\sum_{i \in F} x_{i,j} = 1 \qquad \text{for all } j \qquad (9.2)$$

$$x_{i,j} \in \{0,1\} \qquad \text{for all } i \text{ and } j$$

Constraints 9.1 and 9.2 ensure that each flight is assigned to only one gate and each gate is assigned to exactly one flight.

Special Cases

If there are more gates than arriving flights, then constraint 9.2 becomes:

$$\sum_{i \in F} x_{i,j} \leq 1 \qquad \text{for all } j$$

The above inequality denotes that an arriving gate can be assigned to a flight by taking a value of 1 or will not be assigned to any flight at all by taking a value of zero.

If, on the other hand, there are more flights than arriving gates then mathematically we can write an inequality for constraint 9.1 similar to the previous special case. However, it will not be realistic. Each flight must land and be accommodated at a gate. If there are no gates available for an arriving flight, as sometimes is experienced in busy airports, then the aircraft has to wait on the tarmac or taxiway until a gate becomes available.

References

Bihr, R.A. (1990), A conceptual solution to the aircraft gate assignment problem using 0,1 linear programming. *Computers Ind. Engng.* 19(1-4), 280-284.

Bolat, A. (2000), Procedures for providing robust gate assignments for arriving aircrafts. *European Journal of Operational Research* 120, 63-80.

Gu, Y. and Chung, C.A. (1999), Genetic Algorithm approach to aircraft gate reassignment problem. *Journal of Transportation Engineering.* September/October, 1999, 384-389.

Haghani, A. and Chen, M.C. (1998), Optimizing gate assignments at airport terminals. *Transportation Research-Part A* 32(6), 437-454.

Jo, G.S., Jung, J.J. and Yang, C.Y. (1997), Expert system for scheduling in an airline gate allocation. *Expert Systems with Applications* 13(4), 275-282.

Paelink, M.C.E. (1991), Europe 1992 and gate requirements. A solution using simulation techniques.

Yu, G. and Thengvall, B. (2002), Optimization in the Airline Industry, *Handbook of Applied Optimization*, edited by P.M. Pardalos and M.G.C. Resende, Oxford University Press, New York.

Chapter 10

Airline Irregular Operations

Introduction

Aircraft mechanical problems, severe weather, crew sickness, airport curfews, and security are among the problems that force an airline to delay and even cancel their regular published flights. On an average day in the United States, approximately 15 to 20% of all flights experience significant delays (more than 15 minutes) and approximately 1 to 3% of all flights are cancelled (Yu, et al. 2003). The scheduling methodologies described in Chapters 3 to 6 provide an airline with a very efficient plan, high utilization of resources and very tight aircraft and crew assignments. In many cases a small perturbation in this plan, such as unavailability of an aircraft or crew, results in major disruption to the scheduled flights. The airlines adopt a combination of tactics such as flight delays, flight cancellations, aircraft substitutions, ferry flights (flying an empty aircraft to a point of need) and aircraft diversions to return to their published scheduled flights as soon as possible. Since these activities are not pre-planned and occur only when there is a disruption in the schedule, they are called irregular operations. The recovery time can span from the time the disruption occurs up to the time the airline gets back to its original schedule.

In practice the two problems of aircraft recovery and crew re-assignment are handled separately (Jarrah and Yu 1993). The airlines that are faced with disruption first attempt to develop a feasible flight rerouting through some of the tactics mentioned above. This new rerouting schedule is checked for crew assignment feasibility. If a feasible crew assignment does not exist, a new rerouting schedule is developed. This process continues until a feasible rerouting and crew-reassignment is found. This chapter examines the daily aircraft rerouting schedules for single fleet only. See the list of references for models that examine multi-fleet and crew re-assignment. The aircraft schedule recover problem is basically defined as:

> Given the position of planes at the time of a disruption, the original flight schedule, an estimated length of disruption time and a time frame for recovery, find the "best" assignment of aircraft to flights so that after the recovery time the airline is capable of operating its regular published flights. Some of the objectives for the "best" assignment include minimizing total passenger delays, minimizing cancellations, honoring curfews and regulations and minimizing the total cost to the airline.

The following sections provide the analysis for a case study and the development of the mathematical model.

Case Study

We begin by examining a case study involving a break in the regular schedule. This case and the accompanying methodology discussed in this chapter are adapted from Argüello, et al. (1998) with minor modifications.

This case involves three aircraft, 12 flights and four cities. Table 10.1 presents the routing for each aircraft and departure/arrival times. All times are eastern standard times. According to this table we have one aircraft available at DAB, ORF and IAD to start their daily scheduled flights.

Table 10.1 Flight schedule and aircraft routing

Aircraft ID	Flight ID	Origin	Destination	Departure	Arrival
Aircraft 1	11	DAB	ORF	1410	1520
	12	ORF	IAD	1605	1700
	13	IAD	ORF	1740	1840
	14	ORF	DAB	1920	2035
Aircraft 2	21	ORF	DAB	1545	1700
	22	DAB	ORF	1740	1850
	23	ORF	IAD	1930	2030
	24	IAD	ORF	2115	2215
Aircraft 3	31	IAD	ATL	1515	1620
	32	ATL	IAD	1730	1830
	33	IAD	ATL	1910	2020
	34	ATL	IAD	2100	2205

Now let us assume that one of the aircraft becomes unavailable due to some mechanical problem at an airport. Our objective is to handle all the remaining flights in the network through a series of delays and/or cancellations so that the total cost to the airline is minimized. Thengval et al., 2000 provides an overview of other objective functions considered by researchers.

Before we present the mathematical model, we need to define the underlying transformation of this problem into a time-band model as was proposed by Argüello, et al. (1998). This transformation enables us to use the network structure similar to the time-space network employed in Chapters 4 to represent the mathematical model.

Time-band Approximation Model

The network structure is similar to the time-space network discussed in Chapter 4. The time-space representation of the above case study without any disruption is shown in Figure 10.1.

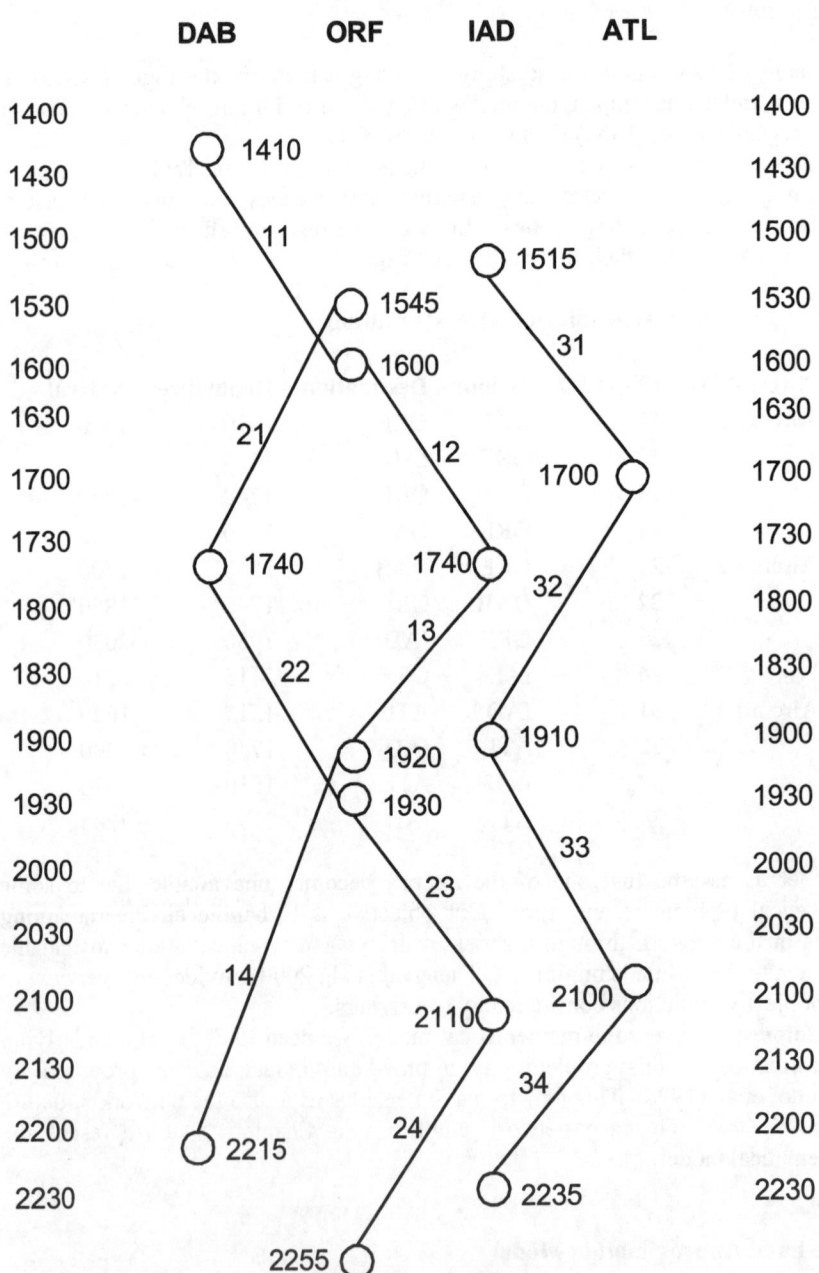

Figure 10.1 Time band network for the case study

In this figure the flight arcs are those that stretch from one airport to another (see for example flight 11). The flight numbers are shown on the flight arcs. The nodes represent an arrival and departure at a specific time. In this network, similar to Chapter 4, the cities and times are represented horizontally and vertically respectively.

In this model the time horizon is partitioned into time bands or discrete intervals of fixed length. Without loss of generality, in our case study as shown in Figure 10.1, this time band is 30 minutes. By partitioning the time horizon into time bands, station activity is aggregated into that time band node.

We also have the following assumptions for our case study:

- Each station requires a minimum of 40 minutes turnaround time;
- Midnight arrival/departure curfew (no arrival or departure after midnight);
- Each minute of delay on any flight costs the airline $20;
- Cancellation cost for each flight leg is as follows.

Table 10.2   Cancellation cost for flight legs

Aircraft ID	Flight ID	Origin	Destination	Cancellation Cost
Aircraft 1	11	DAB	ORF	$7,350
	12	ORF	IAD	$10,231
	13	IAD	ORF	$7,434
	14	ORF	DAB	$14,191
Aircraft 2	21	ORF	DAB	$11,189
	22	DAB	ORF	$12,985
	23	ORF	IAD	$11,491
	24	IAD	ORF	$9,581
Aircraft 3	31	IAD	ATL	$9,996
	32	ATL	IAD	$15,180
	33	IAD	ATL	$17,375
	34	ATL	IAD	$15,624

A major assumption and rule in this model is that during the recovery period, any flight arc from any airport (node) can be made available to other feasible airports (nodes).

Considering the time band intervals, the flight paths and the fact that flight from every node is available to every other feasible node, results in the following time-band network.

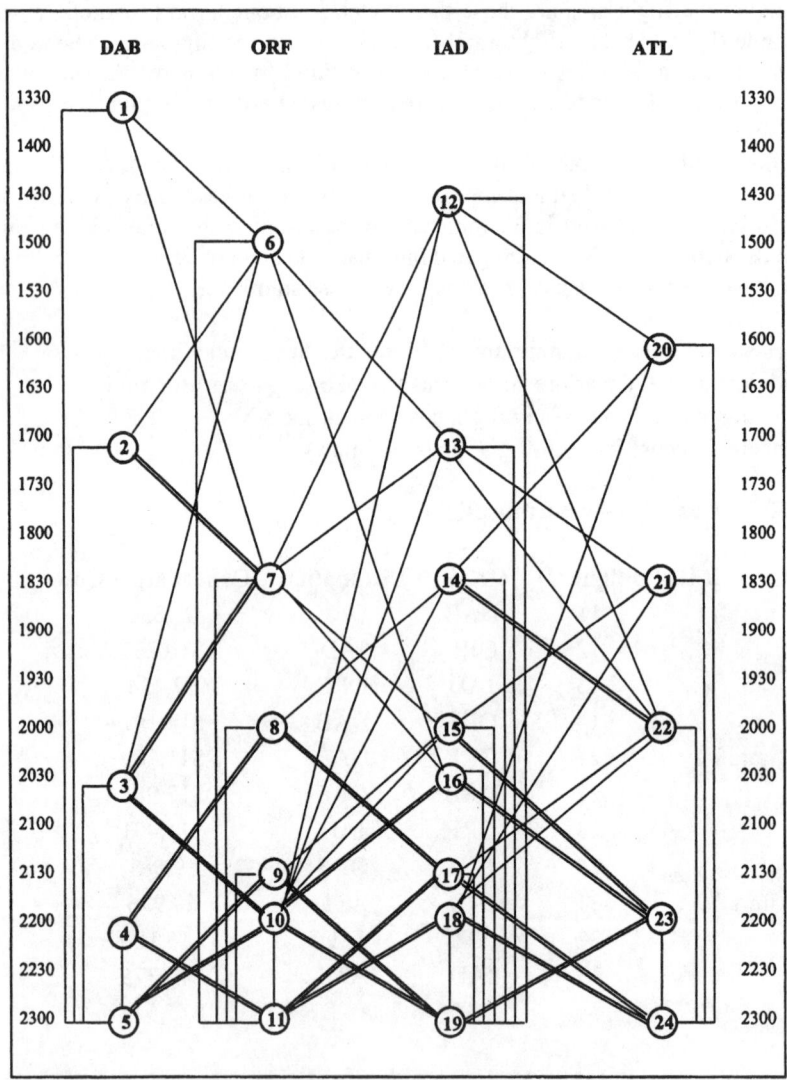

Figure 10.2 Time band approximation network

As the figure suggests, all 30-minute activities within an airport are aggregated in a single node. As an example, node 1 represents all activities from 1:30 pm through 1:59pm. Argüello, et al. (1998) classify the nodes in two groups, transshipment and sink nodes. Transshipment nodes also referred to as station-time nodes, are those nodes that the aircraft arrives into and leaves the node. In Figure 10.2 these nodes include 1,2,3,4,6,7, etc. Sink nodes, also referred to as station sink nodes, represent those nodes that the aircraft arrives into but does not leave until the end of recovery time. These nodes are similar to starting nodes for wrap-around arcs discussed in Chapter 4. In Figure 10.2, nodes 5,11,19 and 24 are station sink nodes.

In this figure we see that for example two arcs are drawn from node 2 to node 7. These two arcs represent flights 11 and 22. For the arc representing flight 11, we have a delay of 210 minutes. This is because flight 11 was scheduled to leave DAB at 1410. If this flight occurs in node 2, we have the departure time of 1700. Considering the nodes are on 30-minute time-bands, this delay spans from 14:00 to 17:30, a total of 210 minutes. Each minute of delay costs the airline $20. So, flight 11, has a delay cost of $4200 if it departs from node 2. The other arc connecting nodes 2 to 7 represents flight 22. By looking at the departure and arrival times of this flight, there is no delay (within 30 minute time-band) for this flight. Table 10.3 presents the non-zero delay costs for all flight arcs in Figure 10.2.

Scenario 1

Let us assume that aircraft 2 in airport ORF becomes grounded due to some mechanical failure at 1400 and is unavailable for the rest of the day. The obvious solution without permitting any rerouting of other aircraft is to cancel flights 21,22,23 and 24 which are conducted by this grounded aircraft for the day. These cancellations cost the airline a total of $45,246 (the sum of all cancellation costs for these four cancelled flights). Let us see how this problem is solved through a series of aircraft rerouting and cancellations in an effort to minimize the total cost to the airline.

Table 10.3 Non-zero delay costs

Flight number	Origin Node	Destination Node	Delay Cost
11	2	7	4,200
11	3	10	8,500
11	4	11	10,300
12	7	15	3,900
12	8	17	5,700
12	9	19	7,800
12	10	19	8,100
13	14	8	1,800
13	15	9	3,900
13	16	10	4,200
13	17	11	5,700
13	18	11	6,100
14	8	4	1,800
14	9	5	3,900
14	10	5	4,200
21	7	3	4,300
21	8	4	6,100
21	9	5	8,200
21	10	5	8,500
22	3	10	4,300
22	4	11	6,100
23	8	17	1,600
23	9	19	3,700
23	10	19	4,000
24	17	11	1,400
24	18	11	1,800
31	13	21	2,900
31	14	22	4,700
31	15	23	6,800
31	16	23	7,100
31	17	24	8,600
31	18	24	9,000
32	21	15	2,300
32	22	17	4,100
32	23	19	6,200
33	15	23	2,100
33	16	23	2,400
33	17	24	3,900
33	18	24	4,300
34	23	19	2,000

Decision Variables

We define the following decision variables:

$$x_{i,j}^k = \begin{cases} 1 \text{ if flight } k \text{ is conducted from station time node } i \text{ to } j \\ 0 \text{ otherwise} \end{cases}$$

$$y_k = \begin{cases} 1 \text{ if flight k is cancelled} \\ 0 \text{ otherwise} \end{cases}$$

z_i = Number of aircraft (integer) terminated at station node i (node i being a station sink node).

The binary Variable $x_{i,j}^k$ is used to identify which flights should be conducted along which routes. For example $x_{1,6}^{11}$ represents the variable for flight number 11 through nodes 1 to 6 (see Figure 10.2). The binary variable y_k is adopted to identify which flight(s) should be cancelled. For example y_{11} represents the decision variable for canceling flight number 11. A value of 1 for this variable means that the flight should be cancelled.

The integer variable z_i is used to keep track of aircraft balance and to have aircraft available at the end of the day for the next day's flight schedule. For example, referring to Figure 10.2, z_1 is the number of aircraft in node 1 (DAB) which is not flown through the day and is carried to the station-sink 5.

Objective Function

The objective function consists of two terms, the delayed cost and the cancellation cost for each flight. Referring to Tables 10.2 and 10.3 we have the objective function as:

Minimize $4200x_{2,7}^{11} + 8500x_{3,10}^{11} + \ldots + 7350y_{11} + 10231y_{12} + \ldots + 15624y_{34}$

Constraints

For this mathematical model, we have three sets of constraints as follows:

Set 1 - Flight Coverage

Each flight must either be flown or be cancelled. As an example to express flight 11's coverage we have:

$$x_{1,6}^{11} + x_{2,7}^{11} + x_{3,10}^{11} + x_{4,11}^{11} + y_{11} = 1$$

The above equation specifies that for flight 11, out of four possible flights (see table 10.3) and a cancellation, only one must be selected.

We write similar equations for every available flight in Table 10.1, a total of 12 constraints for this set.

Set 2 - Station Time Node Flow

For this set we need to write the flow of aircraft at each node. There are some nodes that have aircraft available (supply nodes) to start the flow within the network (such as nodes 1, 6 and 12). Most of the station-time nodes are transshipment nodes signifying that the net flow in these nodes is zero. The net flow for a node is determined as follows:

The number of aircraft in a node = number of outgoing aircraft from the node − (minus) incoming aircraft into the node + (plus) the number of aircraft carried over from this node to sink node (same city) for the next day's operation.

For example, for node 1 we have:

$$x_{1,6}^{11} + x_{1,7}^{22} + z_1 = 1$$

Referring to Figure 10.2 and Tables 10.1 and 10.3, we have two outgoing flights from node 1. These are flights 11 represented by arc 1,6 and flight 22, represented by arc 1,7. There are no incoming flights to node 1. z_1 represents the number of aircraft that are carried over to node 5 which is a sink station node. The purpose of z variables is to allow the flexibility to the model to save the aircraft at some specific cities for the next day's operation. The right hand side of the above equation is 1. This is because at node 1, (DAB) we have one aircraft available to start the flights from DAB (see Table 10.1).

Similarly the flow balance for node 2 (transshipment node) is as follows:

$$x_{2,7}^{11} + x_{2,7}^{22} - x_{6,2}^{21} + z_2 = 0$$

We have two outgoing (flights 11 and 22) and one incoming flow (flight 21) in this node. z_2 is the number of aircraft that are grounded in DAB and are carried over to station-sink 5. The right hand side of this constraint is zero since node 2 is a transshipment node. As the aircraft at node 6 is grounded and not available (scenario 1), the right hand side for this constraint is also zero.

In this case we have 20 station-time nodes resulting in 20 constraints for this set.

Set 3 - Station-Sink Node Flow

We include this set of constraints to insure that there are aircraft available in the designated airports at the end of the day to fly the flights for the next day according to the published schedule. Basically the following rule applies for these sink nodes: Required number of aircraft at any sink-node = Total incoming flight terminating at this sink node + (plus) number of carried over aircraft from previous transshipment nodes at this airport.

In this case study, to be able to fly the published schedule for the next day, we must have one aircraft available in DAB, ORF and IAD each. Therefore we must ensure that the net flow in station sink nodes for these cities is one. Without this set of constraints, the aircraft may end-up at the wrong airports at the end of the day. The following constraint represents the net flow for DAB for station sink node 5 (see Figure 10.2).

$$x_{9,5}^{14} + x_{9,5}^{21} + x_{10,5}^{14} + x_{10,5}^{21} + z_1 + z_2 + z_3 + z_4 = 1$$

There are four arcs coming from other cities to node 5. The first four terms of the above equation represents these four arcs (flights). The other four terms represent the number of aircraft from previous nodes in the same city (DAB) carried over to this sink node. It should be noted that for ORF, we assumed that the aircraft is grounded and not available for the rest of the day. It is assumed, however, that it will be available for the next day.

We have four sink nodes which will result in four constraints for this set.

Solution

The above case study has 64 flight arcs (x variables), 12 flight cancellation (y variables) and 20 termination nodes (z variables), a total of 96 binary/integer variables. It has 36 constraints. The solution to this model is as follows.

Table 10.4 Solution for Scenario 1

Aircraft ID	Flight	Origin	Destination	Origin Node	Destination Node	Delay Cost	Cancellation Cost
Aircraft 1	11	DAB	ORF	1	6	-	-
	21	ORF	DAB	6	2	-	-
	22	DAB	ORF	2	7	-	-
	23	ORF	IAD	7	16	-	-
	24	IAD	ORF	16	10	-	-
	14	ORF	DAB	10	5	4,200	-
Cancel	12	ORF	IAD	-	-	-	10,231
	13	IAD	ORF	-	-	-	7,434
Aircraft 3	31	IAD	ATL	12	20	-	-
	32	ATL	IAD	20	14	-	-
	33	IAD	ATL	14	22	-	-
	34	ATL	IAD	22	18	-	-
Total cost						4,200	17,665

The minimum cost solution for this scenario is two cancellations and one delayed flight at a total cost of $21,865 ($4,200+$17,665). Compare this cost with the trivial solution of $45,246 resulting from canceling all flights operated by aircraft 2.

Note that this model was based on aggregating the activities within an airport in a 30-minute time-band into one single node. The above solution is utilized to fine-tune and determine the actual departure/ arrival times and the actual cost for each flight. The detailed solution for each flight with their revised arrival/departure times is presented in Table 10.5.

Table 10.5 Detailed and final solution for Scenario 1

Aircraft ID	Flight	Origin	Destination	Departure Time	Arrival Time	Delay Cost	Cancellation Cost
Aircraft 1	11	DAB	ORF	1410	1520	-	-
	21	ORF	DAB	1600	1715	300	-
	22	DAB	ORF	1755	1905	300	-
	23	ORF	IAD	1945	2045	300	-
	24	IAD	ORF	2125	2225	200	-
	14	ORF	DAB	2305	0020	4,500	-
cancel	12	ORF	IAD	-	-	-	10,231
	13	IAD	ORF	-	-	-	7,434
Aircraft 3	31	IAD	ATL	1515	1620	-	-
	32	ATL	IAD	1730	1830	-	-
	33	IAD	ATL	1910	2020	-	-
	34	ATL	IAD	2100	2205	-	-
Total cost						5,600	17,665

The above departure/arrival times accommodate for 40-minute aircraft turnaround times. Note that the cost for this schedule is higher than the solution presented in Table 10.4. This is because of the 30-minute aggregation in a single node. The actual total cost for the above feasible solution is $23,265, which is still significantly lower than the trivial cost.

Scenario 2

In scenario 1, we assumed that aircraft 2 was grounded. In scenario 2, we assume that both aircraft 1 and 2 are operational for the day but aircraft 3 is grounded in IAD at 1400 and will be unavailable for the rest of the day. The trivial solution is to cancel all flights conducted by this aircraft, i.e. flights 31, 32, 33, 34 at a total cost of $58,175.

The mathematical model is basically very similar to scenario 1, with the following minor changes:

In set 2 of the constraints, for station-time node 6, the right hand side becomes one since aircraft 2 is available in city ORF. The right hand side for node 12, however, becomes zero because aircraft 3 is grounded in IAD and is unavailable.

Similarly in set 3 of the constraints the right hand sides for nodes 11 and 19 become one and zero respectively.

The solution to this mathematical model is given in Table 10.6:

Table 10.6 Solution for Scenario 2

Aircraft ID	Flight	Origin	Destination	Origin Node	Destination Node	Delay Cost	Cancellation Cost
Aircraft 1	11	DAB	ORF	1	6	-	-
	12	ORF	IAD	6	13	-	-
	33	IAD	ATL	13	22	-	-
	34	ORF	IAD	22	18	-	-
	24	IAD	ORF	18	11	1,800	-
Aircraft 2	21	ORF	DAB	6	2	-	-
	22	DAB	ORF	2	7	-	-
	23	ORF	IAD	7	16	-	-
	13	IAD	ORF	16	10	4,200	-
	14	ORF	DAB	10	5	4,200	
Cancel	31	IAD	ATL	-	-	-	9,996
	32	ATL	IAD	-	-	-	15,180
Total cost						10,200	25,176

The total cost for this solution is $35,376. Table 10.7 shows the conversion of this solution to actual departure and arrival times.

Table 10.7 Detailed and final solution for Scenario 2

Aircraft ID	Flight	Origin	Destination	Departure Time	Arrival Time	Delay Cost	Cancellation Cost
Aircraft 1	11	DAB	ORF	1410	1520	-	-
	12	ORF	IAD	1605	1700	-	-
	33	IAD	ATL	1910	2020	-	-
	34	ORF	IAD	2100	2205	-	-
	24	IAD	ORF	2245	2345	1,800	-
Aircraft 2	21	ORF	DAB	1545	1700	-	-
	22	DAB	ORF	1740	1850	-	-
	23	ORF	IAD	1930	2030	-	-
	13	IAD	ORF	2110	2210	4,200	-
	14	ORF	DAB	2250	0005	4,200	-
Cancel	31	IAD	ATL	-	-	-	9,996
	32	ATL	IAD	-	-	-	15,180
Total cost						10,200	25,176

The total cost for this actual flight schedule is also $35,376 which is similar to the approximation time-node solution.

Scenario 3

In this scenario, we assume that aircraft 2 and 3 in cities ORF and IAD are operational all day. Aircraft 1 in DAB, however, must be grounded at 13:00 for four hours. That is, aircraft 1 is unavailable from 1300 to 1700. The trivial solution is to cancel flights 11 and 12 which are flown by aircraft 1 during 1300 to 1700. The total cost associated with these two cancelled flights is $17,581.

Again with minor modifications to the previous models we can formulate this scenario as follows:

In set 2 of the constraints, for station-time node 6 and 12 the right hand side becomes one. The right hand side for node 1 becomes zero because aircraft 1 is grounded in DAB. This aircraft returns back to service after four hours at 1700. Therefore, the right hand side value for node 2 (representing DAB at 1700) becomes 1 (see Figure 10.2). In set 3 of the constraints, since all the three aircraft are available to station sink nodes, we set the right hand side values for nodes 5, 11 and 19 equal to 1.

The solution to this linear integer programming model is as follows:

Table 10.8 Solution for Scenario 3

Aircraft ID	Flight	Origin	Destination	Origin Node	Destination Node	Delay Cost	Cancellation Cost
Aircraft 1	11	DAB	ORF	2	7	4,200	-
	12	ORF	IAD	7	15	3,900	-
	33	IAD	ATL	15	23	2,100	-
	34	ATL	IAD	23	19	2,000	-
Aircraft 2	21	ORF	DAB	6	2	-	-
	22	DAB	ORF	2	7	-	-
	23	ORF	IAD	7	16	-	-
	24	IAD	ORF	16	10	-	-
Aircraft 3	31	IAD	ATL	12	20	-	-
	32	ATL	IAD	20	14	-	-
	13	IAD	ORF	14	8	1800	
	14	ORF	DAB	8	4	1800	
Total cost						15,800	-

Based on the above solution no flight is cancelled and the total cost to the airline is $15,800. Table 10.9 shows the actual departure and arrival for each flight derived from the above table.

Table 10.9 Detailed and final solution for Scenario 3

Aircraft ID	Flight	Origin	Destination	Departure Time	Arrival Time	Actual Delay Cost	Cancellation Cost
Aircraft 1	11	DAB	ORF	1700	1810	3,400	-
	12	ORF	IAD	1850	1955	3,300	-
	33	IAD	ATL	2035	2145	1,700	-
	34	ATL	IAD	2225	2330	1,700	-
Aircraft 2	21	ORF	DAB	1545	1700	-	-
	22	DAB	ORF	1740	1850	-	-
	23	ORF	IAD	1930	2030	-	-
	24	IAD	ORF	2115	2215	-	-
Aircraft 3	31	IAD	ATL	1515	1620	-	-
	32	ATL	IAD	1730	1830	-	-
	13	IAD	ORF	1910	2010	1,800	
	14	ORF	DAB	2050	2205	1,600	
Total cost						13,500	-

The total actual cost for the above feasible schedule is $13,500.

Mathematical Model

This section formally introduces the integer linear programming model adapted for the case study. This approach is based on the Time-Band Approximation Model by Argüello et al. 1998.

Indices

i, j node indices
k flight index

Sets

F set of flights
$G(i)$ set of flights originating at station-time node i
$H(k,i)$ set of destination nodes for flight k originating at station-node i
I set of station-time nodes
J set of station-sink nodes
$L(i)$ set of flights terminating at node i
$M(k,i)$ set of origination station-time nodes for flight k terminating at node i
$P(k)$ set of station-time nodes from which flight k originates
$Q(i)$ set of station-time nodes at airport containing station-sink I

Parameters

a_i Number of aircraft available at station-time node i

c_k Cost of canceling flight k

$d^k_{i,j}$ Delay cost of flight k from station-node i to node j

h_i Number of aircraft required to terminate at station-sink node j

Decision Variables

$x^k_{i,j} = \begin{cases} 1 \text{ if flight } k \text{ occurs through station time node } i \text{ to } j \\ 0 \text{ otherwise} \end{cases}$

$y_k = \begin{cases} 1 \text{ if flight } k \text{ is cancelled} \\ 0 \text{ otherwise} \end{cases}$

$z_i = $ integer number of aircraft terminated at station time node i to station sink node at that airport

Mathematical Formulation

Minimize $$\sum_{k \in F} \sum_{i \in P(k)} \sum_{j \in H(k,i)} d_{i,j}^k x_{i,j}^k + \sum_{k \in F} c_k y_k$$

Subject to

(flight cover) $$\sum_{i \in P(k)} \sum_{j \in H(k,i)} x_{i,j}^k + y_k = 1 \quad \text{for all } k \in F$$

(station-time node flow) $$\sum_{k \in G(i)} \sum_{j \in H(k,i)} x_{i,j}^k - \sum_{k \in L(i)} + z_i = a_i \quad \text{for all } i \in I$$

(station-sink node flow) $$\sum_{k \in L(i)} \sum_{j \in M(k,i)} x_{i,j}^k + \sum_{j \in Q(i)} z_j = h_i \quad \text{for all } i \in J$$

(binary aircraft flow) $\quad x_{i,j}^k \in \{0,1\} \quad \text{for all } k \in F, i \in P(i) \text{ and } j \in H(k,i)$

(binary cancellation flow) $\quad y_k \in \{0,1\} \quad \text{for all } k \in F$

(integer termination arc flow) $\quad z_i \in Z^+ = \{0,1,2,...\} \quad \text{for all } i \in I$

References

Arguello, M., Bard, J.F. and Yu, G. (1998), "Models and Methods for Managing Airline Irregular Operations." *Operations Research in the Airline Industry*, edited by G. Yu, Kluwer Academic Publishers, Boston, 1-45.

Cao, J.M. and Kanafani, A. (1997), Real-time decision support for integration of airline delay flight cancellations and delays part I: mathematical formulation. *Transportation Planning and Technology* 20, 183-199.

Cao, J.M. and Kanafani, A. (1997), Real-time decision support for integration of airline delay flight cancellations and delays part II: algorithm and computational experiments. *Transportation Planning and Technology* 20, 201-217.

Jarrah, A.I.Z. and Yu, G. (1993), A decision support framework for airline flight cancellations and delays. *Transportation Science* 27(3), 266-280.

Lettovsky, L. (2000), Airline crew recovery. *Transportation Science* 34(4), 337-347.

Luo, S. and Yu, G. (1997), On the airline schedule perturbation problem caused by the ground delay problem. *Tranportation Science* 31(4), 298-311.

Mathaisel, D.F.X. (1996), Decision support for airline system operations control and irregular operations. *Computers Ops. Res.* 23(11), 1083-1098.

Thengvall, B.G., Bard, J.F. and Yu, G. (2000), Balancing user preferences for aircraft schedule recovery during irregular operations. *IE Transactions* 32, 181-193.

Wei, G., Yu, G. and Song, M. (1997), Optimization model and algorithm for crew management during airline irregular operations. *Journal of Combinatorial Optimization* 1, 305-321.

Yan, S. and Lin, C.G. (1997), Airline scheduling for the temporary closure of airports. *Transportation Science* 31(1), 72-82.

Yan, S. and Tu, Y. (1997), Multifleet routing and multistop flight scheduling for schedule perturbation. *European Journal of Opertional Research* 103, 155-169.

Yu, G., Arguello, M., Song, M., McCowan, S. and White, A. (2003), "A New Era for Crew Recovery at Continental Airlines", Interfaces, Vol. 33, No. 1, 5-22.

PART III
COMPUTATION COMPLEXITY AND SIMULATION CASE STUDIES

PART II

Chapter 11

Computational Complexity and Heuristics

Introduction

The case studies and examples that were presented in the previous chapters where integer linear programming models were adopted could be easily solved using an optimization software. This was mainly due to a relatively small number of decision variables and/or constraints. The objective for these cases and examples was to introduce the development of the mathematical model rather than the solution to the problem. We assumed that once the problem is formulated we could use a software to obtain the optimal solutions. Unfortunately the problems that many airlines face involve millions or even billions of decision variables. These huge models cannot be solved using the standard computer packages. Consider the following example:

A cargo airline serves 30 cities within its network with its single fleet type aircraft. Each route on average consists of 7 flights per day. Referring to Chapter 5 (Aircraft Routing), in order to find the optimum solution we need to list all possible routes. The total number of possible routes will be determined by the following permutation formula:

$$^{30}P_7 = \frac{30!}{(30-7)!} = 10,260,432,000$$

In Chapters 5 and 6 we imposed many restrictions to keep the number of decision variables small. Even for our small Ultimate Air case we had more than 6000 decision variables for aircraft routing for the 737-800 fleet!

Now compare and contrast our small size Ultimate Air case study with table 11.1 representing actual crew, equipment sizes and daily number of flights for a select number of airlines.

Complexity Theory

Since the emergence of real world problems and their solution methodologies, there was a constant need to classify and compare them on the basis of the computational tractability. Specifically, we are interested to know how the computational times increase as the size of the problem grows. As an example, if it

Table 11.1 Network and crew size for select airlines

Airline	Daily Flights	Pilots	Total Destinations	Total Fleet
American Airlines	2600	12297	172	771
US Airways	1229	3402	87	261
United Airlines	1800	7992	117	520
Northwest	1500	5534	145	428
Lufthansa	1550	4200	340	240
America West	900	1675	90	137
Southwest	2750	3966	59	383
Air France	1900	4315	199	245
Delta Air Lines	1988	8074	262	509

Source: ATA Airline Almanac 2001

takes 5 seconds to solve a linear program with 100 variables and 50 constraints using a specific software package, how long would it take to solve a similar model with 1000 variables and 500 constraints on the same computer and using the same software? Will it take ten times as much to solve this problem or more? We should note that the computation times are very dependent on the computer processor and programming language adopted. Therefore, instead of time which depends on the computer, we would like to know if there is any other way that presents a general overview of the complexity of the problem as the size of the problem grows. The researchers have instead focused on *number of steps*. That is for a given algorithm how the number of steps to solve a problems increase as the size of the problem increases. Consider the following example adapted from Winston and Venkataramanan, (2003). Assume that you have a sequence of n numbers to sort from smallest to largest. One method (algorithm) to do the sorting is by looking at two neighboring numbers. If they are in the wrong order then swap them. We keep repeating this process until all numbers are in sequence. This method is called bubble sort. The best scenario is that all the numbers are already in the right order (of course we do not know this in advance!). In this case after n comparisons (steps) the algorithm tells us that the numbers are in order. In the worst possible scenario (again not knowing in advance), where all numbers are sorted from largest to smallest, we have to repeat this comparison n^2 times since every number is in the wrong order. We are normally interested in the worst case scenario since it will serve as the upper bound for the number of steps to generate the solution. According to this example the bubble sort has a complexity of order of n^2. It is shown as $O(n^2)$. Where O stands for *order of time*. According to this complexity, if the size of the problem (in this example the numbers to be sorted) is doubled then the number of steps (comparisons) is bounded by four times the numbers of steps for the original problem. This order of complexity provides some guidelines on how the computational complexity will increase for large scale problems, as compared to lower scale ones.

During the 1970s, many researchers in computer science and operations research studied various algorithms in terms of their computational complexity (Daskin 1995). They classified the algorithms based on their computation tractability into two groups, polynomial (P) and non-deterministic polynomial (NP) time algorithms. For polynomial time algorithms, the solution times are bounded by a polynomial order. As an example our bubble sort algorithm is classified as a polynomial time of order of n^2. The polynomial time algorithms are typically considered "good". This is because these algorithms can solve large instances of the problem in reasonable steps and time. For non-deterministic polynomial (NP) time algorithms on the other hand as the name implies, the steps to solve the problem grows exponentially with the problem size. As an example consider that an algorithm is classified as non-deterministic polynomial (2^n) order. If the problem size doubles, then the steps (times) that it takes to solve this problem will be the number of steps for the original problem to power two or $(2^{2n}) = (2^n)^2$. These algorithms are considered 'bad' in the sense that as the problem size increases, the computational times grows very large. Many algorithms that are adopted to solve the combinatorial type problems such as traveling salesman (see Chapter 2) have an order of complexity of $O(n!)$. These problems represent the most challenging in terms of computational complexity. As the order of time implies, in these algorithms the computational complexity grows exponentially with the size of the problem. For more technical details on polynomial and non-polynomial time algorithms, the interested reader is referred to the list of books referenced in this chapter.

Unfortunately the algorithms and methodologies that are adopted to solve integer linear programming models discussed in the previous chapters all belong to this class of NP. For this reason, it is almost impossible for the airlines cited in Table 11.1 to get the optimal solutions for their crew scheduling or aircraft routing in a reasonable computational time.

Note that the computational complexity lies with the solution algorithms, i.e., the way the problems are solved, and not the mathematical models or the way they have been formulated.

Heuristic Procedures

Not being able to obtain the optimum solutions in a timely fashion for NP type algorithms, prompted the researchers to develop other alternatives. These alternative solution methods are generally classified as heuristic methods. Heuristic methods are techniques that do not guarantee or promise the optimum solutions but attempt to provide a "good" and sometimes "near optimum" solutions in a minimal amount of time.

There are many technical papers in the operations research literature that describe different heuristics and their applications to the airline industry. These heuristics and their technical descriptions are however, beyond the scope of this book and we refer the interested readers to the papers referenced in previous chapters.

As for the airlines, they either develop their in-house customized heuristics to solve their linear integer programs in their operations research departments or outsource the service. The website www.airlinetechnology.net provides the names and areas of expertise for some of the companies that provide such services.

References

Ahuja, R., Magnanti, T. and Orlin, J. (1993), *Network Flows, Theory, Algorithm and Applications*, Prentice-Hall.
Anderson, D., Sweeney, D. and Williams, T. (2003), *Quantitative methods for business*, 9th edition, South-Western.
Bazaraa, M., Jarvis, J. and Sherali, H. (1990), Linear programming and network flows, Wiley.
Daskin, M. (1995), *Network discrete location*, Wiley.
Hillier, F. and Lieberman, G. (2001), *Introduction to Operations Research*, 7th edition, McGraw Hill.
Ignizio, J. and Cavalier, T. (1994), *Linear Programming*, Prentice Hall.
Schrage, L. (1997), *Optimization modeling with Lindo*, 5th edition, Duxbury.
Winston, W. and Albright, C. (2001), *Practical Management Science*, second edition, Duxbury.
Winston, W. and Venkataramanan, M. (2003), *Introduction to Mathematical programming*, 4th edition, Duxbury.

Chapter 12

Start-up Airline Case Study

Introduction

It was explained in Chapter 1 that this book is the result of developing a course on airline operation and scheduling. The following case is a real-world case study referred to our class by an entrepreneur to determine the viability of operations so that a business plan can be developed.

A start-up airline plans to operate a fleet of amphibian (capable of landing on both ground and water) aircraft, which would be used to fly leisure passengers between the United States and the Caribbean. The aircraft is the Russian made Beriev Be-200. It has a capacity of 72 passengers, requires 2 crew and 2 service personnel, and has a range of 1200 miles.

The airline plans to start up its operations initially with 4 amphibian aircraft. The proposed flight network for this airline is presented in Figure 12.1. According to this figure the airline flies to 11 cities as follows:

Table 12.1 List of airports and their codes for case study

Airport	Code
Atlanta International Airport	ATL
Nassau International Airport	NAS
Orlando International Airport	MCO
Tampa International Airport	TPA
Palm Beach International Airport	PBI
Fort Lauderdale/Hollywood International Airport	FLL
Miami International Airport	MIA
Key West International Airport	EYW
Providenciales International Airport	PLS
Norman Manley International Airport	KIN
Claremore Regional Airport	GCM

164   *Airline Operations and Scheduling*

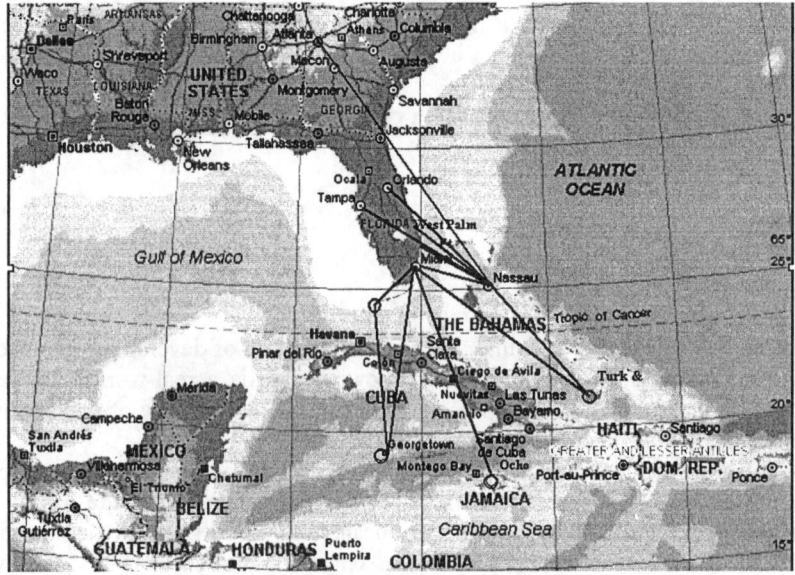

Figure 12.1 Flight network for the start-up airline

The requirements for this airline are as follows:

- Only use 4 airplanes.
- An average load factor of 65% should be assumed for all flights.
- Each aircraft can be utilized for at most 16 hours per day.
- Aircraft turn around time is 43 minutes for all flights.
- At the end of each operation day, the aircraft are to be parked in Miami or Nassau for Maintenance.

Table 12.2 provides information on the airline's network routes as follows:

- Columns 1 and 2 represent the sequence and the proposed routes.
- Columns 3 and 4 show the distance (miles) and flight blocks (minutes) between city pairs.
- Column 5 shows the total time. This time is obtained by adding the flight block + aircraft turn around time (43 minutes).
- Column 6 presents the frequency of flights between city pairs. These frequencies are determined by daily forecasted demand and the required load factor as explained in Chapter 3.

- Columns 7 and 8 show average one-way fare and total expected revenue on each flight. Column 8 is calculated by multiplying column 7 × 72 (aircraft capacity) × .65 (load factor).

The airline realizes that it cannot fly all the flight frequencies in Table 12.2 with its four aircraft in its initial operations. The objective of this case is then to identify and determine valid daily routes for 4 aircraft so that the total revenue generated through these flights is maximized. Note that in this case we do not have the complete flight schedule (arrivals and departures times) as we do not know which flights will be selected, and which frequency they will have. Once these flights are identified, appropriate departure and arrival times will be assigned to them.

Table 12.2 Proposed routes and their frequencies

Seq	Route	Distance (miles)	Block Time min	Total Time (min)	Daily Flights	Avg. Fare	Rev. /Flight
1	ATL-NAS	725	159	202	2	$436	$20,561
2	MCO-NAS	333	87	130	2	$217	$10,233
3	TPA-NAS	373	95	138	1	$186	$8,771
4	PBI-NAS	199	63	106	1	$121	$5,706
5	FLL-NAS	182	60	108	4	$154	$7,262
6	MIA-NAS	183	60	103	7	$149	$7,026
7	MIA-EYW	109	35	78	1	$222	$10,469
8	MIA-PLS	578	122	165	1	$348	$16,411
9	MIA-KIN	585	123	166	3	$342	$16,128
10	MIA-GCM	452	112	155	2	$236	$11,129
11	NAS-ATL	725	159	202	1	$416	$19,618
12	NAS-MCO	333	87	130	2	$218	$10,280
13	NAS-TPA	373	95	138	1	$169	$7,970
14	NAS-PBI	199	63	106	1	$111	$5,234
15	NAS-FLL	182	60	108	6	$167	$7,875
16	NAS-MIA	183	60	103	12	$153	$7,215
17	NAS-PLS	400	98	141	1	$328	$15,468
18	EYW-MIA	109	35	78	1	$214	$10,092
19	EYW-GCM	363	92	135	1	$369	$17,402
20	PLS-MIA	578	122	165	1	$329	$15,515
21	PLS-NAS	400	98	141	1	$309	$14,572
22	KIN-MIA	585	123	166	5	$367	$17,307
23	GCM-MIA	452	112	155	2	$229	$10,799
24	GCM-EYW	363	92	135	0	$339	$15,987

Solution Approach

A modified set-partitioning approach (Chapter 2) with side constraint as discussed in Chapters 5 and 6 is adopted to determine the efficient aircraft routings. The following binary decision variable is used to formulate the problem.

$$R_i = \begin{cases} 1 \text{ if route } i \text{ is selected} \\ 0 \text{ otherwise} \end{cases}$$

By route we mean complete daily aircraft routing. A route generator program (similar to the one in Chapter 5) was developed to generate daily routes with the following characteristics:

- Maximum daily aircraft utilization of 16 hours (16% 60=960 minutes).
- An overnight stay in Miami or Nassau for maintenance checks.
- Since each aircraft stays overnight at Miami or Nassau, they should start and end their daily routings from these two locations.

The program not only generates valid routes but also determines its total flight times and revenue generated over all flights in that route. This program generated more than 1200 routes. Table 12.3 presents three sample valid routes.

Table 12.3 Three sample routes

Route #	Routing	Total Time (Min)	Revenue
R_1	NAS-PLS-NAS-MIA-NAS-PBI-NAS-MIA-NAS	906	$69,462
R_2	MIA-EYW-GCM-MIA-NAS-MIA-GCM-MIA	884	$74,839
R_3	MIA-EYW-MIA-NAS-MCO-NAS-MIA-PLS-MIA	952	$87,241

Objective Function

In the proposed set-partition model, the routes are represented as rows and columns are the daily flights. The mathematical model attempts to maximize the total revenue subject to flight cover and number of available aircraft. The objective function (considering the above routes to be R_1, R_2 and R_3) is as follows:

Maximize $69462R_1 + 74839R_2 + 87241R_3 + ...$

There are two sets of constraints in this problem, flight frequency and aircraft availability.

Flight Frequency Cover

The frequency for each flight must not exceed the daily required frequency of flights (see Table 12.2). As an example we should have at most 7 daily flights between MIA and NAS. By looking at the above three sample routes we see MIA-NAS is repeated twice in R_1, once in R_2 and once in R_3. To automate the search for flights, a simple program can identify how many times each flight is repeated in each route. When we have all the frequencies on each route then we can write the constraint for that flight leg. As an example to address the frequency on MIA-NAS, we write

$$2R_1 + R_2 + R_3 + ... \leq 7$$

In general if a flight leg has N frequency, then the constraint to cover at most N of these frequencies is as follows:

$$\sum_i f_i R_i \leq N$$

Where f_i is the number of times that the specific flight leg is repeated in route i and R_i is the ith route as explained above.

Aircraft Availability

We have a total of four aircraft. Therefore the total number of routes assigned to these aircraft must equal 4. Therefore:

$$R_1 + R_2 + R_3 + ... = 4$$

Solution

We used an optimization software to solve this problem. The solution for this problem with four aircraft is presented in Table 12.4. The total daily revenue is $336,706.

Table 12.4 Solution for the case

Aircraft	Routing	Total flight Time (Min)	Daily Revenue
1	NAS-MCO-NAS-ATL-NAS-TPA-NAS	940	$77,433
2	MIA-KIN-MIA-PLS-NAS-FLL-NAS-MIA	957	$86,770
3	NAS-MIA-GCM-EYW-GCM-MIA-EYW-MIA-NAS	942	$90,119
4	MIA-NAS-PBI-NAS-PLS-MIA-KIN-MIA	953	$82,384

Table 12.5 presents the complete schedule with departure and arrival times incorporating turn around times derived from the above solution.

Figures 12.2 and 12.3 show the time-space network at each airport and frequency of flights between city pairs respectively.

Table 12.5 Flight schedule and aircraft routing for the case study

Aircraft No.	Flight-leg	Flight No.	Route	Departure Time	Arrival Time	Block Time
1	1	172	NAS-MCO	7:00 AM	8:27 AM	1:27
1	2	127	MCO-NAS	9:10 AM	10:37 AM	1:27
1	3	171	NAS-ATL	11:20 AM	1:59 PM	2:39
1	4	117	ATL-NAS	2:42 PM	5:21 PM	2:39
1	5	173	NAS-TPA	6:04 PM	7:39 PM	1:35
1	6	137	TPA-NAS	8:22 PM	9:57 PM	1:35
2	1	2610	MIA-KIN	7:00 AM	9:03 AM	2:03
2	2	2106	KIN-MIA	9:46 AM	11:49 AM	2:03
2	3	269	MIA-PLS	12:32 PM	2:34 PM	2:02
2	4	297	PLS-NAS	3:17 PM	4:55 PM	1:38
2	5	275	NAS-FLL	5:38 PM	6:38 PM	1:00
2	6	257	FLL-NAS	7:21 PM	8:21 PM	1:00
2	7	276	NAS-MIA	9:04 PM	10:04 PM	1:00
3	1	376	NAS-MIA	8:00 AM	9:00 AM	1:00
3	2	3611	MIA-GCM	9:43 AM	11:35 AM	1:52
3	3	3118	GCM-EYW	12:18 PM	1:50 PM	1:32
3	4	3811	EYW-GCM	2:33 PM	4:05 PM	1:32
3	5	3116	GCM-MIA	4:48 PM	6:40 PM	1:52
3	6	368	MIA-EYW	7:23 PM	7:58 PM	0:35
3	7	386	EYW-MIA	8:41 PM	9:16 PM	0:35
3	8	367	MIA-NAS	9:59 PM	10:59 PM	1:00
4	1	467	MIA-NAS	8:00 AM	9:00 AM	1:00
4	2	474	NAS-PBI	9:43 AM	10:46 AM	1:03
4	3	447	PBI-NAS	11:29 AM	12:32 PM	1:03
4	4	479	NAS-PLS	1:15 PM	2:53 PM	1:38
4	5	496	PLS-MIA	3:36 PM	5:38 PM	2:02
4	6	4610	MIA-KIN	6:21 PM	8:24 PM	2:03
4	7	4106	KIN-MIA	9:07 PM	11:10 PM	2:03

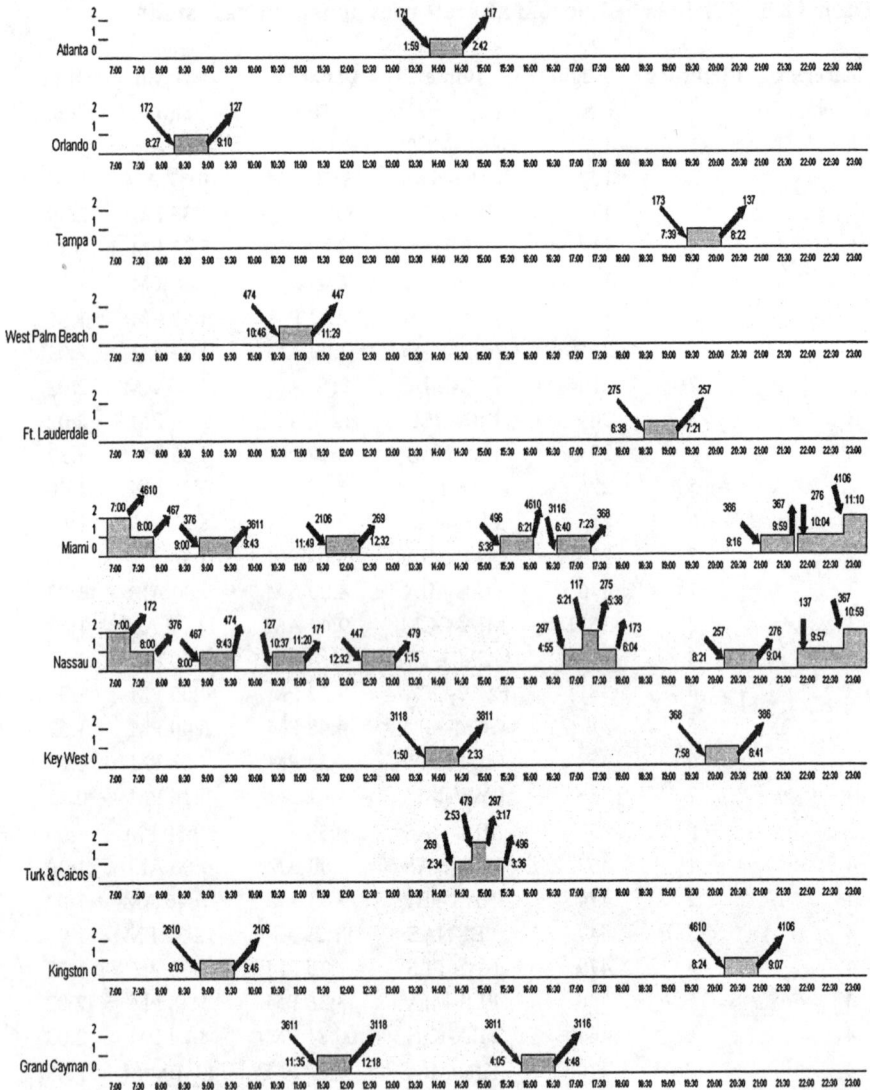

Figure 12.2 Arrival/departure of flights at each airport

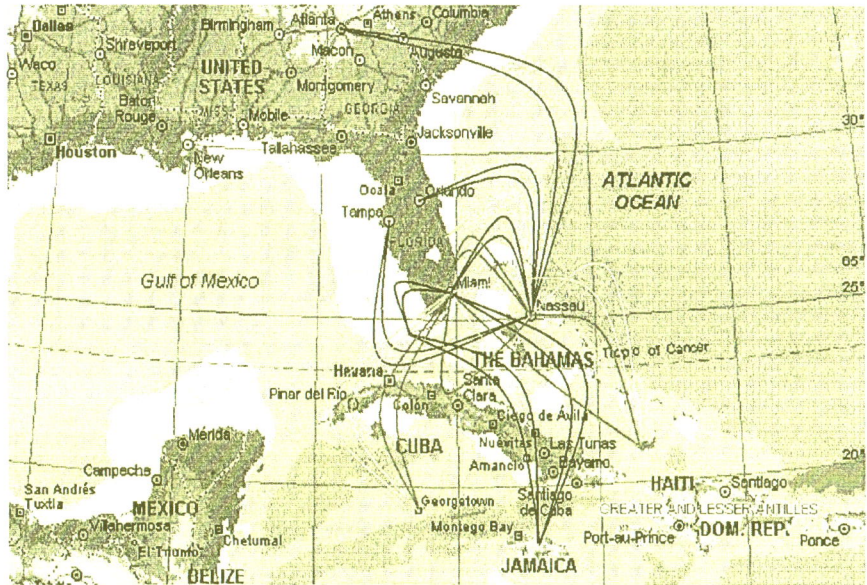

Figure 12.3 Airline's network and aircraft routing

Chapter 13

Simulation Case 1

Introduction

A manufacturing, transport, financial, health or distribution system is frequently in need of upgrading and improvement. How would the new system perform? What are the unforeseen problems that could occur? Would the performance of the projected improvements justify the initial expenditure outlay? What resources should be purchased and how should they be planned so that the new system would generate the expected benefits?

We can answer these questions and study the performance of the organization under the new regime, in advance, through *simulation modeling* without actually investing in the new changes.

Simulation Modeling

Simulation modeling involves a process by which the basic features of the system may be analyzed and simulated by a computer. The model may then be used to view the way in which the system would operate by means of an animation. It is possible to experiment with the model under various conditions to see what might happen under the proposed conditions in which the new system might operate.

Simulation study is proving to be an integrated part and/or alternative way to mathematical modeling where the governing parameters are very complex and dynamic. It allows the user to perform *what-if* analysis under different scenarios.

Both this chapter and Chapter 14 present two simulation case studies for an airline and an airport, respectively. The objective of these chapters is not to introduce the concept of simulation but to introduce how they can be utilized in planning for the aviation industry. For readers not familiar with simulation modeling, Law and Kelton (2000) and Kelton et al. (2003) provide comprehensive descriptions of simulation modeling and its application to various industries.

Simulation in Airlines

A browse through AGIFOR's website (www.AGIFORS.org) and simulation conferences (www.wintersim.org/program.htm) show that a growing number of airlines are now adopting simulation study as an important tool for their planning. A major stream of simulation conferences is now airline planning. Simulation has been applied to manpower planning, fleet assignment, gate assignment, flight scheduling, traffic flow, etc. The simulation modeling is becoming much more popular as the software used for these models are becoming easier to use, and more powerful. The recent integration of meta-heuristics in these simulation software, has enabled them to actually optimize the parameters within the models. This feature is another important factor for the growing popularity and use of these software.

This case concerns the manpower planning for maintenance at Continental Airlines (Bazargan, et. al. 2003). For maintenance capacity planning, simulation provides the capability of changing many variables simultaneously. Gatland et al. (1997) used simulation modeling techniques to solve engine maintenance capacity problems. Duffuaa and Andijani (1999) developed an integrated simulation model for effective planning of maintenance operations for the Saudi Arabian Airlines (SAUDIA).

Manpower Planning for Continental Airlines

This case study describes the development of a simulation model for aircraft line maintenance planning at Continental Airlines for one of their major maintenance stations at Newark airport. The simulation model is used as a tool to support the management of the line maintenance department in solving various capacity planning issues related to its manpower requirement and scheduling.

Line maintenance (commonly referred to as short routine maintenance) includes the regular short haul inspections of aircraft between their arrival, and consecutive departure from the airport. Ninety percent of the cost of line maintenance is attributable to labor (Lam 1995).

Line maintenance is driven by the flight schedule. Once the flight schedule is finalized, a maintenance schedule is assigned to each maintenance station. The maintenance schedule takes into consideration the fleet/equipment type flying to that station, the number and type of maintenance programs to be carried out, the capabilities of the specific station, task standards for each of these maintenance programs, ground time available, and other resources such as tooling, hangars, weather, and events that would conflict with one another.

Mathematical modeling techniques have been used for maintenance planning, and sometimes integrated with other scheduling models. Dijkstra et al. (1991), Clarke et al. (1996), Hane et al. (1995), Rushmeier and Kontogiorgis (1997), Barnhart et al. (1998), Talluri (1998), Sachon and Pate-Cornell (2000) are among the researchers who developed mathematical modeling for aircraft maintenance planning. In most of these mathematical models, maintenance requirements are included as constraints in the problem formulation rather than treating maintenance as the primary goal of study.

Over the past few years it has become apparent that better decision support tools, such as simulation modeling, are needed in the maintenance department. Duffuaa and Andijani (1999) consider that the application of computer simulation to maintenance functions provides a better and more viable alternative to mathematical modeling and analysis. This is because of the difficulty of the mathematical models in capturing the complexities of maintenance operations, uncertainty of parameters in arrivals, sequencing, job contents, and availability of resources.

Line Maintenance Department

This simulation study aims at duplicating the maintenance operations at Continental's major maintenance station at Newark (EWR). AutoMod Simulation Software (Banks 2000) has been used as the developmental platform for the study. The focus of this study is to analyze and recommend efficient manpower staffing models.

Continental Airlines, based in Houston, Texas, is the fifth largest airline in the United States serving 136 Domestic and 87 International destinations from its Newark, Houston and Cleveland hubs with a total of 2,238 daily departures. At the time the study was conducted, Continental Airlines was operating 43 wide-body and 327 narrow-body jet aircraft.

Equipment / Fleet Type

The aircraft equipment/fleet-types operating through Newark are presented in Figure 13.1. Here, the abbreviated three-letter number coding system represents the respective aircraft-types under each size/range classification (e.g., the 733 under narrow-body is a Boeing 737-300, while the 735 represents a Boeing 737-500, etc.).

Maintenance Schedules: Line maintenance includes the regular short-haul inspections of aircraft between their arrival at an airport and their consecutive departure from the airport. An aircraft flying into a station can be classified as a *through, day hold* or *remains overnight* flight.

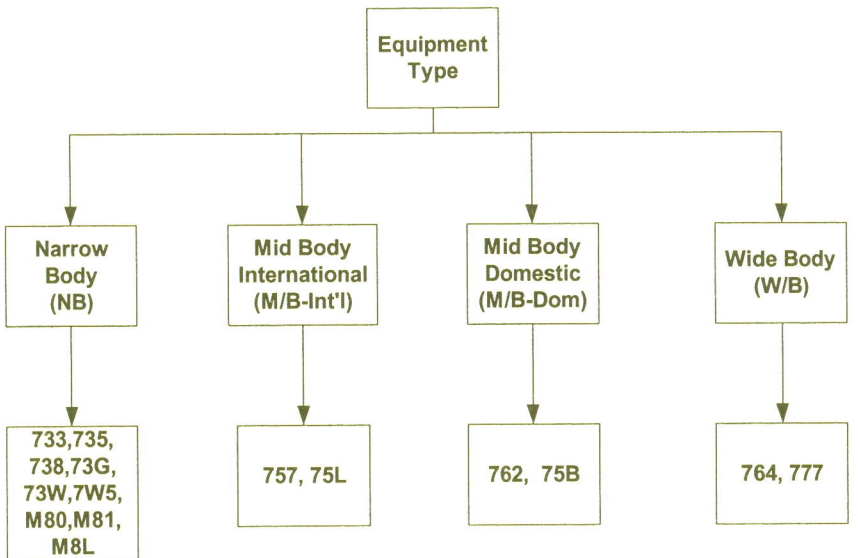

Figure 13.1 Equipment type

Through Flight: The aircraft is in transit through the station with minimal ground time. Every through flight goes through a departure check while it is on the ground. The total number of narrow-body, mid-body (domestic), mid-body (International), and wide-body aircraft flying into Newark are presented in Table 13.1. Figure 13.2 shows the workload of through flights on a typical day at the time of the study.

Day Hold: The aircraft is scheduled for one of the routine checks, held during the daytime, before its subsequent departure.

Remains Overnight (RON): The aircraft remains overnight for one of the routine checks before its subsequent departure.

Table 13.1 Number of through flights in a day

Equipment Type	Number of Through Flights in a Day
Narrow Body	145
Mid Body – Domestic	15
Mid Body – International	16
Wide Body	7

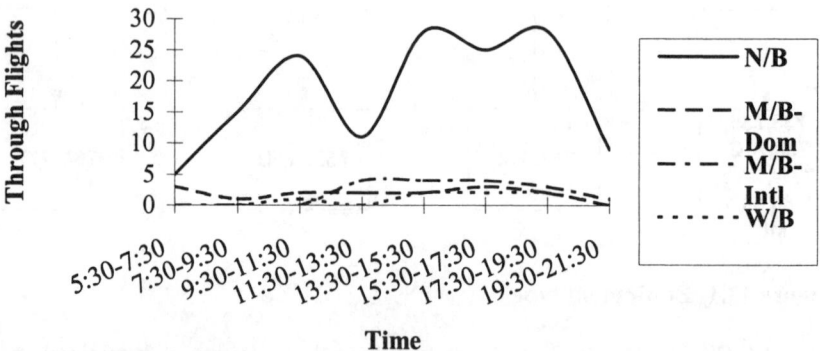

Figure 13.2 Through flights on a typical day

Maintenance Programs

The maintenance programs that an aircraft goes through are as follows:

Service Check (SVC): A walk-around service level and systems check applicable to all fleets, generally done on an overnight basis. Wide-body aircraft get this check done on *day holds* as well as overnights. If an aircraft remains overnight at a station with sufficient ground time, a service check will be performed, regardless of how many days it has been since its last service check, unless a higher-level check being performed supercedes or signs-off the service check.

Level 3 Service Check (SC3): A more in-depth service check applicable to all fleet-types. This check is also done on an overnight basis. It generally takes between 8 to 10 hours for narrow-body aircraft, while wide-body aircraft can have the level 3 service check done on either day or overnight holds of generally 12 hours or more. A level 3 service check is a higher-level check than a service check, so a service check is not performed if a higher-level check is due.

Line Package Visit (LPV): A scheduled check applicable to all narrow-body aircraft, generally done on an overnight basis. It requires 75 man-hours, and generally one line-package visit is scheduled at Newark in a day, and the workload is handled by the night-shift technicians.

Table 13.2 presents the daily demand for various checks for the different fleet-type classifications.

Table 13.2 Total number of checks scheduled on each equipment type daily

Equipment Type	Total Number of Checks		
	SVC	SC3	LPV
Narrow Body	35	7	1
Mid Body-Domestic	4	1	0
Mid Body-International	5	1	0
Wide Body	9	1	0

Standard Maintenance Timings

Table 13.3 gives the standard man-hours (M/H), ground time (in hours), and technician requirements for each maintenance program for *day holds* and *remains overnights* for all fleet types at Newark.

Table 13.3 Man-hours, ground time and technician requirements for *day holds* and *remains overnights* (RON)

Fleet Type	Ground Time	Number of Technicians	Actual Time Worked
N/B	<0.75 hrs	2	Ground Time
	≥0.75 hrs	1	0.75 hrs
M/B-Dom	<0.75 hrs	2	Ground Time
	≥0.75 hrs	1	0.75 hrs
M/B-Int'l	<1.5 hrs	3	Ground Time
	≥1.5 hrs	2	1.5 hrs
W/B	<1.5 hrs	3	Ground Time
	≥1.5 hrs	2	1.5 hrs

Tables 13.4 and 13.5 show the standard man-hours (M/H), , ground time (hours), variability (+/-) and technician requirements for *through flights* for all fleet types at Newark.

Table 13.4 *Service Check (SVC)* **man-hours, ground time and technician requirements for** *through flights*

Fleet Type	M/H	SVC Ground Time (Hrs.)	+/- (Hrs.)	Number of Technicians
N/B	6	6	0.25	1
M/B-Dom	8	8	0.25	1
M/B-Intl	10	5	0.25	2
W/B	25	6.25	0.25	4

Table 13.5 *Level 3 Service Check (SC3)* **man-hours, ground time and technician requirements for** *through flights*

Fleet Type	M/H	SC3 Ground Time (Hrs.)	+/- (Hrs.)	Number of Technicians
N/B	16	8	0.25	2
M/B-Dom	18	9	0.25	2
M/B-Intl	30	7.5	0.25	4
W/B	75	18.75	0.5	4

Shift Schedule

There are three working shifts in a day. They are *day*, *swing* (afternoon) and *night shifts*. Each shift is divided into sub-shifts. Table 13.6 projects the shift and sub-shifts schedules at Newark.

Table 13.6 Shift and sub-shift schedules at Newark

Shifts	Sub-shifts	Start Time	End Time
Day	1	05:30	14:00
	2	06:00	14:30
	3	06:00	16:30
	4	11:00	21:30
Swing	1	13:00	21:30
	2	13:30	22:00
	3	14:00	22:30
	4	14:30	23:00
Night	1	20:30	07:00
	2	21:30	08:00

Manpower Challenge

The challenge that the maintenance department was confronted with, was determining the number of technicians required and their shift schedules based on the flight schedule and the maintenance programs to be carried out.

Management has been using mathematical models to come up with a headcount, but these models were incapable of capturing the peaks and troughs in the arrivals and departures.

A simulation approach therefore seemed promising in capturing the complexity of operations at the maintenance department.

Assumptions of the Simulation Model

The proposed simulation model incorporated the following assumptions:

- The daily flight schedule at Newark was used for the arrival process.
- There are three technician pools - day, swing and night shifts, each divided into several sub-shifts.
- The model extracts the technicians from the requisite pool whenever there is a requirement.
- A technician already assigned to a job cannot be utilized for another job until he/she finishes the job, which has currently begun.
- A technician becomes available to work on a new job immediately after finishing a previous job.
- Every technician is qualified to work on any job. There is no distinction between the technicians who work on *through flights* and *routine checks* (i.e., day holds and remains overnights).

Process Logic

The flowchart in Figure 13.3 presents a sample logic behind the development of the simulation model for *through flights*.

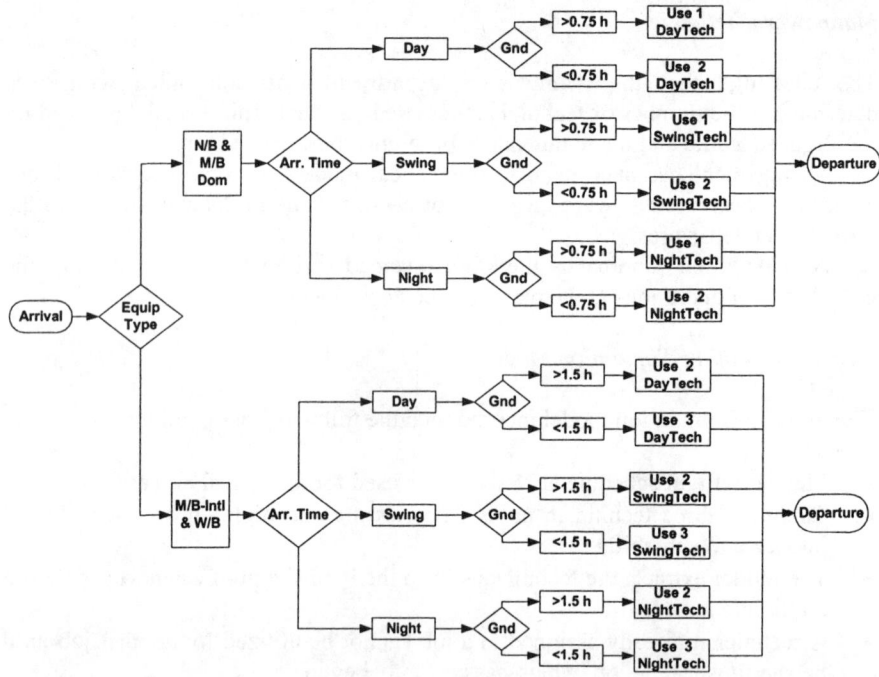

Figure 13.3 Maintenance cycle for *through flights* (narrow body, mid body-domestic, mid body-international and wide body aircraft)

Analysis (Base Scenario)

In the first attempt, the focus was at developing the simulation model for the existing maintenance practices. Meetings with the airline personnel and feedback received from the maintenance department concerning validity of the results convinced us that the simulation model was working properly. The following presents the results for the existing practices at the time of the study, which we refer to as *base scenario*. The AutoStat analysis tool (Banks 2000) was used to derive the various performance measures for the system. The model simulates an entire day of operations. Multiple replications are made for each scenario for increased reliability of the output.

For this study, the airline was interested to identify three performance measures for maintenance technicians namely number of aircraft serviced, utilization and unfinished jobs. The following section describes these performance measures under the base and proposed scenarios.

Total Technician Requirement

Figure 13.4 presents the output of the simulation model for the total technician requirement during each sub-shift for the base scenario. As the figure suggests, there is more demand for technicians during the night shift than other shifts.

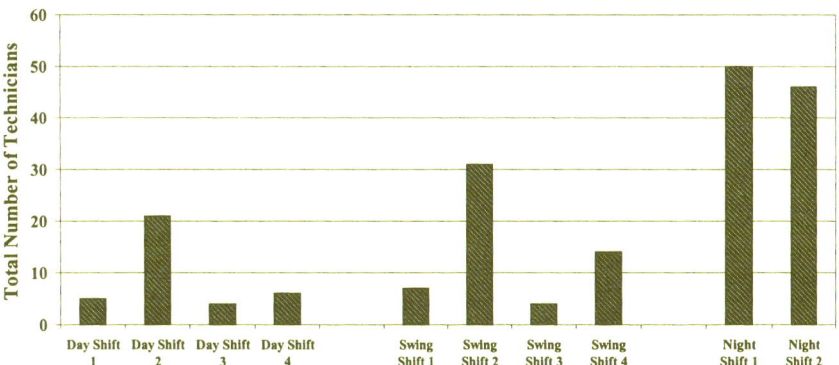

Figure 13.4 Total technician requirements for each sub-shift in a day

Total Number of Aircraft Serviced by each Technician

Table 13.7 summarizes the average workload in terms of number of aircraft serviced by a technician in each shift.

Table 13.7 Average number of aircraft serviced by each technician in each shift

Shift	Average Workload for a Technician
Day	2.5 aircraft
Swing	3.5 aircraft
Night	1.7 aircraft

The number of aircraft serviced by day and swing-shift technicians increases with the major workload of *through flights* during the day and swing shifts, as *through flights* require less time to service. However, the major workload during the night shift consists of *routine checks* that require comparatively more ground time to complete, thus decreasing the total number of aircraft serviced by night shift technicians.

Utilization of Technicians

The *utilization* of each technician is calculated by adding the total amount of time a technician works on each job divided by the total shift time (calculated as a percentage). A technician working near his/her maximum capacity represents a *bottleneck*, and a technician with a low percentage of utilization is considered *underutilized*. Figure 13.5 summarizes the average percentage utilization of technicians in each shift. The day-shift technician utilization is comparatively less than the other shifts. This can be attributed to the nature of the workload for *through flights*, experienced by day shift technicians. The policy requiring a technician to be available to greet an aircraft upon arrival generates underutilized technicians. In reality, these utilization percentages are higher as the technicians can also be utilized elsewhere as needed to work on other *unscheduled jobs*. The introduction of *part-time technicians* could improve the utilization of day-shift technicians.

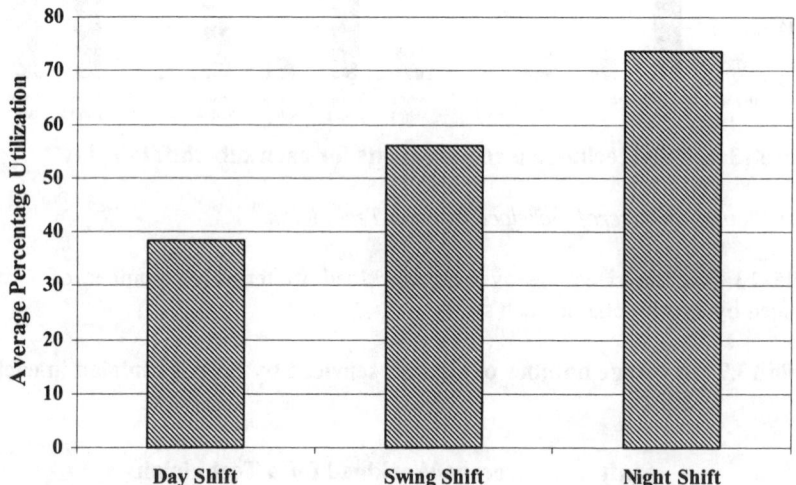

Figure 13.5 Average percentage utilization of technicians in a day

Number of Technicians with Unfinished Jobs

A technician will only take up a job if it arrives between his/her shift start and end-times. If a technician is still busy on a job after the shift end time, the job is transferred to a technician in the next shift. The management considers that the lower the number of jobs transferred to the next shift, the better the spread of workload would be across all shifts. Thus, a required performance measure in evaluating the efficiency of the existing shift schedule was to determine the number of unfinished jobs in each shift.

The total number of technicians with unfinished jobs after their shift end times for each shift is shown in Table 13.8. The number of technicians with unfinished jobs for all other shifts is zero. As it can be observed, the later swing shift and especially the night shifts need to be better scheduled for a more uniform spread of workload.

Table 13.8 Number of technicians with unfinished jobs at the end of each shift

Shift	Number of Technicians with Unfinished Jobs
Swing Shift 4	4
Night Shift 1	8
Night Shift 2	34

Sensitivity Analysis

Various analyses and changes were made to the model in order to answer questions raised by the airline on how the system would perform under different scenarios. These scenarios included changes to daily flight schedules, the number of technicians, the start/end of sub-shifts, etc. Reports detailing the impact of such changes to the operation of line maintenance were submitted to the airline. In this section, a proposed schedule is presented that improves the performance measures.

An interesting feature of recent simulation software is optimization. Through this feature, the model makes changes to a set of parameters within specified boundaries in an effort to optimize some objective function. The optimization algorithm of the AutoMod simulation software automates the process of changing the necessary parameters. It uses meta-heuristics (Banks 2000) to determine these set of parameters.

In this study we adopted the optimal scenario, to determine the start/end of sub-shifts. The optimal scenario corresponds to the situation in which the system uses its resources to achieve the highest point of efficiency. Here, the management was interested to see how we could reduce the number of unfinished jobs (aircraft) carried from one shift to another.

Optimal Shift Schedule

Our study showed that the day, swing and night-shift schedules (starting/ending times) have a major impact on the spread of workload and carrying unfinished jobs to another shift. The software was allowed to make changes to these schedules in an effort to minimize the unfinished jobs. Utilizing the optimization feature of the software, generated the results in Table 13.9, which presents the best start/end time for each shift/sub-shift based on the optimization module of the software.

Table 13.9 Optimal shift schedule

Shifts	Sub-shifts	Start Time	End Time
	Shift 1	05:30:00	14:00:00
Day	Shift 2	06:00:00	14:30:00
	Shift 3	08:00:00	16:30:00
	Shift 4	11:00:00	19:30:00
	Shift 1	13:00:00	21:30:00
Swing	Shift 2	13:30:00	22:00:00
	Shift 3	14:00:00	22:30:00
	Shift 4	15:00:00	23:30:00
Night	Shift 1	22:00:00	06:30:00
	Shift 2	24:00:00	08:30:00

Figure 13.6 presents a comparison of the total number of technicians with unfinished jobs at their shift end-times for the base and the optimal scenarios.

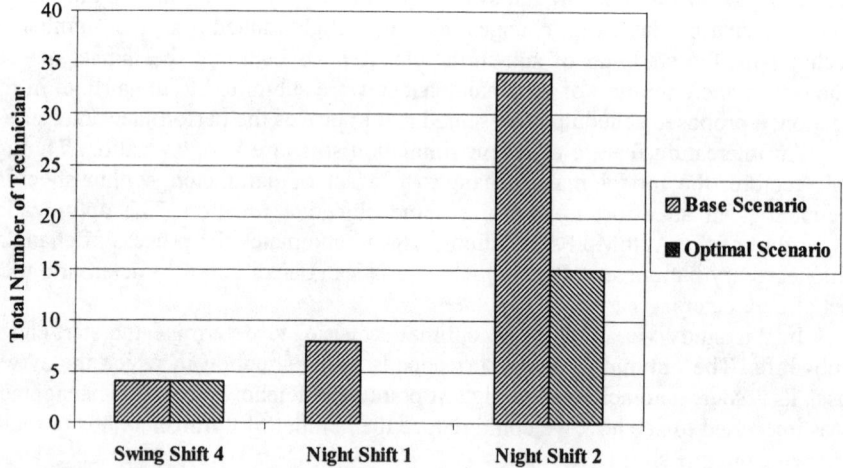

Figure 13.6 Total number of technicians with unfinished jobs in any shift

As the figure shows, the optimal scenario offers a better spread of workload across the shifts by reducing the workload passed on to the next shift.

Conclusions

The simulation model captures the daily operations of the line maintenance facility at Newark. Various system parameters were evaluated, and their validity confirmed by comparison with the airline's existing figures. Some of the benefits of this simulation study include:

- Effective estimation of technician requirement on a sub-shift basis. The model results closely matched actual numbers.
- Simulation analysis generated performance measures, like *technician utilization* and *work overflow*, which could not be estimated earlier.
- Low utilization of technicians, which brings forth the idea of using part-time technicians especially during the day shifts.
- Optimization studies, which show that changing of the shift schedule can greatly enhance the efficiency of the existing system by spreading the workload more uniformly across shifts.

References

Albino, V., Carella, G. and Okogbaa, O.G. (1992), Maintenance Policies in Just-in-Time, Manufacturing Lines. *International Journal of Production Research*. 30, 369-382.

Banks, J. (2000), *Getting Started with AutoMod*. AutoSimulations, Inc.

Barnhart, C., Boland, N.L., Clarke, L.W., Johnson, Nemhauser, G.L. and Shenoi, R.G. (1998), Flight String Models for Aircraft Fleeting and Routing, *Transportation Science*. 32, 208-220.

Bazargan, M., Gupta, P. and Young, S. (2003), A simulation approach to manpower planning, Proceedings of Winter Simulation Conference (WSC 2003), New Orleans, Dec. 7-10, pp. 1677-1685.

Clarke, L.W., Hane, C.A., Johnson, E.L. and Nemhauser, G.L. (1996), Maintenance and Crew Considerations in Fleet Assignment, *Transportation Science*, 30, 249-260.

Dijkstra, M.C., Kroon, L.G., Jo, A.E.E. and van Nunen, Salomon, M. (1991), A DSS for Capacity Planning of Aircraft Maintenance Personnel, *International Journal of Production Economics*, 23, 69-78.

Duffuaa, S.O. and Andijani, A.A. (1999), An Integrated Simulation Model for Effective Planning of Maintenance Operations for Saudi Arabian Airlines (SAUDIA*)*, *Production Planning and Control*, 10, 579-584.

Gatland, R., Yang, E. and Buxton, K. (1997), Solving Engine Maintenance Capacity Problems with Simulation. *Winter Simulation Conference Proceedings*, pp. 892-899.

Hane, C.A., Barnhart, C., Johnson, E.J., Marsten, R.E., Nemhauser, G.L. and Sigisimondi, G. (1995), The Fleet Assignment Problem: Solving a Large-Scale Integer Program, *Math. Program*, 70, 211-232.

Kelton, D., Sadowski, D. and Sadowski, R. (2003), *Simulation with Arena*, 3rd Edition, Irwin McGraw-Hill.

Lam, Michael (1995), An Introduction to Airline Maintenance, The Handbook of Airline Economics, pp. 397-406.

Law, A.M. and Kelton, W.D. (2000), *Simulation Modeling and Analysis*. McGraw-Hill, New York.

Madu, C.N. and Kuei, Chu-Hua (1993), Simulation Analysis of a Maintenance Float Shop. *International Journal of Production Economics*, 29, 149-157.

Mortenson, Robert E. Jr. (1981), Maintenance Planning and Scheduling Using Network Simulations, Winter Simulation Conference Proceedings, pp. 333-340.

Naeem, M. (1994), Integrated Production Planning and Control, *IATA Proceedings*.

Pritsker, A. (1987), *Introduction to Simulation and SLAM II*. West Lafayette, Indiana, USA: Systems Publishing Corporation.

Rushmeier, Russel A. and Kontogiorgis, Spyridon A. (1997), Advances in the Optimization of Airline Fleet Assignment, *Transportation Science*. 31, 159-169.

Sachon, M. and Pate-Cornell, E. (2000), Delays and Safety in Airline Maintenance. *Reliability Engineering and System Safety*, 67, 301-309.

Talluri, Kalyan T. (1998), The Four-Day Aircraft Maintenance Routing Problem, *Transportation Science*. 32, 43-53.

Chapter 14

Simulation Case 2

Introduction

The case study in this chapter concerns the simulation of an airport, rather than an airline. The main objective of this case is to introduce some new, emerging trends in aviation and the way in which they will be integrated in the transportation system. These new trends will impact the short-haul operations of airlines. The following represents some of these new trends that will seriously affect the transportation industry in general and airlines in particular.

- Small Aircraft Transportation System (SATS) - SATS is a new vision that was originally proposed by the National Aeronautics and Space Administration (NASA). SATS represents an innovative program intended to provide travelers with a safe and affordable traveling alternative to current transportation systems. SATS will be discussed in more details later in this chapter.
- Fractional Ownership Programs - because of growing security issues with the airlines and airports, besides the presence of problems and delays caused by these security concerns, some companies have moved to Fractional Ownership Programs. In this program, companies with many business travelers, jointly purchase and maintain small jet(s). Based on their contribution to this program (fraction), these companies, will use the aircraft for their business travels. According to the FAA's definition, the fractional ownership program is possible when an individual or corporation purchases at least 1/16th share of an airplane. The aircraft is then placed in a "pool" to share with other owners of aircraft. The pooled aircraft are managed by a company that provides aviation management services with the necessary expertise for the owners.
- Air Taxis - Because of the growth in the demand of small jet aircraft, we have witnessed an increase in the number of their manufacturers. These companies utilizing advances in aircraft manufacturing, avionics and falling component prices, have been able to offer small jets (4-8 seaters) at very reasonable prices (see for example http://www.eclipseaviation.com). Some of these aircraft are selling for as low as one million dollars. A large number of entrepreneurs have placed orders for these aircraft to start up air-taxis in various parts of the nation. These start up companies use regional airports and provide full service to their passengers. Some of these air-taxis promise a one-hour advance call for the service. Once the passenger(s) calls, the air taxi sends a car to pick-up

the customer(s) from their home or work place. The car then drives the passenger(s) to the nearest regional airport. The waiting jet will fly the passenger(s) to their destination (in most of the cases, another quiet regional airport). At the destination, the process repeats again, with a waiting car taking passenger(s) to their homes or businesses. All this at the price of a first-class airline ticket! It is anticipated that with increased competition, increased demand and falling aircraft prices, this service will be offered at the current airline's economy fares.

Considering these trends, an important question is that can the existing airports and airspace accommodate such increased flow of aircraft? Will there be congestions and delays? The study presented in this chapter, primarily sponsored by the Florida Department of Transportation (FDOT), uses simulation to address the introduction of SATS and its integration with the current traffic for the Tallahassee Regional Airport for the years 2002-2025.

Small Aircraft Transportation System (SATS)

An efficient and reliable transportation system is the backbone of every successful economy (Ashford 1992, Wells 2000, Dempsey 2000). The demand for transportation continues to grow, while current highways and hub-and-spoke systems become more congested. Increasing congestion and delays continue in the current infrastructure, while national investments to reduce these issues are reaching a point of diminishing effectiveness. If these concerns are not addressed, delays in the hub and spoke system will limit economic activity to the few well-connected regions and communities. With 98% of the US population living within a 30-minute drive of over 5000 public-use landing facilities, this infrastructure is an untapped national resource of mobility.

Introduction and commitment to the hub and spoke system of routing, has focused the development of airports to major cities, increasing air traffic congestion to these specific regions (Reynolds-Feighan, et al. 1999, Pitfield, et al. 1999). Conversely, many rural airports and their communities have been suffering a lack of essential air service due to the fact that it has not been financially viable for air carriers to serve these airports. As a result, many major city airports are heavily congested, operating at or above capacity and many rural city airports are increasingly underutilized. This trend has been apparent for some time and is becoming increasingly more significant.

The Small Aircraft Transportation System (SATS) is being introduced as a solution to improve this imbalance by decreasing the congestion at major city airports, and improving rural airport utilization. With such vision, NASA, the U.S. Department of Transportation (DOT), the Federal Aviation Administration (FAA), industry stakeholders, and academia have joined forces to pursue the SATS viability. Its goal is to utilize next generation technology, to improve travel between remote communities and urban transportation centers, and by using general aviation airports. Principled on a new generation of fully automated and affordable small aircrafts, SATS would operate in a fully distributed system of small airports serving thousands of suburban, rural, and remote communities. The idea for SATS is to have the passengers and commuters fly the aircraft. These aircrafts are so advanced and automated that they basically fly by themselves with no or minimum human interaction.

The small aircraft transportation vision is a safe travel alternative, freeing people and products from transportation system delays by creating access to more communities (for more information see http://sats.erau.edu).

The following represent some of the anticipated benefits of SATS:

- Reduction of intercity travel cost on the order of half in many markets, while increasing the number of communities served by air transportation by more than ten-fold in the longer term.
- Distribution of transportation capabilities.
- An alternative to delays imposed by grid-lock, hub-lock, and urban sprawl.
- The potential to ease some of the environmental impacts of the ever-expanding transportation consumption in the nation.
- An increase in the radius of action of daily life by ten-fold, the first increase of such magnitude since the cars replaced horses for intercity travel.

It is not known whether the current infrastructure of small rural airports is capable of accommodating SATS concept without encountering significant operational difficulties. The primary objective of this study is to analyze the operations of the integrated system, identify and evaluate the potential congestion points of airports, runways and terminals, and develop solutions to these problems.

Project Focus

The state of Florida was identified as one of the pioneer states to implement the SATS concept. Seven rural and regional airports including the Tallahassee regional airport in Florida were identified as potential and suitable airports for the SATS program. The Florida Department of Transportation (FDOT), showed their interest, and sponsored a study to examine the integration of SATS with existing traffic to its regional airport at Tallahassee; the states capital. The study was not focused on the technological or economic feasibility of SATS, but on the operation side of it. More specifically, the study should focus on the following for 2002-2025:

- How would the new integrated system perform? What are the unforeseen bottlenecks/problems that could occur?
- What is the impact of SATS on congestions at the airport?
- What facilities, if any should be expanded or created, in order to streamline the integration of SATS?
- How adversely does the existing air traffic will be affected due to sudden and unanticipated SATS growth and expansion rates?

In order to conduct this study, our first attempt was to estimate the future flow (growth) of exiting traffic as well as SATS.

Future Traffic Flow Forecast for KTLH

Three independent aviation forecasts have been prepared for Tallahassee regional airport (KTLH). These forecasts do not consider SATS airplanes. These three forecasts are made by the FAA, an independent consulting group, and KTLH Management; respectively. Figure 14.1 shows the growth of annual operations (without SATS) from 2000-2005 based on these three forecasts. These operations show the number of landing and departure per year. They include commercial, general and military operations. Further research, meetings, interviews, and other issues convinced us that the forecast made by the consulting group to be more realistic.

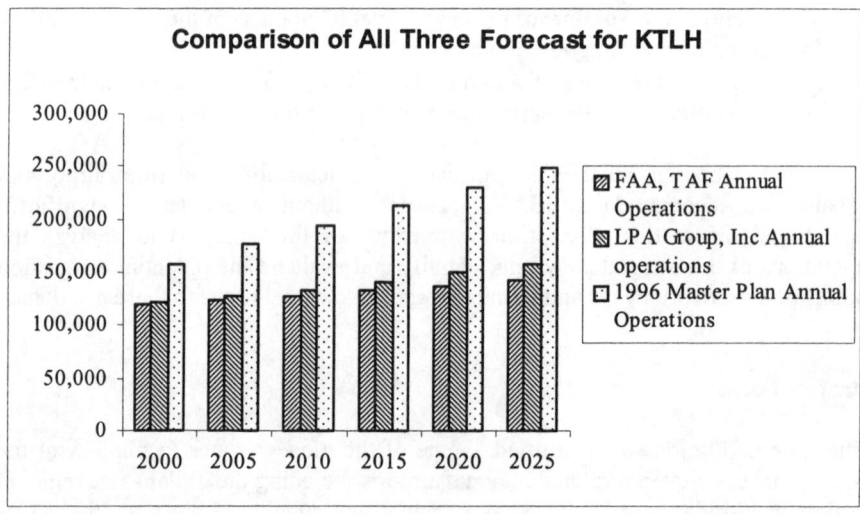

Figure 14.1 Forecasts for number of operations (landings and take-offs) at KTLH on a five-year basis

SATS Traffic Flow Forecast

Currently, the scheduled implementation date of the first set of SATS flight is set for the year 2005. Based on NASA's analysis and forecasts, it is estimated that the total SATS operations at KTLH will be around 3,000 in year 2005. It is also anticipated that it will grow to maturity to 80,000 SATS operations in year 2025.

All new products and services typically follow a life-cycle graph (see Figure 14.2). With any new technology, in the beginning, the demand is relatively low and growing at a slow rate; later on, the demand picks up and grows at a faster rate, until it reaches maturity where the demand either levels off or declines (Tidd, et al., 2001). The SATS program is envisioned to follow this same cycle over the twenty-year projection 2005-2025. A life-cycle curve was fitted to the beginning (2005) and ending (2025) years of this program at KTLH. Figure 14.2 shows the forecasted SATS operations over this 20-year time horizon.

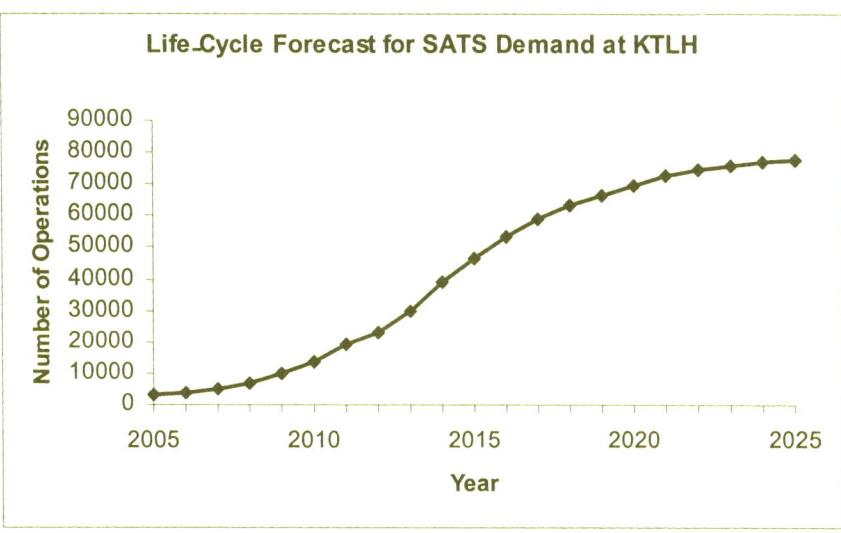

Figure 14.2 Forecast for SATS operations

Figure 14.3 presents the SATS operations, existing traffic and total future operation forecasts for KTLH from 2005-2025 (on a five-year basis).

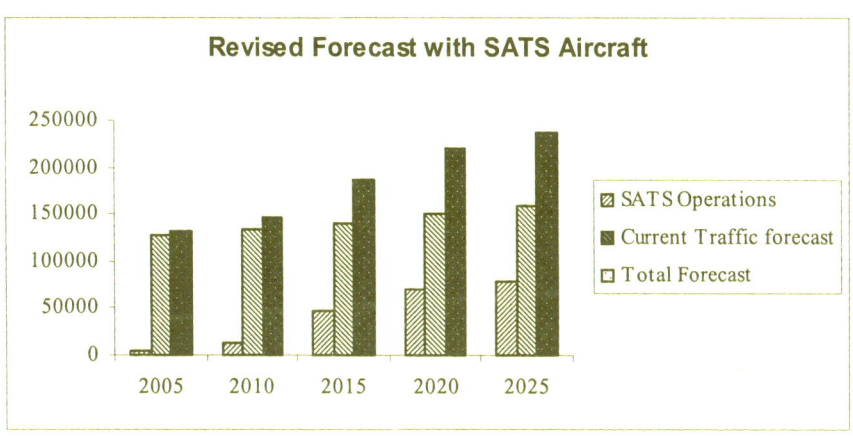

Figure 14.3 Forecast for SATS, existing and total operations for KTLH

Total Airspace and Airport Modeler (TAAM)

TAAM (Total Airspace & Airport Modeler) was developed by The Preston Group (now Preston Aviation Solutions - http://www.preston.net) in cooperation with the Australian Civil Aviation Authority. TAAM is a large scale detailed fast-time simulation software for modeling entire air traffic systems. TAAM is a dedicated simulation software which is primarily used for decision making, planning, design, and analysis of both airport configurations and its surrounding airspace. The scale of simulation can vary, ranging from the local airport or airspace, through a national scale, all the way to intercontinental range.

TAAM has been used in a wide variety of applications including airport capacity estimation (gate, taxiway, runway capacity), planning airport improvements, extensions, noise impact, impact of new air traffic control rules, system wide delays and cost/benefit studies.

TAAM requires comprehensive input data files describing the entire Air Traffic system. The level of detail, however, is variable and can be adapted to suit individual project needs. Typical inputs include the airport layout, air traffic schedule, environment description, aircraft flight plans and air traffic control rules. These are used to investigate the usage of the airport and airspace, conflict detection and resolution, and to compute aggregate metrics using TAAM's internal algorithms and user specified rules. The software generates output on system delay and its distribution costs: fuel, non-fuel; airport movements; operations on taxiways and runways; runway occupancy and airspace operation metrics, such as usage of routes, sectors, fixes and coordination.

Tallahassee Regional Airport (KTLH)

The Tallahassee market contains a total population of more than 1.4 million people. This includes Tallahassee, eleven neighboring Florida counties and twelve southern Georgia counties. The Tallahassee Regional Airport (KTLH) has two runways; runway 27 and runway 36. Figure 14.4 presents the layout of the runways and terminal for this airport.

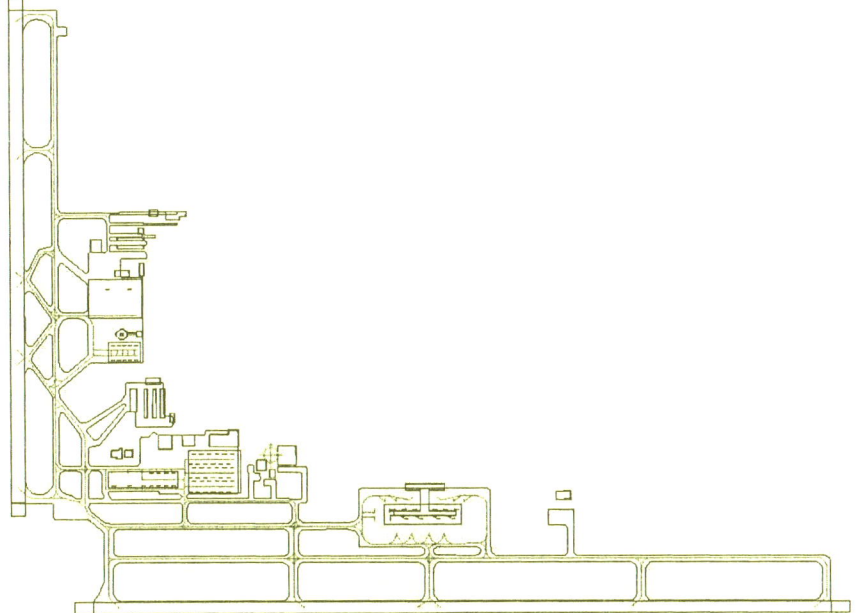

Figure 14.4 KTLH runway, taxiway and terminal layout

Preliminary activities consisted of gathering all initial data and information about Tallahassee Regional Airport (KTLH) from the airport officials. A baseline layout was produced from drawings provided by KTLH. Gate allocation information was also gathered to develop accurate aircraft terminal parking rules. Information from the KTLH tower was used to design reasonable rule assumptions about accurate runway usage. These assumptions included gate and apron rules.

Performance Measures

Similar to many other simulation software, TAAM also generates large amounts of output and reports. We were specifically interested in the following performance measures (Fishburn and Stouppe, 1997):

- System Delays – arrival, departure, airspace and total flight delays;
- Dissection of Delay on a per aircraft basis;
- Peak Movement Rates – Peaks in arrival, departure and total flights;
- Runway Utilization Percentages by aircraft type and market segment.

Baseline Scenario

To capture the logic and to verify the accuracy of the model, initially a simulation model for a typical day in the year of 2002 (the year of this study) was developed. This model did not include any SATS operations. The intention was to check the validity of the model with the actual figures for KTLH. On a typical day in year 2002, there are around 300 daily operations. These operations include commercial, general and military activities. Figure 14.5 presents the TAAM output report for the spread of these 300 operations over different times of the days. As the figure suggests the peak operation time at KTLH occurs between 15:00 and 16:00 with a total of 33 operations.

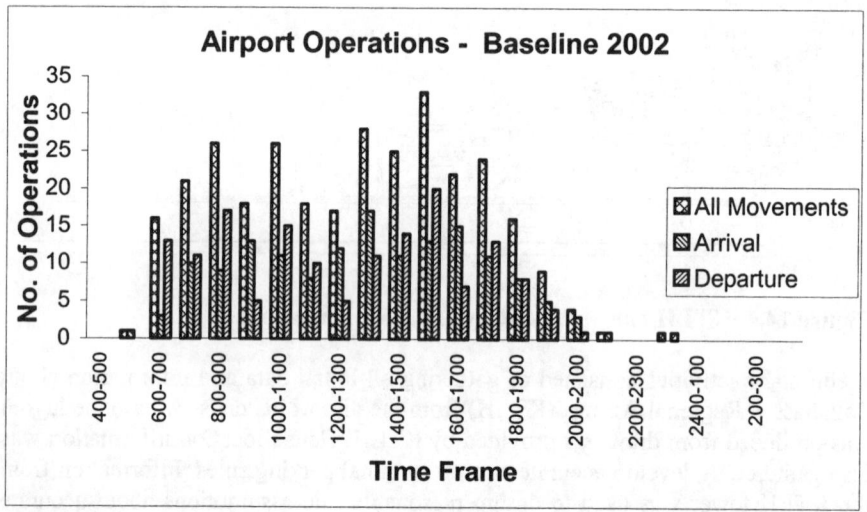

Figure 14.5 Daily arriving, departing and total flight operation at KTLH

Figure 14.6 presents the TAAM report for the delay distribution over the time of the day. This figure shows the total delay in minutes that the arrival and departure flights experience. Note that these delays also consider and include airspace congestion around KTLH. This covers an area within a 20 nautical mile radius of the airfield. According to this figure the peak delay happens between 15:00 and 16:00. The total delay times for all arrivals and departures during this peak hour is 25 minutes. Returning to Figure 14.5 we have 33 operations during this peak hour. This means that during the peak hour, the flights experience on average a delay of less than one minute (25 minute/33 operations).

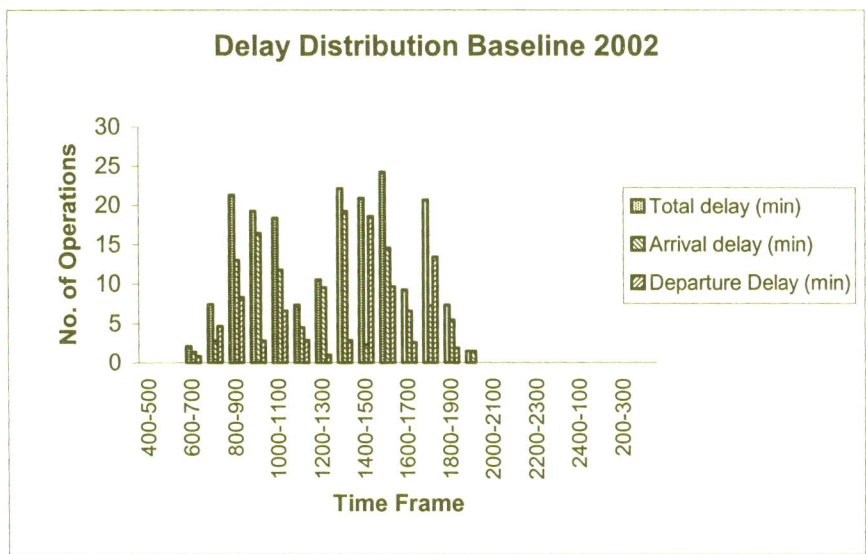

Figure 14.6 Delay distribution for baseline scenario

Figure 14.7 presents the dissection of delays at KTLH. This figure shows how many aircraft experience delays and by how much. According to this figure 250 out of 300 daily operations do not experience any delays at all. Fifty operations experience 3-6 minutes of delay and less than ten operations experience 6-9 minute delays.

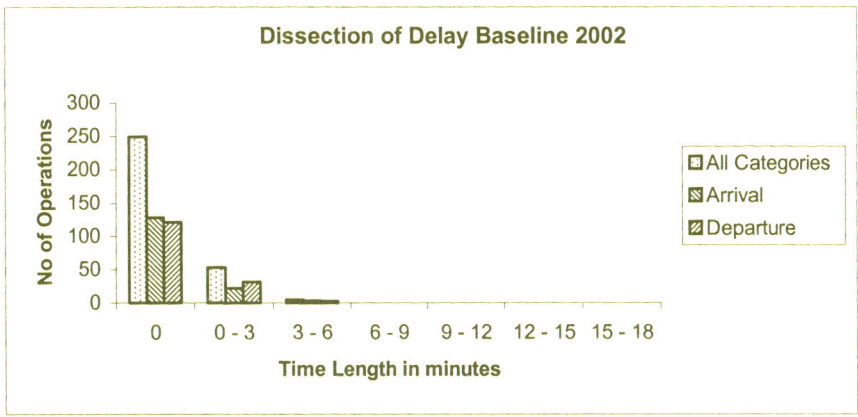

Figure 14.7 Dissection of delays at KTLH

Figure 14.8 presents the TAAM report for number of arriving and departure flights using each of the two runways at the KTLH.

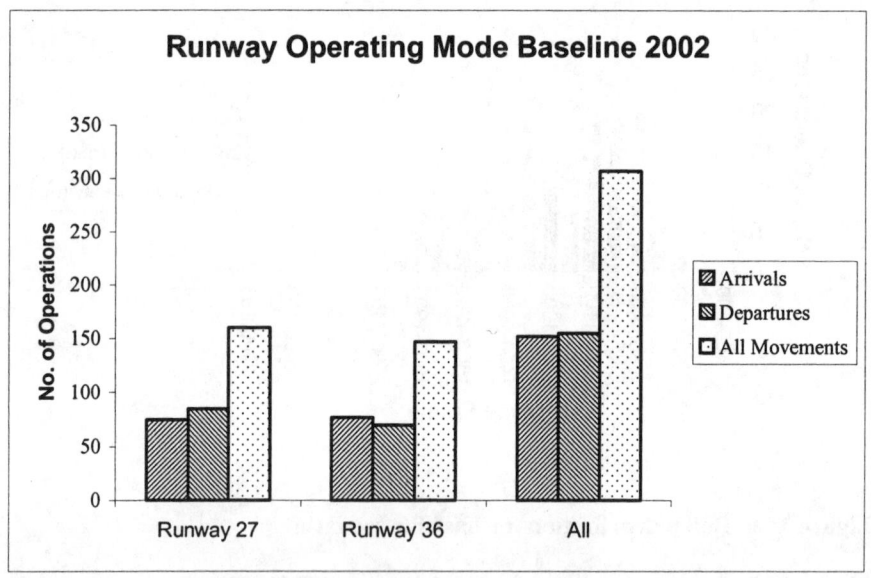

Figure 14.8 Runway usage at KTLH

These results and figures were compared and verified with the actual data. As the figures suggests, KTLH is a quiet airport with no significant flight delays. The FAA defines a significant delay to be those arriving or departure flights that experience more than 15 minutes delay.

Simulation Analysis for 2002-2025

Convinced by the validity of the TAAM model, we started simulating the airport operations for future years. We used the forecasted flow for the SATS and non-SATS traffics at KTLH as was described earlier in this chapter. We adopted the same parameters such as air traffic control rules for arriving and departing flights as the baseline scenario. The only change to the model for the future years was the increased flow. We used guidelines provided by the KTLH to disperse the increased daily flow over different times of the day. Similar performance measures were used to compare the results between the baseline scenario and future operations. The following presents the simulation reports for future operations.

Figure 14.9 presents the peak airport operations from 2002-2025. As we described earlier the peak number for operations in 2002 is 33. This figure will double by 2025 when the current flow is increased and SATS is fully operational.

Simulation Case 2

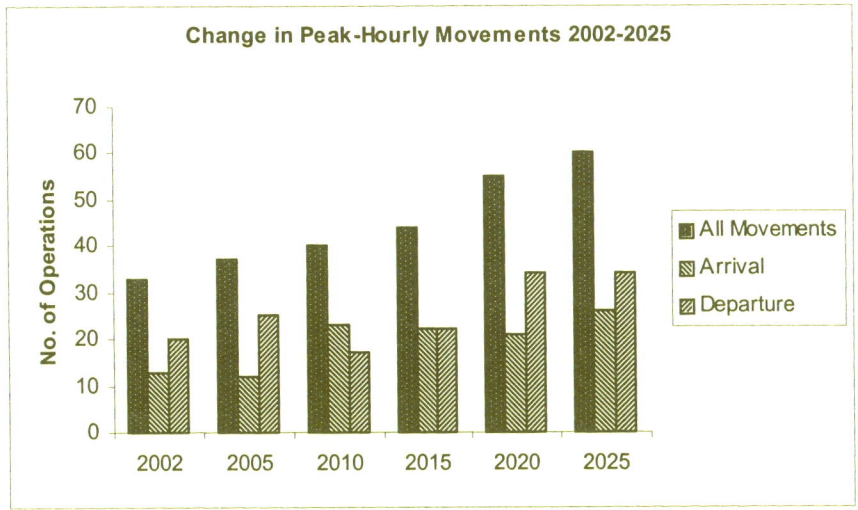

Figure 14.9 Change in peak hourly movements for 2002-2025 study time

Figure 14.10 presents the total delay times in minutes during the peak hour from 2002-2025. According to this figure the peak total time delay in a typical day in 2025 is 150 minutes. This time represents a total delay for 63 flight operations (see Figure 14.9). This total delay translates into an average of less than 3 minutes during the peak time.

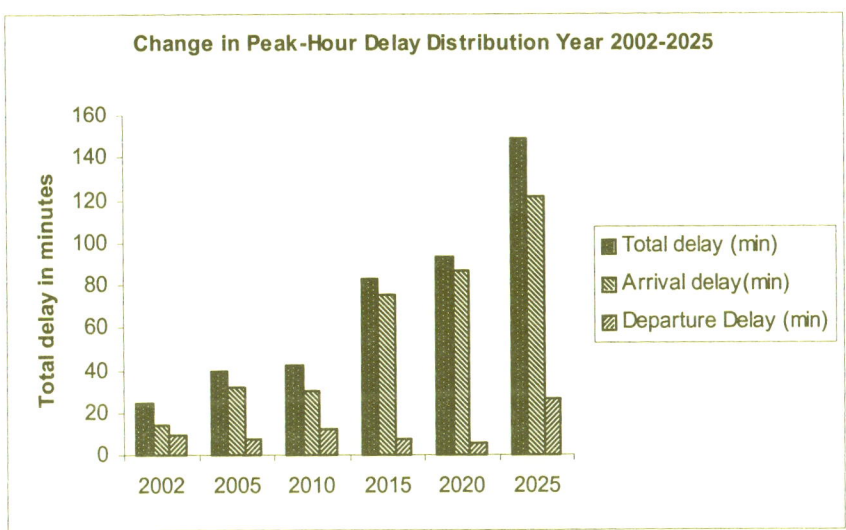

Figure 14.10 Changes in peak delay distribution time for 2002-2025

Figure 14.11 shows the dissection of delays. As the figure suggests there are no significant delays, or they are very minimal (less than two operations in 2025) More than half of the flights do not experience any delays. Again these delays incorporate both ground and airspace congestions.

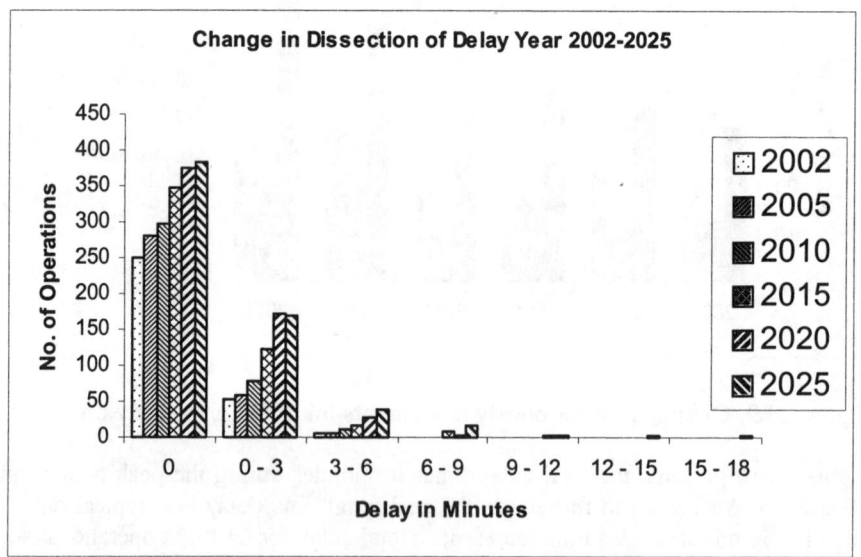

Figure 14.11 Change in dissection of delay 2002-2025

Finally Figure 14.12 shows the number of times each runway is used for the future operations.

Simulation Case 2 199

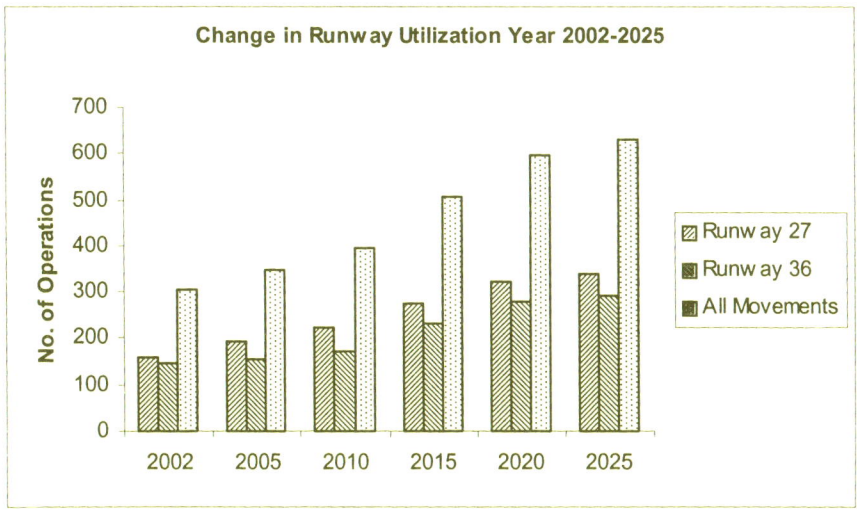

Figure 14.12 Change in runway utilization 2002-2025

As suggested by the above results of the simulation runs, the current infrastructure at Tallahassee Regional Airport is capable of successfully handling the increased traffic demands placed by the forecasted increase in activity, as well as allow for the smooth integration of the SATS program with existing commercial, general, cargo and military operations.

Sensitivity Analysis

In an effort to study the KTLH operations under extreme and unanticipated conditions, we increased the flow of SATS flights in 2025 at peak hour by 40%. Even with these increased flows the flights that experienced significant delays (more than 15 minutes) at peak times remained as less than 2% of all flights. This confirms that the existing infrastructure at KTLH is able to handle unanticipated growth in SATS operations without major bottlenecks or significant delays.

Final Remarks

This study and other similar research work shows that the introduction of SATS is operationally viable. The departure from the hub and spoke concept and change to rural and regional airports looks very promising. These airports are perfectly capable of accommodating increased traffic flow through SATS, fractional ownership programs and air taxis. We believe the airlines should be aware of this trend and consider how these concepts will impact their strategic positions, at least in their short-haul operations.

References

Ashford, N. and Wright, P.H. (1992), *Airport Engineering*. 3rd ed. New York: Wiley.

Dempsey, P.S. (2000), *Airport Planning & Development Handbook: A Global Survey*. New York: McGraw-Hill.

Federal Aviation Administration (2001), *Airport Capacity Benchmark Report*. Washington, D.C.: The Administration.

Fishburn, P.T. and Stouppe, M.S. (1997), Simulation: a powerful planning tool. In Airport Modeling and Simulation, *Conference Proceedings, August 17-20, 1997, Key Bridge Marriot Hotel, Arlington, Virginia*, ed. S.A. Mumayiz and P. Schonfeld, 36-44. Reston, Virginia: American Society of Civil Engineers.

Pitfield, D.E. and Jerrard, E.A. (1999), Monte-Carlo comes to Rome: a note on the estimation of unconstrained runway capacity at Rome Fiumucino International Airport. *Journal of Air Transport Management*, 5:185-192.

Reynolds-Feighan, A.J. and Button, K.J. (1999), An assessment of the capacity and congestion levels at European airports, *Journal of Air Transport Management*, 5:113-134.

Tidd, J., Bessant, J. and Pavitt, K. (2001), *Managing innovation integrating technological, market and organizational change*, John Wiley & Sons.

Wells, A.T. (2000), *Airport Planning & Management*, 4th ed, New York: McGraw-Hill.

Appendix

Airport codes

The following airport codes were used in various chapters of this book. The definition of locations of these airport codes as defined by IATA (International Air Transport Association – see www.IATA.org) and ICAO (International Civil Aviation Organization – see www.icao.org) are presented in this appendix. The IATA airport codes are most common and consist of a three-letter code designating each airport around the world. ICAO airport codes are represented by four letters.

Airport Code	Airport Name
ATL	Atlanta International Airport
BOS	General Edward Lawrence Logan International Airport (Boston)
CVG	Cincinnati/Northern Kentucky International Airport
DAB	Daytona Beach Regional Airport
DTW	Detroit Metropolitan Wayne County Airport
EWR	Newark International Airport
EYW	Key West International Airport
FLL	Fort Lauderdale/Hollywood International Airport
GCM	Claremore Regional Airport
HOU	William P. Hobby Airport (Houston)
IAD	Washington Dulles International Airport
JFK	John F. Kennedy International Airport
KIN	Norman Manley International Airport
KTLH	Tallahassee Regional Airport
LAF	Purdue University Airport (Lafayette)
LAX	Los Angeles International Airport
MCO	Orlando International Airport
MIA	Miami International Airport
MON	Mount Cook Airport (New Zealand)
NAS	Nassau International Airport
ORD	Chicago-O'Hare International Airport
ORF	Norfolk Interantional Airport
PBI	Palm Beach International Airport
PLS	Providenciales International Airport
SFO	San Francisco International Airport
TPA	Tampa International Airport

Index

AGIFORS 1, 172
Air Taxis 187, 199
Aircraft Balance 48-52, 147
Aircraft Routing 2-3, 37, 55, 59-64, 68, 71, 74, 76, 79, 81, 84-85, 89, 92, 141, 159, 161, 166, 169,171
Aircraft Tail Number 59, 74
Aircraft Utilization 166
Airline Deregulation 1, 30
Airline Revenue Management 110
Airport Utilization 188
Amphibian Aircraft 163
Arc Capacity 8, 17
Arcs 8-10, 13, 15-18, 43, 143, 145, 149
ASM (ASK) 41
Automod Simulation 174, 183
Autostat Analysis 180

Bid Line Procedure 92
Booking Request 110-111
Bumped Passengers 128

Cabin Crew 81
Cancellation Cost 143, 145, 147, 150-153
Cancelled Flights 145, 152
Capacity 3, 4, 8, 15, 17-18, 21-22, 32, 35, 40-41, 45-47, 109-110, 114,116, 121-124, 126-128, 132, 163, 165, 173, 182, 185, 188, 192
Cargo 10, 13, 19, 25-26, 104, 159, 199
CASM (CASK) 41
Civil Aeronautics Board 30
Combinatorial 25, 82, 105, 161
Complexity Theory 159
Computational Complexity 159, 161
Congestion 32, 132, 188-189, 194, 198
Connected Network 10
Connecting Flight 15-16, 22, 32, 69, 84
CPLEX 4
Crew Cost 81-82
Crew Pairing 82-94
Crew Rostering 3, 82, 89, 92, 96-97
Crew Scheduling 79, 81-82, 100, 161

Curfew 44, 140, 143
Cyclic 75, 100

Daily Pairing 94
Day Hold 175-177, 179
Deadheading 84
Delay 4, 32, 72, 84, 132, 140-141, 143, 145-147, 150-154, 187-189, 192-199
Delay Cost 150-154
Delayed Flights 150
Delta Airlines 30, 40, 110, 160
Demand Nodes 9
Department of Transportation (DOT) 188-189
Destination Node 12-13, 15, 17-18, 146, 150-151, 153-154
Deterministic Demand 120-121, 124, 127
Directed Arc 8-9
Discount Fare 114-115
Disjoint 24, 27, 95, 102
Dispatch 3
Disruptions 4, 140-141
Duty 82-84, 88-89

Expected Marginal Revenue 112-115, 124, 126
Expected Marginal Seat Revenue (EMSR) 115, 118

FAA 1, 60, 187-188, 190
Fare Class 110-123, 125, 127-128
Fares 1, 33, 110, 114-116, 188
Federal Aviation Regulations (FAR) 82
Ferry Flights 140
Fleet Assignment 3, 18, 37, 40-44, 48-49, 53-54, 56-57, 59-62, 79, 81, 173, 185-186
Fleet Assignment Model 3, 18, 48-49, 56-57
Fleet Diversity 32, 40-41, 45
Fleet Size 52, 55
Flight Cover 148, 167

Flight Coverage   59, 69-70, 88-89, 148
Flight Crew   81-82, 100
Flight Path   143
Flight Scheduling   3, 30, 32-33, 173
Forecast   35-36, 104, 164, 190-191, 196, 199
Fractional Ownership   187, 199
Frequency   32-33, 35, 60, 62, 82, 164-165, 167-168
Full Fare   114-116

Gate Assignment   4, 132, 173
Ground Controller   132
Grounded Aircraft   145

Heuristic Procedures   161
Heuristics   159, 173, 183
Home Base   81, 83-84, 88, 91-92
Hub-and-spoke   22, 30-32, 132, 188

Irregular Operations   4, 140

Life Cycle Forecast   191
Line Maintenance   60, 173-174, 183-185
Load Factor   33, 35-36, 45, 164-165

Maintenance Base   9, 59, 63
Maintenance Planning   173
Maintenance Requirements   59-60, 132, 173
Maintenance Routing   62
Manpower Planning   3-4, 32, 100, 173
Market Evaluation   32
Maximum Flow Problem   15
Minimum Cost Flow Problem   13, 15, 19
Monthly Roster   92, 93
MPL   4
Multi-commodity Problem   18-20
Nested Seat Allocations   128
Network Flows   3, 7
Network Optimization   3
Newsvendor Problem   129
Nodes   7-21, 43, 53, 56, 143-149, 151-154
Non-deterministic Time Algorithms   161
Non-nested Seat Allocations   128
Non-working Day   100
No-shows   42, 128-129

Operating Costs   44-45, 47
Operations   1, 3-4

Operations Research   1, 25, 29, 129, 132, 162
Origin-destination   110, 120-121, 123-125, 128
Overbooking   128-130
Overnight Stay   64-65, 69, 71, 73, 129, 166

Pairings Generators   84
Passenger Flow   134
Passenger Spill Cost   45
Passenger Spills   45-46
Path   9-10, 12-13, 17, 143
Peak Delay   194, 197
Performance Measures   180, 183, 185, 193, 196
Personalized Schedule   92
Polynomial Time Algorithms   161
Probabilistic Demand   124-125
Probability   45, 112-113, 119, 124, 126, 129
Process Logic   179

RASM (RASK)   41
Recapture Rate   47
Recovery Period   143
Remains Overnight (RON)   174-177
Reserve   96
Rest   82-84, 92-93
Revenue Management   2, 3, 33, 34, 109
Route Generators   64, 85
Route System   1, 30
Routing Cycles   62, 64
RPM (RPK)   41

Scheduling   2-3, 30, 81, 100, 104, 140, 161, 163, 173
Seat Inventory Control Problem   110-111, 114
Seat Protection   114, 117
Service Check (SVC)   176, 178
Set-coverings   21-22, 25
Set-partitioning   24-25, 84, 93-94, 166
Shift Schedule   178-179, 182-185
Shortest Path   10, 12-13, 17
Simulation   4, 46, 100, 172, 175, 179-185, 187-189, 192
Simulation Modeling   172-173
Sit Connection   83-85, 128
Small Aircraft Transportation System (SATS)   187-188

Software 4, 14, 20, 33, 46, 53, 67, 71, 89, 95, 104, 123, 136, 159-160, 168, 173-174, 183, 192-193
Source Node 11, 13, 15, 17-18
Start-up airline 4, 163
Station-sink Node Flow 149
Station Time Node Flow 148
Supply Node 8, 13, 148

Technician Requirement 177-178, 181, 185
Through Flight 69, 175-182
Time Block 100, 102-105
Time-band 141, 143, 145, 150, 153
Time-space Network 43-44, 49-50, 141, 168
Total Airspace and Airport Modeler (TAAM) 192
Traffic Flow Forecast 190
Transportation 1, 13, 18-19, 187-189
Transshipment Node 9, 11, 13-14, 17-18, 144, 148-149

Traveling Salesman Problem 25-28
Turn Around Time 62-63, 65, 71-72, 75, 84, 164, 168

Undirected Arc 8
United Airlines 101, 104, 160
Utilization 45, 59, 67-68, 83, 87, 92, 100, 140, 166, 182, 185, 188, 193, 199

Valid Routings 62, 68-69

Walking Distance 132, 134-137
Weekly Roster 95
Working Shift 101, 178
Workload 92, 175, 177, 181-185

Yield 41-42, 109
Yield Management 109